5.00

WITH

D1209799

MAY 9 1988

TIME AND NARRATIVE VOLUME 2

TIME AND
NARRATIVE VOLUME 2

PAUL RICOEUR

Translated by Kathleen McLaughlin and David Pellauer

The University of Chicago Press · Chicago and London

PAUL RICOEUR has been the dean of the faculty of letters and human sciences at the University of Paris X
(Nanterre) for many years and is currently the John Nu-
veen Professor Emeritus in the Divinity School, the
Department of Philosophy, and the Committee on Social Thought at the University of Chicago.

Originally published as *Temps et Récit*, vol. 2,
© Editions du Seuil, 1984

The University of Chicago Press, Chicago 60637
The University of Chicago Press, Ltd., London

Library of Congress Cataloging in Publication Data
Ricoeur, Paul.
    Time and narrative.

    Translation of: Temps et récit.
    Includes index.
    1. Narration (Rhetoric)   2. Time in literature.
3. Mimesis in literature.   4. Plots (Drama, novel, etc.)
5. History—Philosophy.   I. Title.
PN212.R5213   1984   809'.923   83-17995
ISBN 0-226-71331-8 (v. 1)
ISBN 0-226-71333-4 (v. 2)

Contents

Preface   vii

PART III: THE CONFIGURATION OF TIME
IN FICTIONAL NARRATIVE   3

   1. The Metamorphoses of the Plot   7
   2. The Semiotic Constraints on Narrativity   29
   3. Games with Time   61
   4. The Fictive Experience of Time   100

Conclusion   153

Notes   161
Index   203

Preface

Volume 2 of *Time and Narrative* requires no special introduction. This volume contains Part III of the single work sketched out in the opening pages of volume 1. Furthermore, the theme of Part III, the configuration of time by fictional narrative, corresponds strictly to the theme of Part II in volume 1, the configuration of time by historical narrative. Part IV, which will make up my third and final volume, will bring together under the title *Narrated Time* the threefold testimony that is provided by phenomenology, history, and fiction concerning the power of narrative, taken in its indivisible wholeness, to refigure time.

This brief preface allows me the opportunity to add to the acknowledgments made at the beginning of Volume 1 of *Time and Narrative* an expression of my gratitude to the directors of the National Humanities Center in North Carolina. The exceptional conditions offered to the Fellows there, allowed me, in large part, to carry out the research that led to this volume.

Part III
The Configuration of Time
in Fictional Narrative

In this third part of *Time and Narrative* the narrative model I am considering under the title *mimēsis*₂ is applied to a new region of the narrative field which, to distinguish it from the region of historical narrative, I am designating as fictional narrative.[1] This large subset of the field of narrative includes everything the theory of literary genres puts under the rubrics of folktale, epic, tragedy, comedy, and the novel. This list is only meant to be indicative of the kind of text whose temporal structure will be considered. Not only is this list of genres not a closed one, their provisional titles do not bind me in advance to any required classification of literary genres. This is important because my specific concerns do not require me to take a stand concerning the problems relative to the classification and the history of such genres.[2] So I shall adopt the most commonly accepted nomenclature as often as the status of my problem allows. In return, I am obligated from this point on to account for the characterization of this narrative subset as "fictional narrative." Remaining faithful to the convention concerning vocabulary I adopted in my first volume, I am giving the term "fiction" a narrower extension than that adopted by the many authors who take it to be synonymous with "narrative configuration."[3] This equating of narrative configuration and fiction, of course, has some justification inasmuch as the configurating act is, as I myself have maintained, an operation of the productive imagination, in the Kantian sense of this term. Nevertheless I am reserving the term "fiction" for those literary creations that do not have historical narrative's ambition to constitute a true narrative. If we take "configuration" and "fiction" as synonyms we no longer have a term available to account for the different relation of each of these two narrative modes to the question of truth. What historical narrative and fictional narrative do have in common is that they both stem from the same configurating operations I put under the title mimesis₂. On the the hand, what opposes them to each other does not have to do with the structuring activity invested in their narrative structures as such, rather it has to do with the "truth-claim" that defines the third mimetic relation.

3

It will be useful to linger awhile on the level of this second mimetic relation between action and narrative. Unexpected convergences and divergences will then have an opportunity to take shape concerning the fate of narrative configuration in the areas of historical narrative and fictional narrative.

The four chapters of which Part III is composed themselves constitute stages along a single itinerary: by broadening, radicalizing, enriching, and opening up to the outside the notion of emplotment, handed down by the Aristotelian tradition, I shall attempt correlatively to deepen the notion of temporality handed down by the Augustinian tradition, without at the same time moving outside the framework provided by the notion of narrative configuration, hence without crossing over the boundaries of mimesis$_2$.

1. To broaden the notion of emplotment is first of all to attest to the fact that the Aristotelian *muthos* has the capacity to be transformed without thereby losing its identity. The breadth of narrative understanding is measured by this mutability of emplotment. Several questions are implied by this: (a) Does a narrative genre as new as the modern novel, for example, maintain a tie with the tragic *muthos*, synonymous with emplotment for the Greeks, so that it can still be placed under the formal principle of concordant discordance by which I defined narrative configuration? (b) Does emplotment, through all these mutations, offer a stability that would allow it to be situated in terms of the paradigms that preserve the style of traditionality characteristic of the narrative function, at least in the cultural sphere of the Western world? (c) What is the critical threshold beyond which the most extreme deviations from this style of traditionality force upon us the hypothesis not only of a schism in relation to the narrative tradition but the death of the narrative function itself?

In this initial inquiry the question of time is dealt with only marginally, through the intervention of concepts such as "novelty," "stability," and "decline," by which I shall attempt to characterize the identity of the narrative function without giving in to any sort of essentialism.

2. To deepen the notion of emplotment I shall confront narrative understanding, forged by our familiarity with the narratives transmitted by our culture, with the rationality employed nowadays by narratology, and in particular by the narrative semiology characteristic of the structural approach.[4] The quarrel over priority that divides narrative understanding and semiotic rationality—a dispute we shall have to arbitrate—offers an obvious parallel with the discussion that arose in Part II concerning the epistemology of contemporary historiography and philosophy of history. We may, in fact, place on the same level of rationality both nomological explanation, which some theorists of history have claimed to substitute for the naive art of narrating, and the apprehension of the deep structures of a narrative in narrative semiotics, with respect to which the rules of emplotment are considered mere surface structures. The question arises whether we can provide the same response to this

conflict over priority that we gave in the similar debate concerning history, namely, that to explain more is to understand better.

The question of time thus comes up again, but in a less peripheral manner than above. To the extent that narrative semiotics does succeed in conferring an achronic status on the deep structures of a narrative, the question arises whether its change of strategic level allows it to do justice to the most original features of narrative temporality, those I characterized in Part I as discordant concordance, by combining Augustine's analyses of time with Aristotle's analysis of muthos. The fate of diachrony in narratology will help us to uncover the difficulties resulting from this second cycle of questions.

3. To enrich the notion of emplotment, along with the notion of time that is related to it, is still to explore the resources of narrative configuration that seem peculiar to fictional narrative. The reasons for according this privilege to fictional narrative will appear only later, when we shall be in a position to carry through the contrast between the time of history and the time of fiction on the basis of a phenomenology of time-consciousness broader than that of Augustine.

Anticipating this great three-way debate between lived experience, historical time, and fictional time, I shall base my remarks on a noteworthy property of narrative "utterance": its ability to present, within discourse itself, specific marks that distinguish it from the "statement" of the things narrated. The result of this, for time, is a parallel capacity of being divided into the time of the act of narrating and the time of the things narrated. The discordances between these two temporal modalities do not stem from the alternative of either achronic logic or chronological development, the two branches to which our earlier discussion was in danger of limiting itself. These discordances in fact present nonchronometric aspects which invite us to decipher in them an original—even a reflective—dimension of the distension of Augustinian time, one the division into utterance and statement is best suited to throw into relief in fictional narrative.

4. To open up the notion of emplotment—and the notion of time that corresponds to it—to the outside is to follow the movement of transcendence by which every work of fiction, whether verbal or plastic, narrative or lyric, projects a world outside of itself, one that can be called the "world of the work." In this way, epics, dramas, and novels project, in the mode of fiction, ways of inhabiting the world that lie waiting to be taken up by reading, which in turn is capable of providing a space for a confrontation between the world of the text and the world of the reader. The problems of refiguration, belonging to the level of mimesis$_3$, begin, strictly speaking, only in and through this confrontation. This is why the notion of the world of the text seems to me still to be part of the problem of narrative configuration, although it paves the way for the transition from mimesis$_2$ to mimesis$_3$.

A new relation between time and fiction corresponds to this notion of the world of the text. And it is, to my mind, the most decisive one. I shall not hesitate to speak here, despite the obvious paradox of the expression, of the "fictive experience of time" in order to express the properly temporal aspects of the world of the text and the ways of inhabiting the world that the text projects outside of itself.[5] The status of the expression "fictive experience" is most precarious. On the one hand, in effect, our temporal ways of inhabiting the world remain imaginary to the extent that they exist only in and through the text. On the other hand, they constitute a sort of transcendence within immanence that is precisely what allows for the confrontation with the world of the reader.[6]

I

The Metamorphoses of the Plot

The precedence of our narrative understanding in the epistemological order, as it will be defended in the following chapter in light of the rationalizing ambitions of narratology, can only be attested to and maintained if we initially give this narrative understanding a scope such that it may be taken as the original which narratology strives to copy. It follows that my task is not an easy one. The Aristotelian theory of plot was conceived during an age when only tragedy, comedy, and epic were recognized as "genres" worthy of philosophical reflection. But new types have appeared even within the tragic, comic, and epic genres, types that may make us doubt whether a theory of plot appropriate for the poetic practice of ancient writers still works for such new works as *Don Quixote* or *Hamlet*. What is more, new genres have appeared, in particular the novel, that have turned literature into an immense laboratory for experiments in which, sooner or later, every received convention has been set aside. We might ask, therefore, whether "plot" has not become a category of such limited extension, and such an out-of-date reputation, as has the novel in which the plot predominates. Furthermore, the evolution of literature has not been confined to producing new types in old genres or even new genres within the constellation of literary forms. Its adventure seems to have brought it to blur the limits between genres, and to contest the very principle of *order* that is the root of the idea of plot. What is in question today is the very idea of a relationship between an individual work and every received paradigm.[1] Is it not true that plot is disappearing from the horizon of literature inasmuch as the very contours of the most basic distinction among the modes of composition, the one having to do with mimetic composition, are being wiped out?

It is a matter of some urgency therefore that we test the capacity of the plot to be transformed beyond its initial sphere of application in Aristotle's *Poetics*, and that we identify the threshold beyond which this concept loses all its discriminating value.

This investigation of the boundaries within which the concept of plot remains valid finds a guide in the analysis of mimesis₂ that I proposed in Part 1 of this work.[2] That analysis contains rules for generalizing the concept of plot that now have to be made explicit.[3]

BEYOND THE TRAGIC MUTHOS

Plot was first defined, on the most *formal* level, as an integrating dynamism that draws a unified and complete story from a variety of incidents, in other words, that transforms this variety into a unified and complete story. This formal definition opens a field of rule-governed transformations worthy of being called plots so long as we can discern temporal wholes bringing about a synthesis of the heterogeneous between circumstances, goals, means, interactions, and intended or unintended results. This is why a historian such as Paul Veyne could assign to a considerably enlarged notion of plot the function of integrating components of social change as abstract as those brought to light by non-event-oriented history and even by serial history. Literature should be able to present expansions of the same scale. The space for this interplay is opened by the hierarchy of paradigms referred to above: types, genres, forms. We may formulate the hypothesis that these metamorphoses of the plot consist of new instantiations of the formal principle of temporal configuration in hitherto unknown genres, types, and individual works.

It is within the realm of the modern novel that the pertinence of the concept of emplotment seems to have been contested the most. The modern novel, indeed, has, since its creation, presented itself as the protean genre par excellence. Called upon to respond to a new and rapidly changing social situation, it soon escaped the paralyzing control of critics and censors.[4] Indeed, it has constituted for at least three centuries now a prodigious workshop for experiments in the domains of composition and the expression of time.[5]

The major obstacle the novel had first to confront, then completely overcome, was a doubly erroneous conception of plot. It was erroneous first because it was simply transposed from two of the already constituted genres, epic and drama, then because classical art, especially in France, had imposed on these two genres a mutilated and dogmatic version of the rules from Aristotle's *Poetics*. It will suffice here to recall, on the one hand, the limiting and constraining interpretation given the rule about the unity of time, as it was understood in chapter 7 of the *Poetics*, and, on the other hand, the strict requirement to begin *in media res*, as Homer did in the *Odyssey*, then to move backward to account for the present situation, so as to distinguish clearly the literary from the historical narrative, which was held to descend the course of time, leading its characters uninterruptedly from birth to death, filling all the intervals of its time span with narration.

Under the eye of these rules, frozen into a supercilious didacticism, plot could only be conceived of as an easily readable form, closed in on itself, symmetrically arranged in terms of an ending, and based on an easily identifiable causal connection between the initial complication and its denouement; in short, as a form where the episodes would clearly be held together by the configuration.

One important corollary of this overly narrow conception of plot especially contributed to the misunderstanding of the formal principle of emplotment. Whereas Aristotle had subordinated characters to plot, taken as the encompassing concept in relation to the incidents, characters, and thoughts, in the modern novel we see the notion of character overtake that of plot, becoming equal with it, then finally surpass it entirely.

This revolution in the history of genres came about for good reasons. Indeed, it is under the rubric of character that we may situate three noteworthy expansions within the genre of the novel.

First, exploiting the breakthrough that had occurred with the picaresque tale, the novel considerably extends the social sphere in which its action unfolds. It is no longer the great deeds or misdeeds of legendary or famous characters but the adventures of ordinary men and women that are to be recounted.

The English novel of the eighteenth century testifies to this invasion of literature by ordinary people. Furthermore, the story seems to have moved toward the episodic form through its emphasis on the interactions arising out of a much more differentiated social fabric, in particular through the innumerable imbrications of its dominant theme of love with money, reputation, and social and moral codes—in short, with an infinitely ramified praxis.[6]

The second expansion of character, at the expense of the plot, or so it seems, is illustrated by the *Bildungsroman*, which reached its high point with Schiller and Goethe and which continued into the opening third of the twentieth century.[7] Everything seems to turn on the self-awakening of the central character. First, it is his gaining maturity that provides the narrative framework; then, more and more, his doubts, his confusion, his difficulty in finding himself and his place in the world govern the development of this type of story. However, throughout this development, what was essentially asked of the narrated story was that it knit together social and psychological complexity. This new enlargement proceeds directly from the preceding one. Narrative technique in the golden age of the novel in the nineteenth century, from Balzac to Tolstoy, had anticipated this by drawing on the resources of an old narrative formula which consisted of deepening a character by narrating more and drawing from the richness of a character the exigency of a greater episodic complexity. In this sense, character and plot mutually influence each other.[8]

Another new source of complexity has appeared in the twentieth century, in particular with the stream-of-consciousness novel, so marvelously illustrated by a work of Virginia Woolf, a masterpiece from the point of view of the perception of time, which I shall look at in more detail below.[9] What now holds

9

the center of attention is the incompleteness of personality, the diversity of the levels of the conscious, the subconscious, and the unconscious, the stirring of unformulated desires, the inchoative and evanescent character of feelings. The notion of plot here seems to be especially in trouble. Can we still talk about a plot when the exploration of the abysses of consciousness seems to reveal the inability of even language to pull itself together and take shape?

Yet nothing in these successive expansions of character at the expense of the plot escapes the formal principle of configuration and therefore the concept of emplotment. I will even dare to say that nothing in them takes us beyond the Aristotelian definition of muthos as the imitation of an action. As the breadth of the plot increases, so does that of action. By "action" we have to understand more than the behavior of the protagonists that produces visible changes in their situation or their fortune, what might be called their external appearance. Action, in this enlarged sense, also includes the moral transformation of characters, their growth and education, and their initiation into the complexity of moral and emotional existence. It also includes, in a still more subtle sense, purely internal changes affecting the temporal course of sensations and emotions, moving ultimately to the least organized, least conscious level introspection can reach.

The concept of an imitation of action can thus be extended beyond the "action novel," in the strict sense of the term, to include novels oriented toward character or toward an idea, in the name of the encompassing nature of plot in relation to the more narrowly defined categories of incident, character, or thought. The sphere delimited by the concept of *mimēsis praxeōs* extends as far as does the capacity of narrative to "render" its object by strategies giving rise to singular wholes capable of producing their "particular pleasure" through an interplay of inferences, expectations, and emotional responses on the reader's part. In this sense, the modern novel teaches us to extend the notion of an imitated or represented action to the point where we can say that a *formal* principle of composition governs the series of changes affecting beings similar to us—be they individual or collective, the bearers of a proper name as in the nineteenth-century novel, or just designated by an initial (K) as in Kafka, or even, at the limit, unnameable as in Beckett.

The history of the genre "novel" does not require us, therefore, to give up the term "plot" as designating the correlate of narrative understanding. However we must not stop with these historical considerations concerning the extension of this genre if we are to understand the apparent defeat of the plot. There is a less obvious reason for this reduction of the concept of plot to that of mere story-line—or schema or summary of the incidents. If the plot, once reduced to this skeleton, could appear to be an external constraint, even an artificial and finally an arbitrary one, it is because, since the birth of the novel through the end of its golden age in the nineteenth century, a more urgent problem than that of the art of composition occupied the foreground: the problem of verisimilitude. The substitution of one problem for the other was facilitated by the fact that the conquest of verisimilitude took place under the banner of the struggle against "conventions," especially against what plot was supposed to be, on the basis of epic, tragedy, and comedy in their ancient, Elizabethan, and "classical" (in the French sense of this term) forms. To struggle against these conventions and for verisimilitude constituted one and the same battle. It was this concern for being true—in the sense of being faithful—to reality, or for equating art and life, that most contributed to covering over the problems of narrative composition.

And yet these problems were not abolished. They were only displaced. To see this, it suffices to reflect upon the variety of novelistic procedures used to satisfy this requirement to depict life in its everyday truth in the early days of the English novel. For example, Defoe, the author of *Robinson Crusoe*, made recourse to a pseudo-autobiographical form, through imitation of the innumerable diaries, memoires, and genuine autobiographies published during the same period by people shaped by the Calvinist discipline of daily self-examination. Following him, Richardson, in *Pamela* and *Clarissa*, believed he could depict private experience—for example, the conflicts between romantic love and the institution of marriage—with even greater fidelity by using as artificial a device as the exchange of letters, despite its evident disadvantages: little selective power, the encroachment of insignificant matters and garrulity, much marching in place and repetition.[10] But, to Richardson, the advantages won out without any need for discussion. By having his heroine immediately write things down, he could convey the impression of great closeness between writing and feeling. Moreover, use of the present tense contributed to this impression of immediacy, thanks to the almost simultaneous transcription of what was felt and its circumstances. At the same time, the unsolvable difficulties of the pseudo-autobiography, dependent as it was on the resources of an unbelievable memory, were eliminated. Finally, this method allowed the reader to participate in the psychological situation presupposed by the very use of an exchange of letters, the subtle mixture of retreats and outpourings that occupy the mind of anyone who decides to confide in writing her or his intimate feelings. On the side of the reader, we find in response to this, the no less subtle mixture arising from the indiscretion of peeking through the keyhole, so to speak, and the impunity that goes with solitary reading.

No doubt what prevented these novelists from reflecting upon the artifice of these conventions, which was the price to be paid in their quest for the probable, was the conviction they shared with empiricist philosophers of language from Locke to Reid that language could be purged of every figurative and decorative element and returned to its original vocation—the vocation, according to Locke, "to convey the knowledge of things." This confidence in the spontaneously referential function of language, returned to its literal usage, is no less important than the will to return conceptual thought to its presumed origin in experience of the particular. In truth, this will could not exist without this confidence. How, indeed, render the experience of the particular by language, if language cannot be brought back to the pure referentiality attached to its presumed literalness?

It is a fact that, once transposed into the realm of literature, this return to experience and to simple and direct language led to the creation of a new genre, defined by the proposal to establish the most exact correspondence possible between the literary work and the reality it imitates.[11] Implicit in this project is the reduction of mimesis to imitation, in the sense of making a copy, a sense totally foreign to Aristotle's *Poetics*. It is not surprising, therefore, that neither the pseudo-autobiography nor the epistolary formula really provided any problem for their users. Memory was not suspected of being fallacious, whether the hero recounted something after the fact or as directly from the scene. For Locke and Hume themselves, memory was the support for causality and for personal identity. Hence to render the texture of daily life as closely as possible was taken to be an accessible and, finally, not problematic task.

It is no small paradox that it was reflection on the highly conventional character of such novelistic discourse that finally led to reflection on the formal conditions of this very illusion of proximity and, thereby, led to the recognition of the basically fictive status of the novel itself. After all, the instantaneous, spontaneous, and frank transcription of experience in the epistolary novel is no less conventional than the recalling of the past by a supposedly infallible memory in the pseudo-autobiographical novel. The epistolary genre presupposes, in fact, that it is possible to transfer through writing, with no loss of persuasive power, the force of representation attached to the living voice or theatrical action. To the belief, expressed by Locke, in the direct referential value of language stripped of ornaments and figures is added the belief in the authority of the printed word substituted for the absence of the living voice.[12] Perhaps it was necessary that at first the declared aim of being probable had to be confused with the aim of "representing" the reality of life so that too narrow and too artificial a conception of plot could be wiped out, and that subsequently the problems of composition should be brought out by reflection on the formal conditions of a truthful representation. In other words, perhaps it was necessary to overthrow the conventions in the name of the probable in order to discover that the price to be paid for doing so is an increase in the refinement of composition, hence the invention of ever more complex plots, and, in this sense, ones more and more distant from reality and from life.[13] Whatever may be said about this alleged cunning of reason in the history of the genre of the novel, the paradox remains that it was refinement in narrative technique, called for by the concern for faithfulness to everyday reality, that brought attention to what Aristotle called, in the broad sense, the "imitation of an action" in terms of "the organization of the events" in a plot.

What conventions or what artifices are not required to put life into writing, that is, to compose a persuasive simulacrum in writing?

It is a great paradox, one that will not be fully unfolded until we consider the connection between configuration and refiguration, that the empire of conventions should grow in proportion to the representative ambition of the novel during its longest period, that of the realistic form. In this sense, the three steps broadly defined above—the novel of action, of character, of thought—mark out a twofold history: that of the conquest of new regions by the formal principle of configuration, but also that of the discovery of the increasingly conventional character of this undertaking. This second history, this history in counterpoint, is the history of the *prise de conscience* of the novel as the art of fiction, to use Henry James's famous title.

During the first phase, formal vigilance remained subordinated to the realist motivation that engendered it. It was even concealed by the representative intention. Verisimilitude is still a province of truth—its image or its semblance. And the best resemblance was what best approximated the familiar, the ordinary, the everyday, in opposition to the amazing deeds of the epic or the sublime ones of classical drama. The fate of the plot thus depended upon this almost desperate effort to bring the artifice of novelistic composition asymptotically close to a reality that slipped away in proportion to the formal exigencies of composition that it multiplied. Everything happened as though only ever more complex conventions could approach what was natural and true, as if the growing complexity of these conventions made this very reality recede into an inaccessible horizon that art wanted to equal and to "render." This is why the call for verisimilitude could not long hide the fact that verisimilitude is not just resemblance to truth but also a semblance of truth. This fine distinction was to deepen into an abyss. Indeed, insofar as the novel was recognized as the art of fiction, reflection on the formal conditions for the production of this fiction entered into open competition with the "realistic" motivation behind which these conditions first lay concealed. The golden age of the novel in the nineteenth century may be characterized by a precarious equilibrium between the always more strongly affirmed aim of faithfulness to reality and the ever sharper awareness of the artifice behind a successful composition.

One day this equilibrium had to be lost. If, indeed, resemblance is only a semblance of truth, what then is fiction under the rule of this semblance but the ability to create the belief that this artifice *stands for* genuine testimony about reality and life? The art of fiction then turns out to be the art of illusion. From here on, awareness of the artifice involved undermines from within the realist motivation, finally turning against it and destroying it.

Today it is said that only a novel without a plot or characters or any discernible temporal organization is more genuinely faithful to experience, which is itself fragmented and inconsistent, than was the traditional novel of the nineteenth century. But this plea for a fragmented, inconsistent fiction is not justified any differently than was the plea for naturalistic literature. The argument for verisimilitude has merely been displaced. Formerly, it was social complexity that called for abandoning the classical paradigm; today, it is the presumed incoherence of reality that requires abandoning every paradigm. But then literature, by reduplicating the chaos of reality by that of fiction, returns mimesis to its weakest function—that of replicating what is real by copying it. Fortunately, the paradox remains that in multiplying its artifices fiction seals its capitulation.

We may then ask whether the initial paradox has not been turned upside down. In the beginning, it was the representative intention that motivated the convention. At the end, the awareness of the illusion subverts the convention and motivates an effort to break away from every paradigm. The questions of the limits and perhaps of the exhaustion of the metamorphoses of plot stem from this reversal.

PERENNIALITY: AN ORDER OF PARADIGMS?

The preceding discussion bore on the capacity for expansion of the formal principle of figuration as this functions in the plot, beyond its initial exemplification in Aristotle's *Poetics*. This discussion required some recourse to literary history as it applied to the beginnings of the novel. Does this mean literary history can take the place of criticism? In my opinion, criticism can neither identify itself with such history nor ignore it. Criticism cannot eliminate this history because it is familiarity with literary works, as they have appeared in the succession of cultures to which we are the heirs, that instructs narrative understanding, before narratology constructs an atemporal simulacrum of it. In this sense, narrative understanding retains, integrates within itself, and recapitulates its own history. Criticism, nevertheless, may not confine itself to listing, in their pure contingency, the appearance of individual works. Its proper function is to discern a style of development, an order in movement, that makes this sequence of developments a significant heritage. This undertaking is at least worth attempting if it is true that the narrative function already contains its own intelligibility long before semiotic rationality undertakes to rewrite its rules. In my programmatic chapter 3 in volume 1, I proposed comparing this prerational intelligibility to the intelligibility of the schematism from which, according to Kant, proceed the rules of the categorial understanding. This schematism is not atemporal, however. It itself proceeds from the sedimentation of a practice with a specific history. It is this sedimentation that gives this schematism the unique historical style I called "traditionality."

Traditionality is that irreducible phenomenon that allows criticism to stand half-way between the contingency of a mere history of genres, or types, or works arising from the narrative function, and an eventual logic of possible narratives that would escape history. The order that can be extricated from this self-structuring of tradition is neither historical nor ahistorical but rather "transhistorical," in the sense that it runs through this history in a cumulative rather than just an additive manner. Even if this order includes breaks, or sudden changes of paradigms, these breaks are not themselves simply forgotten. Nor do they make us forget what preceded them, and what they separate us from. They too are part of the phenomenon of tradition and its cumulative style.[14] If the phenomenon of tradition did not include this force for order, it would not be possible to evaluate the phenomena of deviation I shall discuss in the next section of this chapter. Nor would it be possible to pose the question of the death of the narrative art through exhaustion of its formative dynamism. These two phenomena of deviation and death are just the obverse side of the problem I am considering now, the problem of an order of paradigms at the level of the schematism of the narrative understanding rather than at the level of semiotic rationality.

Consideration of this problem drew me to Northrop Frye's *Anatomy of Criticism*.[15] The theory of modes we find there in the first essay, and even more the theory of archetypes in the third essay, are incontestably systematic. However, the systematic character does not work on the same level as the rationality characteristic of narrative semiotics. Instead it stems from narrative understanding in its traditionality. It aims at extricating a typology of this schematism which is always being formed. This is why it does not justify itself by its coherence or its deductive virtues but by its capacity for providing an account, by an open, inductive process, of the greatest possible number of works included in our cultural heritage. Elsewhere I have attempted a reconstruction of *Anatomy of Criticism* that illustrates how the system of narrative configurations proposed by Frye stems from the transhistorical schematism of the narrative understanding, not from the ahistorical rationality of narrative semiotics.[16] Here I shall draw upon several parts of that essay that contribute to my argument.

Let us first consider the theory of modes, which corresponds most closely to what I am calling here the narrative schematism, and, among these modes, those that Frye calls fictional modes to distinguish them from thematic modes. These fictional modes have to do only with the internal structural relations of the fable, to the exclusion of its theme.[17] Their distribution is governed by a single basic criterion: namely, the hero's power to act, which may be, as we have seen in Aristotle's *Poetics*, greater than our own, less than our own, or comparable to our own.

Frye applies this criterion in terms of two parallel tables of modes, that of the tragic and that of the comic, which in fact are not modes but classes of modes. In the tragic modes, the hero is isolated from society (to which isolation corresponds a comparable aesthetic distance on the side of the spectator, as is seen in the "purged" emotions of terror and pity). In the comic modes, the hero is reincorporated into society. It is under these two headings of the tragic and the comic that Frye applies his criterion of degrees of the power to act. He distinguishes under each heading five modes, divided into five columns. In the first column, that of myth, the hero is superior to us "in kind." Myths, broadly speaking, are stories about the gods. On the tragic side, we find the Dionysian myths, celebrating dying gods; on the comic side, the Apollonian myths where the divine hero is received into the society of the gods. In the second column, that of romance, the hero's superiority is no longer in kind but in degree as regards other human beings and their common environment. To this category belong folktales and legends. On the tragic side, we have amazing tales with a elegiac tone—the death of a hero or of a martyr saint, for example. Corresponding to this on the side of the listener is a special quality of fear and pity appropriate to such amazement. On the comic side, are marvelous tales with an idyllic tone—the pastoral or the western, for example. In the third column, that of high mimetic, the hero is superior to other people but not to their environment, as can be seen in the epic and in tragedy. On the tragic side, the poem celebrates the hero's fall. Here *catharsis* gets its specific note of pity and fear from the tragic *harmartia*. On the comic side, we find the old comedy of Aristophanes, to whose ridicule we respond with a mixture of sympathy and punitive laughter. In the fourth column, that of low mimetic, the hero is superior to neither his environment nor his fellow human beings. He is their equal. On the tragic side, we find the pathetic hero, isolated externally and internally, from the imposter or *alazon* to the "philosopher" obsessed with himself in the manner of Faust and Hamlet. On the comic side stands the new comedy of Menander, the erotic plot, based on fortuitous encounters and recognition scenes—the domestic comedy, the picaresque tale that tells of a knave's rise in society. Here is where we should put the realistic fiction described in the preceding section. Finally, in the fifth column, that of irony, the hero is inferior to us in strength and intelligence. We look down on him from above. To this mode also belongs the hero who pretends to be lower than he is in reality, who undertakes to say less in order to signify more. On the tragic side, we have a whole collection of models who respond in different ways to the vicissitudes of life with temperaments devoid of passion and who lend themselves to the study of tragic isolation as such. The range here is vast, running from the *pharmakos* or scapegoat, to the hero whose fault was inevitable (Adam in Genesis, K in Kafka's *The Trial*) to the innocent victim (Christ in the gospels and nearby, between the irony of the inevitable and the irony of the incongruous, Prometheus). On the side of comedy, we have the expelled *pharmakos* (Shylock, Tartuffe), punitive comedy which avoids becoming a lynching party only through the element of play, "the barrier that separates art from savagery" (p. 46), and all the parodies of tragic irony, whose resources are exploited in the murder mystery and in science fiction.

Two other theses correct the appearance of a taxonomical rigidity offered by this sort of classification. According to the first one, fiction, in the West, has ceaselessly shifted its center of gravity from above to below, that is, from the divine hero toward the hero of tragedy and ironic comedy, including the parody of tragic irony. This law of descent is not necessarily a law of decadence, if we consider its counterpart. First of all, as the sacred aspect of the first column and the marvelous aspect of the second column decrease, we see the mimetic tendency increase, first in the form of high mimetic, then of low mimetic, and the values of plausibility and of verisimilitude also increase (see pp. 51–52). We meet again here one of the important features of my preceding analysis of the relationship between convention and verisimilitude. What is more, thanks to the diminution of the hero's strength, the values of irony are liberated and given free reign. In one sense, this irony is potentially present as soon as there is any muthos in the broad sense of this term. That is, every muthos implies an "ironic retreat from reality" (p. 82). This explains the apparent ambiguity of the term "myth." In the sense of a sacred myth, the term designates stories of heroes superior to us in every way; in the sense of the Aristotelian muthos, it covers the whole realm of fiction. These two senses are tied together by irony. Hence the irony inherent in any muthos seems to be linked to the whole set of fictional modes. It is implicitly present in every muthos but only becomes a "distinct mode" with the decline of sacred myth. Only at this price does irony constitute a "terminal mode" following the law of descent referred to above. This first appended thesis thus introduces an orientation to the taxonomy.

According to the second thesis, irony, in one way or another, moves back toward myth (see pp. 42–43, 48–49). Frye is anxious to catch sight of some indication, at the bottom of the scale of ironic comedy, across the irony of the *pharmakos*—whether it be the irony of the inevitable or the irony of the incongruous—of a return toward myth underlying those specimens of what he calls "ironic myth."

This orientation of the taxonomy, following from the first thesis, along with its circularity, owing to the second thesis, defines the style of European or Western traditionality for Northrop Frye. In fact, these two rules for reading would appear to be entirely arbitrary if the theory of modes did not find its hermeneutic key in the theory of symbols that informs the other three essays of *Anatomy of Criticism*.

A literary symbol, in essence, is a "hypothetical verbal structure" (p. 71)— in other words, it is an assumption, not an assertion—in which the orientation "toward the inside" is more important than the orientation "toward the outside," which has to do with signs having an extroverted and realist vocation.[18]

So understood, the symbol provides a hermeneutic key for the interpretation of the line of fictional modes. When set in the appropriate literary contexts, symbols, in effect, pass through a series of "phases," comparable to the four senses of medieval biblical exegesis, which have been so magnificently reconstructed for us by Henri De Lubac.[19]

The first phase, called the literal one, corresponds to the first sense in this biblical hermeneutics. It is defined by our taking the hypothetical character of the poetic structure seriously. To understand a poem literally is to understand everything that constitutes it "as it stands" (p. 77). It is to interest ourselves in the unity of its structure, to read it as a poem. In this respect, the realistic novel is the form that best satisfies the criteria of the literal phase of the symbol.

With the second phase, called the formal one, which recalls the allegorical sense of medieval exegesis, the poem gets a structure from its imitation of nature, without losing anything of its hypothetical quality. From nature, the symbol draws an imagery that places all of literature in an oblique, indirect relationship with nature, thanks to which it can be not only pleasing but instructive.[20]

The third phase is that of the "symbol as archetype" (p. 95). We should not rush to denounce the latent "Jungianism" of the archetypal criticism proper to this stage. What is first emphasized by this term is the recurrence of the same verbal forms, stemming from the eminently communicable aspect of poetic art, which others have designated with the term "intertextuality." It is this recurrence that contributes to the unification and integration of our literary experience.[21] In this sense, I see in Frye's concept of an archetype an equivalent of what I have called the schematism issuing from the sedimentation of tradition. What is more, the archetype integrates into this stable conventional order the imitation of nature that characterizes the second stage. This imitation brings along its own recurrences: day and night, the four seasons, life and death. To see the order of nature as imitated by a corresponding order of words is a perfectly legitimate enterprise, if we know how to construct it on the basis of the mimetic conception that is itself built upon the hypothetical conception of the symbol.[22]

The final phase of the symbol is the one where the symbol is a "monad." This phase corresponds to the anagogical sense of medieval biblical exegesis. By a monad, Frye means imaginative experience's capacity to attain totality in terms of some center. There can be no doubt that Northrop Frye's whole enterprise hangs on the thesis that the archetypal order finally refers to a "still center of the order of words" (p. 117). Our whole literary experience points toward it. In any case, we would misconceive the whole point of archetypal criticism, and even more so of anagogical criticism, if we saw in it some kind of will to mastery, as in rationalizing reconstructions. On the contrary, the schemata arising out of these two phases testify to an order we cannot master in its cyclical composition. In fact, the imagery whose secret order we seek to discern—for example, that of the four seasons—is dominated from above by the apocalyptic imagery that, in forms difficult to enumerate, turns upon the idea of reconciliation in unity—the unity of a one yet triune God, the unity of humanity, the unity of the animal world in the symbol of the lamb, of the vegetative world in the symbol of the tree of life, of the mineral world in the symbol of the heavenly city. Furthermore, this symbolism has its demonic side in the figures of Satan, the tyrant, the monster, the barren fig tree, and the "primitive sea," the symbol of "chaos." And finally, this polar structure is itself unified by the strength of the desire that configures both the infinitely desirable and its contrary, the infinitely detestable, at the same time. From an archetypal and an anagogical perspective, all imagery is inadequate in relation to this apocalyptic imagery of fulfillment and yet at the same time is in search for it.[23] The symbol of the apocalypse can polarize the literary imitations of the cycle of the seasons because, with the tie to the natural order cut, this order can only be imitated, so that it then becomes an immense storehouse of images. Literature as a whole may thus be globally characterized as a quest, in the romantic modes, the high and low mimetic modes, as well as in the ironic mode represented by satire.[24] And it is as a quest that our whole literary experience is in relation to this "still center of words." [25]

For Frye, the progression from the hypothetical toward the anagogical is a never completed approximation of literature as a system. It is this telos, in return, that makes plausible an archetypal order that configures the imaginary and finally organizes the hypothetical into a system. In a sense, this was Blake's dream and even more so that of Mallarmé who said, "Tout au monde existe pour aboutir à un livre." [26]

At the end of this review of one of the more powerful attempts to recapitulate the literary tradition of the West, the philosopher's task is not to discuss its execution but, accepting it as plausible, to reflect upon the conditions of possibility of such a passage from literary history to criticism and the anatomy of criticism.

There are three points relative to our inquiry about emplotment and time that merit emphasizing.

First, it is because cultures have produced works that may be related to one another in terms of family resemblances, which operate, in the case of the narrative modes, on the very level of emplotment, that a search for some order is possible. Next, this order may be assigned to the productive imagination for which it constitutes the schematism. Finally, as an order of the imaginary, it includes an irreducible temporal dimension, that of traditionality.

Each of these three points allows us to see in emplotment the correlate of a genuine narrative understanding that precedes, both in fact and by right, every reconstruction of narrating in terms of a second-order rationality.

DECLINE: AN END TO THE ART OF NARRATION?

We have come as far as possible with the idea that the schematism ruling the narrative understanding unfolds in a history that maintains a single style. We need now to consider the opposite idea: does this schematism allow for deviations that, today, make this style differ from itself to such an extent that its identity is no longer recognizable? Must we include within the style of the traditionality of narrative the possibility of its dying out?

One aspect of the very idea of traditionality—that is, of the epistemological aspect of "making a tradition"—is that identity and difference are inextricably mixed together in it. The identity of style is not the identity of an achronic logical structure. Rather it characterizes the schematism of the narrative understanding, such as it becomes constituted through a cumulative and sedimented history. This is why this identity is transhistorical rather than atemporal. It thus becomes possible to conceive how the paradigms set up by the self-configurating of this tradition could have engendered and still continue to engender variations that threaten its identity of style to the point of announcing its death.

In this regard, the problems posed by the art of ending a narrative work may serve as an excellent touchstone. Because the paradigms of composition in Western tradition are at the same time paradigms of endings, we may anticipate that the eventual exhaustion of these paradigms may be seen in the difficulty of concluding a narrative. Linking these two problems together is all the more justified by the fact that the one formal feature of the Aristotelian notion of muthos that has to be preserved, beyond its successive instantiations in genres (for example, tragedy or the novel) and types (for example, Elizabethan tragedy or the nineteenth-century novel) is the criterion of unity and completeness. Muthos, we recall, is "an imitation of an action that is whole and complete in itself" (*Poetics*, 50b23–25).[27] And an action is whole and complete if it has a beginning, a middle, and an end; that is, if the beginning introduces the middle, if the middle with its reversals and recognition scenes leads to the end, and if the end concludes the middle. Then the configuration wins out over the episodic form, concordance overcomes discordance. Hence it is legitimate to take as a symptom of the end of the paradigmatic tradition of emplotment the abandonment of the criterion of completeness and therefore the deliberate choice not to end a work.

It is important at the beginning to be clear about the nature of the problem and not to confuse two questions, the first of which stems from mimesis$_2$ (configuration) and the second from mimesis$_3$ (refiguration). In this regard, a work may be closed with respect to its configuration and open with respect to the breakthrough it is capable of effecting on the reader's world. Reading, I shall say in Part IV, is precisely the act that brings about the transition between the effect of closure for the first perspective and the effect of openness for the second. To the extent that every work does something, it adds something to the world which was not there previously. But the pure excess we may attribute to the work as an act, its power of interrupting repetition, as Roland Barthes puts it, in his "Introduction to the Structural Analysis of Narrative," does not contradict the need for closure. "Crucial" endings are perhaps the ones that best combine these two effects.[28] So it is not a paradox to say that a well-closed fiction opens an abyss in our world, that is, in our symbolic apprehension of the world.

Before we turn to the magisterial work of Frank Kermode, *The Sense of an Ending*, it will be useful to say a few words about the perhaps insurmountable difficulties that confront any inquiry into a criterion of poetic closure.

Some authors—for example, J. Hillis Miller—take this problem to be undecidable.[29] Others, such as Barbara Herrnstein Smith, have sought help in the solutions proposed for the problem of closure in the adjoining region of lyric poetry.[30] There the rules for closure are easier to identify and to describe. Such is the case for the endings with a gnomic, sententious, or an epigrammatic aspect. What is more, the evolution of the lyric poem from the Renaissance sonnet to the free verse and the visual poem of today, by way of the Romantic poem, allows us to follow with precision the fate of these rules. And finally, the technical solutions brought by lyric poetry to the problem of closure can be related to the reader's expectations created by the poem, expectations for which the closure brings about a "sense of finality, stability, and integrity" (*Poetic Closure*, p. viii). The ending has this effect only if the experience of configuration is not just dynamic and continuous but also capable of retrospective rearrangements that make the resolution itself appear as the final approbation that seals a good form.

Yet however illuminating this parallel between poetic closure and the law of a good form may be, it reaches its limit in the fact that in the case of poetic closure the configuration is a work of language, and from the fact that the feeling of completion may be obtained by very different means. It follows that the completion itself admits of many different forms, including surprise—and it is difficult to say just when an unexpected ending justifies itself. Even a disappointing ending may be appropriate to the structure of a work, if it is intended to leave the reader with residual expectations. It is equally difficult to say in which cases the deception is required by the very structure of the work rather than just being a "weak" ending.

Transposed to the narrative plane, the lyric model suggests the need for a careful study of the relation between the way of ending a narrative and the degree of integration as regards the more or less episodic aspect of the action, the unity of the characters, the argumentative structure, and what below I shall call the strategy of persuasion that constitutes the rhetoric of fiction. The evolution of lyric closure also has its parallel in narrative closure. From the tightly knit adventure novel to the systematically fragmented one, the structural principle goes through a complete cycle that, in a way, leads back, in a very subtle manner, to the episodic form. The resolutions called for by these structural changes are consequently very difficult to identify and to classify. One difficulty stems from the always possible confusion of the end of the imitated action and the end of the fiction as such. In the tradition of the realistic novel, the end of the work tended to be confused with the end of the represented action. It thus tended to simulate the coming to rest of the system of interactions that formed the framework of the story. This was the sort of ending that most novelists of the nineteenth century sought. So it is relatively easy, in confronting the problem of composition and its solution, in these cases, to say if the end succeeds or not. But this is no longer the case once the literary artifice, by virtue of the reflexivity I spoke of above, turns back upon its fictive aspect. The ending of the work is then the ending of the fictive operation itself. This reversal of perspective characterizes contemporary literature. Here the criterion of a good closure is much more difficult to manage, especially when it has to agree with the tone of irresolution of the work as a whole.

Finally, the satisfaction of the expectations created by the dynamism of the work takes on, here too, varying, if not opposed, forms. An unexpected conclusion may frustrate our expectations modeled on older conventions but reveal a more profound principle of order. And if every closure responds to expectations, it does not necessarily fulfill them. It may leave behind residual expectations. An inconclusive ending suits a work that raises by design a problem the author considers to be unsolvable. It is nonetheless a deliberate and a concerted ending, which sets in relief in a reflexive way the interminable character of the theme of the whole work. Its inconclusiveness declares in a way the irresolution of the problem posed.[31] However I am in agreement with Barbara Herrnstein Smith when she says that "anticlosure" reaches a threshold beyond which we are confronted with the alternative: either exclude the work from the domain of art or give up the most basic presupposition of poetry, that it is an imitation of the nonliterary uses of language, which include the ordinary use of narrative as a means to arrange systematically what happens in life.[32] In my opinion we must choose the first alternative. Beyond every possible suspicion, we must have confidence in the powerful institution of language. This is a wager that brings its own justification.

It is this alternative—and, in the strict sense of the word, this question of confidence—that Frank Kermode treats in his excellent book *The Sense of an Ending*.[33] Without seeking to do so, he takes up the problem again where Northrop Frye left it when he related the desire for a completeness of discourse to the apocalyptic theme, considered on the anagogical level. It is also beginning with the avatars of the apocalyptic theme that Kermode undertakes to contribute to the discussion of the art of closure, concerning which literary criticism has much difficulty reaching any agreement. However the framework now is that of a theory of fiction quite different from Frye's theory of the symbol and the archetype.

Admitting that it is the reader's specific expectations that govern our need to give a meaningful end to a poetic work, Kermode turns toward the myth of the

Apocalypse, which in the traditions of the West has most contributed to structuring these expectations, by giving the term "fiction" a range that overflows the domain of literary fiction. It is a term that is theological by way of Judeo-Christian eschatology, historical-political by way of the strong imperial ideology that continued up to the fall of the Holy Roman/Germanic Empire, epistemological by way of the theory of models, and literary by way of the theory of the plot. At first sight, this set of reapprochements seems incongruous. Is not the Apocalypse a model of the world, while Aristotle's *Poetics* proposes only the model of a verbal work? The passage from one plane to the other, in particular from a cosmic stance to a poetic one, nevertheless finds some justification in the fact that the idea of the end of the world comes to us by means of the text that, in the biblical canon received in the Christian West, at least, concludes the Bible. Apocalypse can thus signify both the end of the world and the end of the book at the same time. This congruence between the world and the book extends even further. The beginning of the book is about the beginning and the end of the book is about the end. In this sense, the Bible is the grandiose plot of the history of the world, and each literary plot is a sort of miniature version of the great plot that joins Apocalypse and Genesis. In this way, the eschatological myth and the Aristotelian muthos are joined together in their way of tying a beginning to an ending and proposing to the imagination the triumph of concordance over discordance. It is not so out of place, therefore, to link the Aristotelian peripeteia to the torments of the last days in the Apocalypse.

It is precisely at this intersection of discordance and concordance that the transformations of the eschatological myth may clarify our problem of poetic closure. Let us note, in the first place, the remarkable power that the apocalyptic has long illustrated of surviving every denial in terms of how events have turned out. The Apocalypse, in this respect, offers the model of a prediction that is continually invalidated without ever being discredited, hence of an end that is itself constantly put off. Moreover, and by implication, the invalidation of the prediction concerning the end of the world has given rise to a truly qualitative transformation of the apocalyptic model. From being imminent, it has become immanent. The Apocalypse, therefore, shifts its imagery from the last days, the days of terror, of decadence, of renovation, to become a myth of crisis.

This radical transformation of the apocalyptic paradigm has its equivalent in the crisis that affects literary composition. And this crisis takes place on the two levels of the closure of a work and of the wearing out of the paradigm of concordance.

Kermode sees anticipatory signs in Elizabethan tragedy of this substitution of crisis, now become an indefinitely extended peripeteia, for the imminent end. This form of tragedy seems to him to have deeper attachments to Christian apocalyptic than to Aristotle's *Poetics*. Even if Shakespeare might still be taken as "the greatest creator of confidence" (p. 82), his tragedies testify to the moment when apocalypse turns from imminence to immanence. Tragedy "assumes the figurations of apocalypse, of death and judgment, heaven and hell; but the world goes forward in the hands of exhausted survivors" (ibid.). However the final restoration of order seems feeble in comparison with the terrors that precede it. It is indeed the time of crisis that bears the features of the quasi-eternal, which in the Apocalypse belong only to the end, that becomes the actual dramatic time.[34] In *King Lear*, for example, Lear's torment tends toward a continually postponed conclusion. Beyond the apparent worst, there is still worse, and the end is itself only an image of the horror of the time of crisis. *King Lear* is thus the tragedy of the sempiternal within the order of misfortune. And with *Macbeth*, peripeteia becomes a parody of prophetic ambiguity, "a play of prophecy" (p. 84). Here again the equivocal ravages time, as can be seen in those famous verses where the hero sees his decisions as coming together in the same juncture of time.[35] In this way, "the play of crisis" engenders a time of crisis that bears the marks of sempiternity, even if this eternity "between the acting of a dreadful thing and the first motion" is only a simulacrum of the eternal present and a usurpation of it. There is hardly need to recall how *Hamlet* too can be taken as "another play of protracted crisis" (p. 87).

This transition from Apocalypse to the Elizabethan tragedy points the way toward one part of the situation of contemporary culture and literature, the one where crisis replaces the end, where crisis becomes an endless transition.[36] The impossibility of concluding thus becomes a symptom of the invalidation of the paradigm itself. It is in the contemporary novel that we may best see the combination of these two themes: the decline of paradigms—hence the end of fiction; the impossibility of ending a poem—hence the ruin of the fiction of the end.[37]

This description of the contemporary situation, which is a well-known one, is less important than the judgment the critic can make concerning it in light of the fate of the Apocalypse. The fiction of the end, we have said, has continually been invalidated, and yet it has never been discredited. Is this also the fate of literary paradigms? Does crisis equally signify for us catastrophe and renovation? This is Kermode's deep conviction and it is one that I fully share.

Crisis does not indicate the absence of every end but the conversion of the imminent end into an immanent end.[38] We may not, according to Kermode, stretch the strategy of invalidation and of peripeteia to the point where the question of closure would lose all meaning. But, we may ask, what is an immanent end when the end is no longer an ending?

This question leads to a point of perplexity in Kermode's analysis, a point that we will not be able to go beyond if we consider just the *form* of a work, neglecting the reader's *expectations*. Here is where the paradigm of consonance takes refuge because here is where it originates. What seems unsurpassable in the last analysis is the reader's expectation that some form of consonance will finally prevail. This expectation implies that not everything will be a peripeteia, otherwise peripeteia itself becomes meaningless, and our expectation of order would be totally frustrated. If the work is to capture our interest as readers, the dissolution of the plot has to be understood as a signal to us to cooperate with the work, to shape the plot ourselves. We have to expect some form of order if we are to be deceived when we do not find it, and this deception can lead to a kind of satisfaction only if the reader, taking over from the author, makes the work what the author uses all his/her ingenuity not to make it. Frustration cannot be the last word. The reader's work of composition cannot be made completely impossible. This interplay of the expectation of deception and the work of bringing about order is not practical unless the conditions for its success are incorporated into the tacit or express contract the author makes with the reader. "I will distort this work, you give it shape—to your advantage." If this contract is itself not to be a deception, the author, far from abolishing every law of composition, has to introduce new conventions that are more complex, more subtle, more concealed, and more cunning than those of the traditional novel; in short, conventions derived from these forms by means of irony, parody, or derision. In this way the most audacious blows to our paradigmatic expectations do not get beyond the interplay of "rule-governed deformations" by means of which innovation has always been the reply to sedimentation. A leap beyond every paradigmatic expectation is impossible.

This impossibility is particularly striking as regards the treatment of time. Rejecting chronology is one thing, the refusal of any substitute principle of configuration is another. It is not conceivable that the narrative should have moved beyond all configuration. The time of a novel may break away from real time. In fact, this is the law for the beginning of any fiction. But it cannot help but be configured in terms of new norms of temporal organization that are still perceived as temporal by the reader, by means of new expectations regarding the time of fiction which I shall explore in Part IV. To believe that we are done with the time of fiction because we have overturned, disarticulated, reversed, telescoped, or reduplicated the temporal modalities the conventional paradigms of the novel have made familiar to us, is to believe that the only time conceivable is precisely chronological time. It is to doubt that fiction has its own resources for inventing temporal measurements proper to it. It is also to doubt that these resources encounter expectations in the reader concerning time that are infinitely more subtle than rectilinear succession.[39]

I agree, therefore, with Kermode's conclusion to his first study, which is confirmed by his fifth study: expectations whose import is comparable to those engendered by the Apocalypse persist even though they change and even though in changing they change their pertinence.

This conclusion is strikingly illuminating with regard to my own thesis about the style of the traditionality of our paradigms. Further, it provides a criterion for "a discrimination of modernisms" (p. 114). For the older form of modernism—that of Pound, Yeats, Wyndham Lewis, Eliot, and even Joyce (cf. Kermode's illuminating pages [pp. 113–14] devoted to Joyce)—the past remains a source of order, even when it is railed against and decried. For the newer form of modernism, which Kermode calls the schismatic form, order itself is what must be denied. Beckett illustrates this "shift towards schism." He is "the perverse theologian of a world which has suffered a Fall, experienced an Incarnation which changes all relations of past, present, and future, but which will not be redeemed" (p. 115). In this respect, he preserves an ironic and parodic tie to Christian paradigms, whose order, even when inverted through the author's irony, preserves its intelligibility, "and whatever preserves intelligibility is what prevents schism" (p. 116). "Schism is meaningless without reference to some prior condition; the absolutely New is simply unintelligible, even as novelty" (ibid.), for "novelty of itself implies the existence of what is not novel, a past" (p. 117). In this sense, "newness is a phenomenon that affects the whole of the past; nothing on its own can be new" (p. 120). Gombrich said it better than anyone: "The innocent eye sees nothing." [40]

These powerful maxims bring us to the threshold of what I will call the question of confidence. (Below we shall see there is no better way of phrasing it.) Why may we—must we—not go beyond every paradigm of order, however refined, convoluted, or labyrinthine it might be?

Kermode does not make the answer easy, inasmuch as his own conception of the relationship of literary fiction to the religious myth in apocalyptic thought runs the risk of undercutting the foundations of his confidence in the survival of the paradigms that govern the reader's expectation of closure. The passage from the imminent end to the immanent end is, in fact, for Kermode, the work of the "skepticism of the clerisy" opposed to naive belief in the reality of the expected end. The status of the immanent end, as a consequence, is that of a demythologized myth, in Rudolf Bultmann's sense, or, as I would put it, in the sense of a broken myth, following Paul Tillich. If we transfer to literature the fate of the eschatological myth, all fiction, including literary fiction, also receives thereby the function of being a broken myth. It certainly conserves a cosmic intention, as we saw in the work of Northrop Frye, but the belief that underlays it is corroded by the skepticism of the clerisy. The difference here between Frye and Kermode is total. Where Frye sees the orientation of the whole universe of discourse toward the still center of words, Kermode suspects, in a Nietzschean way, a need for consolation in the face of death that in one way or another makes fiction a form of trickery. [41] An insistent theme throughout Kermode's book is that the fictions of the end, in their various forms—theological, political, and literary—have to do with death as a mode of consolation. Whence the ambiguous and troubling tone—the *Unheimlich-keit* I would say—that gives *The Sense of an Ending* its fascination.[42]

A divorce is thus established between truthfulness and consolation. The result is that Kermode's book ceaselessly oscillates between the inescapable suspicion that fictions lie and deceive, to the extent that they console us,[43] and the equally invincible conviction that fictions are not simply arbitrary, inasmuch as they respond to a need over which we are not the masters, the need to impress the stamp of order upon the chaos of existence, of sense upon nonsense, of concordance upon discordance.[44]

This oscillation explains why Kermode responds to the hypothesis of schism, which after all is only the most extreme consequence of the skepticism of the clerisy with regard to every fiction of concordance, by a simple "and yet . . ." (p. 43). For example, having referred to what Oscar Wilde called "the decay of lying," he writes, "And yet, it is clear, this is an exaggerated statement of the case. The paradigms do survive, somehow. If there was a time when, in Stevens's words, 'the scene was set,' it must be allowed that it has not yet been finally and totally struck. The survival of the paradigms is as much our business as their erosion" (ibid.).

If Kermode finds himself in such an impasse, is it not because he has imprudently posed, and prematurely resolved, the problem of the relations between "fiction and reality" (a whole essay is devoted to this topic), instead of holding it in suspense, as I am attempting to do here, by isolating the problems of configuration in terms of mimesis$_2$ from the problems of refiguration in terms of mimesis$_3$. Northrop Frye seems to me to have been much more prudent in his statement of the problem, in according the apocalyptic myth only a literary status, without passing judgment about the religious significance it may bear from the eschatological perspective of a history of salvation. At first, Frye seems more dogmatic than Kermode with his definition of the eschatological myth as a "still center." In the end, he turns out to be more reserved than Kermode in that he does not allow literature and religion to become mixed or confused with each other. It is on the hypothetical order of symbols, we saw, that their analogical assemblage is constructed. For Kermode, the constant contamination of literary fiction by the broken myth gives his book both its force and its weakness—its force from the scope given to the realm of fiction, its weakness due to the conflict between confidence in the paradigms and the skepticism of the clerisy, which the linking together of fiction and broken myth entails. As for his solution, which I said is premature, this is so in the sense that it leaves no other perspective for the effort to give meaning to life than that recommended by Nietzsche in *The Birth of Tragedy*, namely, the necessity of throwing an Apollonian veil over the Dionysian fascination for chaos, if we are not to die for having dared to contemplate pure nothingness. It seems legitimate to me, at this stage of our meditation, to hold in reserve other possible relationships between the fiction and the reality of human acting and suffering than that of consolation reduced to a vital lie. Transfiguration, as well as defiguration; transformation, as well as revelation, also have their right to be preserved.

If therefore we confine ourselves to speaking of the apocalyptic myth only in terms of literary fiction, it is necessary to find other roots for the need for the configuration of narrative than the horror of the unformed. For my part, I hold that the search for concordance is part of the unavoidable assumptions of discourse and of communication.[45] Either discourse or violence, Eric Weil has said in his *Logique de la Philosophie*.[46] The universal pragmatics of discourse says what amounts to the same thing. Intelligibility always precedes itself and justifies itself.

Having said this, one may always refuse the possibility of coherent discourse. This too we can read in Weil's work. Applied to the sphere of narrative, this refusal signifies the death of every narrative paradigm, the death of narrative.

It is this possibility that Walter Benjamin refers to with such awe in his well-known essay "The Storyteller."[47] Perhaps we are at the end of an era where narrating no longer has a place, he says, because human beings no longer have any experience to share. And he sees in the rule of advertising the sign of this retreat of narrative, a retreat without return.

Perhaps, indeed, we are the witnesses—and the artisans—of a certain death, that of the art of telling stories, from which proceeds the art of narrating in all its forms. Perhaps the novel too is in the process of dying as a form of narration. Nothing, in fact, prevents our excluding the possibility the cumulative experience that, at least in the cultural space of the West, provided a historically identifiable style might be dying today. The paradigms that were spoken of heretofore are themselves only the sedimented deposits of a tradition. Nothing, therefore, excludes the possibility that the metamorphosis of the plot will encounter somewhere a boundary beyond which we can no longer recognize the formal principle of temporal configuration that makes a story a whole and complete story. And yet . . . and yet. Perhaps, in spite of everything, it is necessary to have confidence in the call for concordance that today still structures the expectations of readers and to believe that new narrative forms, which we do not yet know how to name, are already being born, which will bear witness to the fact that the narrative function can still be metamorphosed, but not so as to die.[48] For we have no idea of what a culture would be where no one any longer knew what it meant to narrate things.

2

The Semiotic Constraints on Narrativity

The confrontation between narrative understanding, stemming from an unbroken familiarity with the modes of emplotment throughout history, and the rationality claimed by narrative semiotics was placed under the sign of a "deepening" of the problem in my introductory remarks to this volume. By a deepening, I mean the search for "deep" structures whose manifestation would be the concrete narrative configurations on the surface of the narrative.

It is easy to see the reason for such an undertaking. The preceding analyses have set before us the paradoxes concerning the style of traditionality of the narrative function. If a certain perenniality may be claimed for these paradigms, this is by no means identical with the atemporality attributed to essences. Such perenniality remains instead caught up in the history of forms, genres, and types. The reference at the end of the previous chapter to an eventual death of the art of narration even revealed the precariousness whose shadow accompanies this perenniality of the narrative function, which is nevertheless present in the many different ethnic cultures identified by cultural anthropology.

What motivates semiotic inquiry, in the face of this instability of what endures, is essentially the ambition to ground this perenniality of the narrative function on rules not dependent upon history. In its eyes, the preceding inquiry must appear tainted by a thoroughgoing historicism. If, through its style of traditionality, the narrative function may claim some perenniality, this has to be based upon some achronological constraints. In short, it is necessary to pass from history to structure.

How? By a methodological revolution comparable to the one in the epistemology of history that tries to superimpose a logical type of rationality on the intelligibility that already lies in the production of narratives. This methodological revolution may be characterized in terms of three major features.

It is first of all a question of trying to approach as nearly as possible a purely deductive procedure, on the basis of a model constructed in an axiomatic manner. This choice finds its justification in the fact that we are confronted with an almost uncountable variety of narrative expressions (oral, written, drawn, acted) and of classes of narrative (myths, folklore, fables, novels, epics, tragedies, dramas, films, comic strips, to say nothing of history, painting, and conversation). This situation renders any inductive approach impractical. Only the deductive way is left; that is, the construction of a hypothetical model of description from which at least some of the fundamental subclasses ought be derivable.[1]

And in what discipline having to do with the facts of language is this ideal of rationality best satisfied, if not in linguistics? The second characteristic of narrative semiotics, therefore, will be to construct its models as closely as possible on the basis of the one used in linguistics. This rather broad formulation allows us to embrace very different efforts, the most radical of which undertake to derive the structural values of units longer than a sentence, starting from structures of language at an even lower level than the sentence. What linguistics proposes here may be summed up in the following way. It is always possible in any given language to separate the code from the message, or, to speak as Saussure does, to isolate *langue* from *parole*. The code, or *langue*, is what is systematic. And to say that *langue* is systematic is also to admit that its synchronic—that is, its simultaneous—aspect can be isolated from its diachronic or successive and historical aspect. As for its systematic organization, it can in turn be mastered if it is possible to reduce it to a finite number of basic differential units, the system's signs, and to establish the set of combinatory rules that give rise to all its internal relations. Under these conditions, a structure may be defined as a closed set of internal relations between a finite number of units. The immanence of these relations—that is, the system's indifference to any extralinguistic reality—is an important corollary of this closure rule that characterizes a structure.

As is well known, these structural principles were first applied with great success to phonology, then to lexical semantics and syntactical rules. The structural analysis of narrative can be considered as one of the many attempts to extend or to transpose this model to linguistic entities above the level of the sentence, the sentence being the last entity dealt with by linguistics. Beyond the sentence we find *discourse* in the strict sense of the word, that is, a succession of sentences presenting their own rules of composition. (For a long time it was one of the tasks of classical rhetoric to deal with this ordered aspect of discourse.) Narrative, as we just said, is one of the broadest classes of discourse, that is, of sequences of sentences put in a certain order.

Now, the extending of the structural principles of linguistics may signify diverse kinds of derivations stretching from vague analogy to strict homology. It was this latter possibility that was defended by Roland Barthes during the period of his "Introduction to the Structural Analysis of Narrative." A "narrative is a long sentence, just as every constative sentence is in a way the rough outline of a short narrative" (p. 256). Taking this idea to its limits, he even declared, "nor does the homology suggested here have merely a heuristic value: it implies an identity between language and literature" (p. 257).

A third general characteristic, which has immense implications in the case of narrative, runs as follows. Among the structural properties of a linguistic system, the most important is its organic character. By this we are to understand the priority of the whole over the parts, and the hierarchy of levels that results from it. It should be observed at this point that French structuralists have attached more importance to this integrative capacity of linguistic systems than have the upholders of purely distributional models in American structuralism. "Whatever the number of levels we propose, and whatever definition we give them, it may not be doubted that a narrative is a hierarchy of instances." [2]

This third characteristic is by far the most important one. It corresponds exactly to what I have described on the level of narrative understanding as the configurating operation. This is what semiotics will try to reconstruct with the hierarchizing and integrating resources of a logical model. Following Todorov, one may distinguish the level of the story (which itself includes two levels of integration, that of the actions with its logic and that of the characters with its syntax) and the level of the discourse, which includes the tenses, the aspects, and the modes of the narrative. [3] Or one may follow Barthes and speak of "functions" (that is, segments of action formalized à la Propp and Bremond), [4] then of actions, and actants (as Greimas also does). Or even, with Todorov again, one may separate out the level of "narration," where the narrative is what is at stake in an exchange between a sender and a receiver of the narrative. In all these cases, narrative is said to present the same combination as does language between the two fundamental processes of articulation and integration, form and meaning. [5]

Essentially, it is this conjunction of articulation and integration that I am going to explore in the following pages, on the basis of this methodological revolution which ends up by eliminating history to the profit of structure. The guideline for this inquiry will be the progress semiotics has made in reconstructing both the articulated and integrated character of emplotment on a level of rationality where the relationship between form and meaning is disconnected from any reference to the narrative tradition. The substitution of achronological constraints for the style of traditionality of the narrative function will be the touchstone for this reconstruction. Narrative semiotics will have better satisfied its three major characteristics when it has succeeded, in Barthes' words, in "dechronologizing" and "relogicizing" narrative. [6] It will try to do so by subordinating every syntagmatic (and therefore temporal) aspect of narrative to a corresponding paradigmatic (and therefore achronological) aspect. [7]

To comprehend what is at stake in the debate begun by this extension of linguistics to narrative semiotics, we have to take into account the revolution that the strategic change of level it brings about constitutes. We cannot over-emphasize the transformation that structural analysis implies in the very object under study, once it is transferred from phonology or lexical semantics to narratives such as myths, tales, and heroic stories. In its application to units smaller than the sentence—from the phoneme to the moneme and lexeme—it does not deal with objects already caught up in frameworks that are symbolically elaborated. It does not enter into competition therefore with any other form of practice where its object of study would already count as a distinct cultural object.[8] Fictional narrative, on the other hand, has already, as a narrative, been made the object of both a practice and a form of understanding before semiotics comes on the scene. In this regard, the situation here is the same as in history, where inquiry of a scientific character and ambition was preceded by legends and chronicles. This is why a comparison can be made between the signification that may attach to semiotic rationality in relation to narrative understanding and the outcome assigned to the covering law model in historiography in Part II in volume 1. What is at stake in the discussion in narratology concerns, in fact, and in a similar manner, the degree of autonomy that should be accorded to the process of logicization and dechronologization in relation to understanding the plot and the time of the plot.

As for the logicization, the question is whether a solution similar to that proposed for historiography may also hold for narratology. My thesis, it will be recalled, was that nomological explanation cannot be substituted for narrative understanding but only interpolated, in light of the adage: to explain more is to understand better. And if nomological explanation may not be substituted for narrative understanding, this is because, I said, it borrows from this understanding those features that preserve the irreducibly historical character of history. Must we also say then that semiotics, whose right to exist is not in question, only conserves its narrative aspect insofar as it borrows from our prior understanding of narrative, whose scope was seen in the preceding chapter?

As for dechronologization, which is the reverse side of this logicization, it once again fundamentally calls into question the relationship between time and fiction.[9] It is no longer just a matter of the historicity of the narrative function (as it was in the preceding chapter), what I called its style of traditionality, but of the diachronic character of the story that is narrated in its relationship to the synchronic (or rather, achronic) dimension of the deep structures of narrativity. In this respect, the change in vocabulary concerning narrative time is not an innocent one. To speak of synchrony and diachrony is already to place ourselves within the fiefdom of that new rationality that rules over narrative understanding,[10] which so marvelously accommodates itself to both the Aristotelian and the Augustinian characterization of time as a discordant concordance. Logicization poses the same question as dechronologization: can the diachrony of a narrative be reinterpreted just using the resources of the grammar of the deep structures of semiotics? Or does it too depend upon the temporal structure of narrative, described in Part I, as a declared autonomy and an unspoken dependence, like the one I have attempted to establish between explanation and understanding on the level of historiography?

Propp's Morphology of the Folktale

Two reasons lead me to open this debate over the logicization and the dechronologization of narrative structures with Propp's *Morphology of the Folktale*.[11] First, it is on the basis of a morphology, that is, of "a description of the tale according to its component parts and the relationships of these components to each other and to the whole" (p. 19), that the project of logicization is set forth by the master of Russian formalism. This morphology openly links itself with Linnaeus, which is to say with a taxonomic conception of structure, but also, more discretely, with Goethe, which is to say, with an organic conception of structure.[12] So we may already just on this basis ask whether the resistance of the organic point of view to the taxonomic one does not testify, within this morphology, to a principle of configuration not reducible to formalism. Second, the linear conception of the organization of the fairy tale proposed by Propp leaves his attempt only half-way to a complete dechronologization of the narrative structure. So we may also ask whether the reasons that prevented him from completely abolishing the chronological dimension of the fairy tale do not rejoin those that prevented the organic point of view from being absorbed into the taxonomic one, and hence prevented his morphology from satisfying a more radical demand for logicization.

Propp's morphology is essentially characterized by the primacy it gives to functions over characters. By a "function," he means segments of action, or more exactly, abstract forms of action such as abstention, interdiction, violation, reconnaissance, delivery, trickery, and complicity, to name the first seven of them. These same functions occur in all the fairy tales, in innumerable concrete guises, and they can be defined independently of the characters who accomplish these actions.

The first of the four basic theses stated at the beginning of this work defines quite clearly this primacy of the function in Propp's morphology: "Functions of characters serve as stable, constant elements in a tale, independent of how and by whom they are fulfilled. They constitute the fundamental components of a tale" (p. 21). In the commentary that follows this definition we can see the competition I have referred to between the organic and the taxonomic points of view break out. A function "is understood as an act of a character, defined from the point of view of its significance for the course of the action" (ibid.). This reference to the plot—"the course of the action"—as a teleological whole corrects in advance the purely additive conception of the relations between functions within the fairy tale.

33

However it is this latter conception that is progressively affirmed in the theses that follow. Here is the second of them: "The number of functions known to the fairy tale is limited" (ibid.). Here we touch upon a postulate common to all the formalists. Appearances are innumerable but the basic components are finite in number. Leaving aside the question of the characters, which we shall see below are quite limited in number (Propp reduces them to seven), it is to the functions that he applies this principle of finite enumeration. Only a high degree of abstraction in the definition of the functions allows him to reduce their number to slightly more than two dozen, thirty-one to be exact.[13] Here our initial question reappears in a new form: what is the principle of closure for the series? Does it have something to do with what has been called the plot or with some other factor of integration of a serial nature?

The third thesis clearly decides this question in favor of the second interpretation: "The sequence of functions is always identical" (p. 22). The identity of the succession gives the identity of the fairy tale. It is true that this thesis marks the irreducible place of chronology in Propp's model, and that it is this aspect of his model that will divide his successors. Some, the ones closest to him, will preserve a chronological element in their model; others, following the example of Lévi-Strauss, will seek to reduce the chronological aspects of narrative to an underlying combinatory system, as free as possible of any chronological aspect. However, if due to its third thesis Propp's model remains, as I have said, only half-way along the road of the dechronologicization and relogicization of narrative, we must immediately emphasize that the temporality preserved on the level of this model remains precisely a chronology, in the sense of a regular succession. Propp never asks in what time his functions succeed one another. He is only interested in the absence of arbitrariness in the sequence. This is why the axiom of succession is immediately taken as an axiom of order. An identical succession suffices to ground the identity of the fairy tale.

The fourth thesis completes this third one by affirming that all the Russian fairy tales, in presenting the same functions in the same order, constitute but one and the same fairy tale. "All the functions known to the tale will arrange themselves within a *single* tale" (p. 22, his emphasis). Consequently, "all fairy tales are of one type in regard to their structure" (p. 23). In this sense, every Russian fairy tale in the collection Propp works with is only a variant of a single fairy tale, which is a unique entity made from the succession of functions that are themselves generic in essence. The series of thirty-one functions merits being called the archetype of the fairy tale for which all these fairy tales are variants. This last thesis will authorize Propp's successors to oppose structure and form. The form is that of the single story underlying all the variants; the structure will be a combinatory system much more independent of plot in comparison with the cultural configuration particular to the Russian fairy tale.[14]

Propp's four theses each pose in their own way the question of the persistence of the organic thought inherited from Goethe in the taxonomic discourse received from Linnaeus. The same question recurs whether it be a matter of the circular relation between the definition of the functions and the unfolding of the plot they contribute to (as in thesis 1); the closure principle for the enumerating of the functions (as in thesis 2); the kind of necessity presiding over their interconnection (as in thesis 3); or finally the status of the archetype, which is singular and typical at the same time, to which the unique sequence of thirty-one functions reduces (as in thesis 4).

The detailed demonstration that follows the stating of these theses clearly makes this latent conflict between a more teleological concept of the order of the functions and a more mechanical concept of their interconnection stand out.

First of all, it is surprising that beginning with "some sort of initial situation" (p. 25) is not counted as a function, even though "it nevertheless is an important morphological element" (ibid.). Which one? Precisely the one that opens the narrative. This opening, which corresponds to what Aristotle calls the "beginning," can only be defined teleologically, in relation to the plot considered as a whole. This is why Propp does not count it in his enumeration of functions arising out of a strict principle of linear segmentation.

Next we may observe that the first seven functions, as listed above, are both identified individually and defined as forming a subset, "the *preparatory part* of the tale" (p. 31, his emphasis). Taken as a set, these functions introduce the villainy or its equivalent, a lack. This new function is not just one more function, "since by means of it the actual movement of the tale is created" (ibid.). It corresponds exactly to what Aristotle calls the complication (*desis*) of the plot that calls for its denouement (*lusis*). "Therefore the first seven functions may be regarded as the *preparatory part* of the tale, whereas the complication [of the plot] is begun by the act of villainy" (p. 31).

In this respect, then, the villainy (or lack) constitutes the pivot point of the plot considered as a whole. The considerable number of species of villainy—Propp lists nineteen!—suggests that the high degree of abstraction here depends not so much on the generic extension, which is broader than for the other functions, as on this function's key position at the turning point of the plot. And in this regard it is noteworthy that Propp does not propose a generic term inclusive of villainy and lack. What they do have in common is that they give rise to a quest. In relation to this quest, both villainy and lack have the same function: "In the first instance, a lack is created from without; in the second, it is realized from within. . . . This lack can be compared to a zero which, in a series of figures, represents a definite value" (p. 35). (So we ought not to think here of Claude Lévi-Strauss's "empty case" in his well-known "Introduction à l'oeuvre de Marcel Mauss.") The villainy (or lack) is in its way a beginning (p. 34), precisely that of the quest. This quest is not properly speaking any one of the functions but rather creates what was said above to be the "actual movement" of the tale. This notion of a quest is henceforth never absent. Propp goes so far as to extend to the subset of functions 8 to 11 (from the hero's entry to his departure) the power, already attributed to the villainy, of complicating the action. The elements of this subset, he notes, "represent the complication. Later on the course of action is developed" (ibid.). So this notation bears witness to the affinity between complication and quest in the interconnections among the functions. The following subset (11–14) (from the testing of the hero to his acquisition of a magical object) dramatizes his taking possession of a means to redress the initial wrong. The first function has a preparatory value, the last one that of an accomplishment, and numerous combinations are available for bringing them together, as may be seen in the chart Propp gives (p. 47), which anticipates the combinatory efforts of Greimas's first model.

The next functions, from some spacial transference to victory over the aggressor (15–18), also form a subset in that they lead to the liquidation of the initial misfortune or lack (19). Propp says of this function that it "constitutes a pair" with the initial misfortune or lack. "The narrative reaches its peak in this function" (p. 53). This is why the hero's return (20) is not noted by a letter but by a downward-pointing arrow (↓) corresponding to the departure designated by (↑). There is no better way of underscoring the prevalence of the principle of teleological unity over that of the segmentation and the simple succession of functions. Similarly, the next functions (20–26) only delay the denouement by introducing new dangers, new struggles, and new assistance, marked by the intervention of a false hero and the real hero's undertaking of a difficult task. These figures repeat the pattern of misfortune, complication, denouement. As for the last functions—recognition of the hero (27), exposure of the false hero (28), transfiguration of the hero (29), punishment of the false hero (30), and the hero's wedding (31)—they form a final subset that plays the role of a conclusion with regard to the plot taken as a whole and with regard to the complication: "At this point the tale draws to a close" (p. 64). But why is it necessary to end in this way? It is noteworthy that Propp speaks here of "logical and artistic necessity" to characterize the interconnections of the sequence. However, it is thanks to this double necessity that the "scheme" constituted by the unilinear sequence of thirty-one functions will play the role of "a measuring unit for individual tales" (p. 65).[15] But what confers a unity such as this on the sequence?

Part of the answer lies in the role played by the characters in the synthesis of the action. Propp distinguishes seven classes of them: the villain, the donor (or provider), the helper, the sought-for person, the dispatcher, the hero, and the false hero. It will be recalled that he began by dissociating the characters from the functions in order to define the fairy tale solely in terms of the sequence of these functions. However, no function can be defined unless it is attributed to some character. The reason for this is that the substantive terms that define the function (interdiction, misfortune, and so on) refer back to action verbs that always require an agent.[16] Furthermore, the way in which these characters are tied to the functions goes in the opposite direction of the segmentation that governs the distinguishing of the functions. The characters are related to groups of functions that constitute the *spheres of action* of their respective performers. This concept of a sphere of action introduces a new synthetic principle into the distribution of the functions: "many functions logically join together into certain spheres. These spheres in toto correspond to their respective performers. They are spheres of action" (p. 79). "The problem of the distribution of functions may be resolved on the plane of the problem concerning the distribution of the spheres of action among the characters" (p. 80). There are three possibilities: a sphere of action exactly corresponds to a character (the donor sends the hero), or one character occupies several spheres of action (three for the villain, two for the donor, five for the helper, six for the sought-for person, four for the hero, three for the false hero), or a single sphere of action is divided among several characters (for example, setting out on the quest brings into play the hero and the false hero).

Hence it is the characters who mediate the quest. That the hero suffers from the villain's action just at the moment that the plot thickens, that he agrees to undertake to repair the villainy or to fill the lack, that the donor provides the hero with the means to redress the wrong that has been done, in each of these cases it is the characters who preside over the unity of the subset of functions that allows the action to become more complicated and the quest to develop further. We might ask in this respect whether all emplotment does not really arise out of the mutual genesis of a character's development and the development of a story.[17] This is why it is not surprising that Propp also names, beyond functions and characters, other elements that bind the tale together, such as motivations and the way characters are introduced, along with their attributes or their accessories. "These five categories of elements define not only the construction of a tale, but the tale as a whole" (p. 96). But is it not the function of emplotment, derived from Aristotle's definition of muthos, to join together such diverse elements, such as those even more complex examples which historiography provided us with?

Propp's final considerations are applied to "the tale as a whole" (pp. 92–117) and confirm the competition we have seen throughout this work between the two conceptions of order I have placed under the aegis, respectively, of Goethe and Linnaeus. The tale is both a series (or, as Propp also calls it, a scheme) and a sequence. A series: "A fairy tale is a story built upon the proper alternation of the above-cited functions in various forms, with some of them absent from each story and with others repeated" (p. 99). A sequence: "Morphologically, a tale may be termed any development proceeding from villainy (A) or a lack (*a*), through intermediary functions to marriage (W*), or to other functions employed as a denouement. . . . This type of development is termed by us a *move* (*xod*). Each new act of villainy, each new lack creates a new move. One tale may have several moves, and when analyzing a text, one must first of all determine the number of moves of which it consists" (p. 92).[18] To my mind, this unit of the tale (the move), which gives rise to a new combinatory system, does not result from the segmentation into functions but rather precedes it.[19] It constitutes the teleological guide for distributing the functions along the sequential line and governs such subsets as preparatory section, complication, delay, and denouement. When related to this one impulse, the discontinuous segments of the sequence take on the roles of reversal and recognition in the tragic muthos. In short, they constitute the "middle" of the plot. And the narrative time is thus no longer the simple succession of segments external to one another but the extended duration between a beginning and an ending.

I do not conclude from this critical review that Propp's archetypal tale coincides with what I have been calling a plot. This archetype reconstructed by Propp is not a tale that is told by anyone to anyone. It is a product of a certain sort of analytic rationality. The fragmentation into functions, the generic defining of these functions, and their placement along a single axis in succession are operations that transform an initial cultural object into a scientific one. This transformation is obvious as soon as the algebraic rewriting of all the functions, by effacing any remaining names borrowed from ordinary language, leaves room only for a pure sequence of thirty-one juxtaposed signs. This sequence is no longer even an archetypal tale, for it is no longer a tale. It is a sequence, the linear track for a "move."

The rationality that produces this sequence, on the basis of the fragmentation of the initial cultural object, cannot be substituted for the narrative understanding inherent in the tale's production and reception because it continues to draw upon this understanding in constituting itself. No segmenting operation, no placing of functions in a sequence can do without some reference to the plot as a dynamic unity and to emplotment as a structuring operation. The resistance of an organic and teleological conception of order, in the Goethean style, to a taxonomic and mechanical conception of the interconnection of functions, in the style of Linnaeus, as I have indicated, appeared to me to be one symptom of this indirect reference to the plot. So despite the epistemological break made by narratological rationality, we can find between it and narrative understanding an indirect filiation comparable to the one I brought to light in Part II of this work between historiographical rationality and narrative understanding.[20]

FOR A LOGIC OF NARRATIVE

We can take a further step along the road toward logicization and dechronologization by beginning with the characters rather than the actions, and by formalizing in an appropriate fashion the roles that these characters are capable of taking in any narrative. Then a logic of narrative becomes conceivable, one that would begin with a systematic inventory of the *possible* principal narrative roles, that is, those capable of being assumed by some character in any narrative whatever. This is what Claude Bremond has attempted to do in his *Logique du récit*.[21] For us, the question here will be about the status given to the plot and its temporality in a logic of narrative grounded upon a choice opposite to Propp's.

In fact, the logical aim of the model proposed by Bremond stems from a critical reflection upon Propp's work.

Basically Bremond contests Propp's way of interconnecting the functions in his model. This interconnection, he thinks, is done in a rigid, mechanical, and constraining manner owing to a failure to make room for alternatives and choices (pp. 18–19). It is this constraint this explains why Propp's schema only applies to the Russian fairy tale, which is precisely that sequence of thirty-one identical functions. Propp's model is limited to ratifying the cultural choices that constituted the Russian fairy tale as one species in the field of "storytelling." To regain the formal intention of the model it is necessary to reopen the alternatives closed off by the one-way sequence of the Russian fairy tale and to substitute for its linear trajectory a map of possible itineraries.

But how can we reopen the closed-off alternatives? By calling into question, says Bremond, the teleological necessity that moves back from the ending toward the beginning—to punish the villain, the tale has him commit the villainy. The regressive necessity of a law of temporal finality blinds us, so to speak, to the alternatives that a progressive reading, on the contrary, encounters—struggle leads either to victory or to defeat, but the teleological model only recognizes victorious struggles (pp. 31–32). "That struggle is implied in victory is a logical requirement, that victory is implied by struggle is a cultural stereotype" (p. 25).

If we do not want to remain prisoners of a plot-type like Propp's series, we have to adopt as our basic unit what Bremond calls an "elementary sequence." It is shorter than Propp's sequence but longer than a function. If we are to narrate anything at all, it is both a necessary and a sufficient condition that some action be guided through three phases: a situation opening some possibility, the actualization of that possibility, the ending of this action. Each of these three moments opens an alternative (p. 131):

$$
\text{Possibility}
\begin{cases}
\text{Passage to the act}
\begin{cases}
\text{Completion} \\
\text{Noncompletion}
\end{cases} \\
\text{No passage to the act}
\end{cases}
$$

This series of dichotomous options satisfies the double character of retroactive necessity and progressive contingency.

39

Once the elementary sequence is chosen as the narrative unit, the problem is to pass from these elementary sequences to complex ones. Here logical necessity ends and the obligation arises to "restore their mobility and their maximum variability to the fixed syntagms that serve as the material of the Russian fairy tale" (p. 30).[22]

The notion of a "role" remains to be formulated before we can put together the vast repertory of possible roles that are to be substituted for the limited sequential schema, as found in Propp, that of a plot type. This reformulation proceeds from a reflection upon the very notion of a "function," which was the pivotal term in Propp's analysis. We recall Propp's initial basic thesis that functions are to be defined without taking into consideration the characters of the action, therefore in abstraction from any specific agent or passive sufferer. But, Bremond says, action is inseparable from the one who undergoes it or who does it. And he presents two arguments in favor of this assertion. A function expresses an interest or an initiative that brings into play a sufferer or an agent. Also, several functions become interconnected if the sequence concerns the story of a single character. It is necessary therefore to conjoin a subject-noun and a process-predicate into a single term, the role. Bremond thus defines a role as follows: "The attribution of some contingent, occurring, or occurred predicate-process to a subject-person" (p. 134). As we see, the elementary sequence is incorporated into the role through the intermediary predicate-process. Bremond's revision of Propp's model is complete. For the concept of a "sequence of actions," he substitutes that of an "organization of roles" (p. 133).

Here the logic, properly speaking, of narrative begins. It consists of "the systematic inventory of the *principal narrative roles*" (p. 134, his emphasis). This inventory is systematic in a twofold sense. First, because it gives rise to more and more complex roles, either by specifying them or by successive determinations, whose linguistic representation requires a more and more articulated form of discourse. Second, because it gives rise to groupings of roles by correlating them, often on a binary basis.

The first dichotomy opposes two types of roles: sufferers, affected by modifying or conserving processes, and, correlatively, the agents who initiate these processes (see p. 145). It is noteworthy that he begins with the roles of sufferers, taken as the most simple ones, and defined as follows. "We shall define as playing the role of a sufferer anyone whom the narrative presents as affected, in one way or another, by the course of narrated events" (p. 139). These roles of being a sufferer are not just the most simple ones but also the most numerous ones because a subject may be modified in other ways than through the initiative of an agent (see pp. 174–75).[23]

A new dichotomy allows us to distinguish two types of roles for sufferers, depending upon the way in which they are affected. On the one hand, we have those influences that affect the subjective awareness the subject has of his fate.

These include "information" (which governs the series: concealment, refutation, confirmation) and "affects" (satisfactions or dissatisfactions, governing, through the addition of a temporal variable, hope and fear). On the other hand, there are actions that objectively affect the sufferer's fate, either by modifying it (amelioration or deterioration) or by keeping it in the same state (protection or frustration).

The nomenclature for agents in part repeats that for sufferers: modifier or preserver, ameliorator or degrader, protector or frustrator. However one series of types of specific agents is tied to the notion of influence on the sufferer. Bremond's study of this group is certainly one of the more noteworthy contributions of the *Logique du récit* (see pp. 242–81). In the sufferer, an influence is addressed to the eventual agent for whom it will tend to set off some reaction. Persuasion and dissuasion, for example, operate on the level of information about what needs to be done, the means to be used, or obstacles to be surmounted, as well as on the feelings the influencer can excite or inhibit. If we add that information or an impulse can be well or poorly founded, we then arrive at some very important roles that center around the notion of a trap and which make the influencer a seducer and a deceiver, a dissimulator and a poor counselor.

This second dichotomy enriches the concept of a "role" in a number of ways. It introduces this concept, in the first place, into the field of "evaluations" by means of the concepts of amelioration or degradation and protection or frustration. In this way, the agent and the sufferer find themselves elevated to the rank of persons. Beyond this, a subjectivity capable of taking account of information and of being affected by it reaches a new field, that of "influences." Finally, the role of an agent capable of an initiative stems from a new field, that of "actions" in the strong sense of the term.

This inventory is completed by the addition of the concepts of esteem and disesteem, along with, on the side of the sufferer, the new roles of beneficiary of esteem and victim of disesteem, and, on the side of the agent, the roles having to do with the distribution of rewards and punishments. A new field is thereby opened for the exercising of roles, one added to the field of evaluations, influences, and actions—the field of "retributions."

Such, broadly speaking, is the schematism underlying this inventory aimed at defining the principal narrative roles. This inventory is equivalent to a nomenclature, a classing together of roles. In this sense, Bremond's enterprise keeps its promise. He does not present a table of plots, as does Northrop Frye, but a table of possible places occupied by the contingent characters of contingent narratives. In this sense, the inventory does constitute a "logic."

The question that arises at the end of this brief summary of the *Logique du récit* is whether a logic of roles succeeds any better than does a morphology of functions in formalizing the concept of narrative at a level of rationality above that of narrative understanding, without borrowing, more or less tacitly, from the concept of a plot the features that assure the properly narrative character of the supposed logic.

Compared to Propp's morphology of the fairy tale, the logic of roles undoubtedly reaches a higher degree of abstract formality. Whereas Propp confined himself to the schema of one plot type, that of the Russian fairy tale, Bremond can take credit for the fact that his nomenclature may be applied to the roles in every species of narrative message, including historical narration (cf. p. 7). His field of investigation is indeed that of possible narratives. Furthermore, the table of narrative roles does immediately attain a more complete dechronologization of narrative inasmuch as the nomenclature of roles is equivalent to filling in the paradigmatic table of principal roles capable of being assumed by any character in a narrative. Bremond's model can, indeed, claim these two titles: a more complete formalization and a more complete dechronologization.

However, we may wonder whether the absence of any syntagmatic consideration in the inventory of roles does not deprive the role of its properly narrative character. In fact, neither the concept of a role nor the nomenclature of roles as such has any narrative character, except by tacit reference to their situations in a narrative, which is never thematized in an explicit way. Lacking this setting within the plot, the logic of roles still stems from a semantics of action prior to a logic of narrative.

Let me make this argument more precise by following the order of exposition used above. We recall that the concept of a role was preceded by that of an "elementary sequence," which encounters the three stages that any action may go through, from contingency to occurrence to success. I agree that this sequence, by means of the alternatives and choices it opens, does constitute one condition of narrativity that is missing in Propp's model. But a condition of narrativity is not equivalent to a narrative component. It only becomes one if some plot traces out an itinerary made up of all the choices between the successive alternative branches. Bremond rightly says that the "process taken up by the elementary sequence is not amorphous. It already has its own structure, which is that of a vector" (p. 33). But is not this "vectoriality" which imposes itself upon a narrator who "takes hold of it to create the initial content of his narrative" (ibid.) borrowed from the plot, which transforms the logical conditions of "making something" into the actual logic of narrative? Is not the series of optional choices projected upon the logic of action by the conduct of the narrative?

It is true that Bremond completes his notion of an elementary sequence with that of a complex series, but under what condition do these series make up a narrative? To specify one sequence by another sequence, as in the case of enclosure, is not yet to make a narrative but rather a table for a logic of action, as in the analytic theory of action.[24] To make a narrative, that is, concretely to lead a situation and characters from some beginning to some ending, requires the mediation of what here is taken as a simple cultural archetype (Bremond, p. 35), which is nothing else than the plot. Making a plot is to extricate a "good form" both on the plane of sequence and on that of configuration.[25] Narrative, to me, introduces into doing anything supplementary constraints other than those of a logic of possible narratives. Or to say the same thing another way, a logic of possible narrative units is still only a logic of action. To become a logic of narrative it has to turn toward recognized cultural configurations, toward that schematism of narrative constituted by the plot-types handed down by tradition. Doing something becomes recountable only through this schematism. It is the function of a plot to bend the logic of *possible* acts toward a logic of *probable* narratives.

This doubt concerning the properly narrative status of the elementary sequence and complex series affects the very notion of a narrative role, which Bremond compares with Todorov's "narrative statement."[26] This is a good place to recall once again what Arthur Danto has said about narrative sentences. To have a narrative sentence, there must be two events mentioned, one that is referred to and one that provides the description in terms of which the first is considered. Hence it is only within a plot that a role is narrative. The linking of an action to an agent is the most general datum of a semantics of action, but it concerns the theory of narrative only to the extent that the semantics of action obviously conditions this theory.

As for the systematic inventory of principal roles, it has to do with the theory of narrativity to the extent that, in Bremond's own words, the roles listed in this way are ones "that can appear not just *in* a narrative, but *through* the narrative and *for* the narrative, in the sense that the appearance or the repression of a role, at some instant of the narration, is always left to the discretion of the narrator, who chooses whether to keep silent or to speak. *For the narrative*, in the sense that the definition of roles works in the narrative, as Propp wanted, 'from the point of view of its significance for the course of action'" (p. 134, his emphases). There is no better way to affirm the circular relationship between role and plot. Unfortunately, the systematic inventory of principal roles takes no account of it and is not, moreover, capable of replacing it.[27] What is missing is "the synthesis of the roles in the plot" (p. 322) for which Bremond only indicates the empty place. In fact, this synthesis does not come from the logic of narrative taken in the sense of a lexicon and syntax of roles, that is, of a grammar. The synthesis of the roles in the plot does not lie at the end of a combinatory system of roles. The plot is a movement. The roles are the places, the positions taken up in the course of the action. To know all the places capable of being assumed—to know all the roles—*is not yet to know any plot whatsoever.* A nomenclature, however ramified it may be, does not make a story. Chronology and configuration, muthos and dianoia, must also be brought into play. This operation, as Louis O. Mink has

observed, is an act of judgment, one arising from an act of "grasping together." Or to put it another way, plot stems from a *praxis* of narrating, hence
from a pragmatics of speaking, not from a grammar of *langue*. This pragmatics is presupposed by, but cannot be produced within, the framework of
the grammar of roles.[28]

The result of this effacing of the connection between the role and the plot
is that the "conceptual necessities immanent in the development of roles"
(p. 133) stem more from a semantics and a logic of action than from a true
logic of narrative. As we have seen, the progressive enrichment of the table of
roles, through the interplay of specifications and correlations that pass suc-
cessively from the field of evaluations to that of influences, then to that of
initiatives, and finally to that of retributions, is easily placed under the aegis
of a semantics of action borrowed from ordinary language.[29] However, the effacing of the connection between role and plot does not go so far as to abolish
it. Is it not the fit of roles to their emplotment that secretly orients the ordering
of the system of roles in terms of successive fields which they may enter into?
Is it not the narrative praxis at work in all emplotment that recruits, so to
speak, by way of the semantics of action, the predicates capable of defining
narrative roles due to the capacity of bringing the structures of human action
within the realm of narrative?

If this hypothesis is correct, the lexicon of narrative roles does not constitute a system prior to and higher than all emplotment. And the plot is not the
result of the combinatory properties of the system but rather of the selective
principle that makes the difference between the theory of action and that of
narrative.

THE NARRATIVE SEMIOTICS OF A.-J. GREIMAS

The narrative semiotics of A.-J. Greimas, which we find in his books *Du Sens*
and *Maupassant*, was preceded by an initial effort to formulate such a model
in his *Structural Semantics*, first published in 1966.[30] There we can already
see his ambition to construct a rigorously achronological model, along with
an attempt to derive the irreducibly diachronic aspects of narrative, such as
we relate them or receive them, through the introduction of appropriate transformation rules. This ambition governs his first strategic decision, the choice
to begin, not as Propp does with functions or segments of formalized actions,
which, as we have seen, obey a sequential order, but with the actors, who are
called "actants" in order to distinguish them from the concrete characters who
incarnate their roles. The advantage of this choice is twofold. As we have already seen in Propp's work, the list of actants is shorter than that of the functions—recall that the definition of the Russian fairy tale was that of a narrative with seven characters. Furthermore, the interactions of actants lend themselves directly to a paradigmatic representation rather than a syntagmatic one.

I shall discuss below how this actantial model is both radicalized and enriched by subsequent formulations of narrative semiotics. But, even in its initial stage, this model reveals the major difficulties of any achronic model as regards the treatment of *narrative time*.

The first thing the actantial model is intended to do is to ground the inventory of actantial roles, whose listing may appear to be purely contingent, on some universal characteristics of human action. And if we cannot proceed to an exhaustive description of the combinatory possibilities of human action on the surface level, then we must locate the deep principle of their construction in discourse itself. Here Greimas is following a suggestion from the French linguist Lucien Tesnières that the simplest sentence is already a miniature drama implying a process, actors, and circumstances. These three syntactical components give rise to the classes: verbs, nouns (those who take part in the process), and adverbs. And this basic structure makes the sentence "a drama which *homo loquens* produces for himself" (*Structural Semantics*, p. 198). There are many advantages to Tesnière's model. First, it is rooted in a structure of language. Next, it offers stability due to the permanence of the distribution of the roles among the syntactic components. Finally, it presents a kind of limitation and closure that fits well with systematic inquiry. It is tempting therefore to extrapolate to the syntax of discourse from this syntax of the elementary statement, thanks to the axiom of homology between language and literature we referred to above.

That the actantial model does not yet fully satisfy the systematic requirements of structuralism is betrayed, however, by the fact that the extrapolation from the syntax of the statement to that of discourse requires inventories of roles drawn by earlier analysts from diverse, empirically given collections—Propp's fairy tales and Etienne Souriau's 200,000 dramatic situations.[31] The actantial model thus stems from a mutual adjustment of a deductive approach, governed by syntax, and an inductive one, stemming from already established inventories of roles. Whence comes the composite character of the actantial model as a mixture of a systematic construct and various "arrangements of a practical order" (*Structural Semantics*, p. 198).

This mutual adjustment finds its equilibrium in a model with six roles resting on three pairs of actantial categories, each of which constitutes a binary opposition. The first category opposes subject and object. Its syntactic base lies in the form A *desires* B. Moreover, it finds support in the inventories consulted (the hero sets out in search of someone, as with Propp). The second category rests upon a relationship of *communication*. A sender is opposed to a receiver. Here again there is a syntactic basis. Every message ties together a transmitter and a receiver. In this way, we meet up again with Propp's donor (the king who charges the hero with a mission, etc.) and the receiver amalgamated to the hero. The third axis is *pragmatic*. It opposes the helper and the opponent. This axis blends with the relation of desire or with that of communication, either of which can be aided or hindered. Greimas grants that the syntactic basis is less evident in this case, although certain adverbs (willingly, nevertheless), circumstantial particles, or aspects of the verb in some languages take the place of this syntactic basis. In the world of fairy tales this pair is represented by the benevolent and malevolent forces. In short, the model combines three relations—of *desire, communication,* and *action*—each resting upon a binary opposition.

Whatever may be said about the laborious character of the elaboration of this model, it recommends itself through its simplicity and its elegance. What is more, unlike Propp's model, this one is distinguished by its capacity for being applied to micro-universes that are as diverse as they are heterogeneous. However, what the theoretician finds interesting is not these thematic instances of the model but the systems of relations among the various positions.

The fate of this model lies in the passage from characters to actions, or in more technical terms from actants to functions. It will be recalled that Propp halted at an inventory of thirty-one functions in terms of which he defined the spheres of action, of characters, and the characters themselves. In an actantial model, the enterprise that Greimas characterizes as one of "reduction" and "structuration" rests upon the transformation rules for the three relations of desire, communication, and action (see p. 223). Anticipating his second model, the one in *Du Sens*, he proposes to characterize all the transformations resulting from any one "semic" category as instances of conjunction and disjunction. In any corpus considered, the narrative on the syntagmatic level is taken as a process starting from the establishment of a contract that then proceeds to its breaking and its restoration. The reduction of this syntagmatic level to the paradigmatic one is obtained by assimilating the establishing of the contract to a conjunction between a mandate and its acceptance, the breaking of the contract to a disjunction between interdiction and violation, and the restoration of the contract to some new conjunction—the reception of the helper in the qualifying test, the liquidating of the lack in the principal test, and the recognition in the glorifying test. Within this general schema, numerous conjunctions and disjunctions can be introduced on the basis of the three basic relations of desire, communication, and action. But, overall, between the lack and its liquidation, there are only "identities to conjoin and oppositions to disjoin" (p. 226). The whole strategy thus amounts to a vast attempt to do away with diachrony.

However, in a purely actantial model, this strategy does not reach its goal. Instead it contributes to underlining the irreducible role of temporal development in narrative insofar as it sets into relief the concept of the test.[32] This notion constitutes the critical moment of narrative, characterized on the diachronic level as a quest. The test, in effect, brings into relation confrontation and success. But the passage from the former to the latter is perfectly aleatory. This is why the relationship of succession cannot be reduced to one of necessary implication.[33] And the same thing must be said as regards the pair mandate/acceptance, which launches the quest, and hence of the quest itself considered in terms of its unity.

The quest, for its part, gets it aleatory character from the highly axiological aspect introduced by the very concepts of a contract, violation, and restoration. As a negation of the acceptance, the violation is an axiological negation as much as it is a logical disjunction. Greimas himself sees one positive feature in this rupture of the contract: "the affirmation of the individual's freedom" (p. 423).[34] So the mediation that the narrative brings about as a quest cannot be simply a logical one. *The transformation of the terms and their relations is really a historical one.* The test, the quest, and the struggle may not therefore be reduced to the role of being the figurative expression of a logical transformation.[35] The latter is instead the ideal projection of an eminently temporalizing operation. In other words, the mediation realized by the narrative is essentially practical, either, as Greimas suggests, in that it aims at restoring a prior order that is threatened, or in that it aims at projecting a new order that would be the promise of salvation. Whether the story explains the existing order or projects another order, it posits, as a story, a limit to every purely logical reformulation of its narrative structure. It is in this sense that our narrative understanding, our understanding of the plot, precedes any reconstruction of the narrative on the basis of a logical syntax.

Our meditation on narrative time finds valuable enrichment here. From the moment that the diachronic element does not allow itself to be dealt with as a residue of the analysis, we may ask what temporal quality is concealed under the word "diachrony," whose dependence on the notions of synchrony and achrony I have already emphasized. In my opinion, the movement from the contract to the struggle, from alienation to the reestablishment of order, the movement constitutive of the quest, does not imply just a successive time, a chronology which it is always tempting to dechronologize and logicize, as we said above. The resistance of the diachronic element in a model whose vocation is essentially achronic seems to me to be the indication of a more basic kind of resistance, that of narrative temporality to simple chronology.[36] If chronology can be reduced to a surface effect, it is because the alleged surface has already been deprived of its own dialectic, namely, the competition between the sequential and the configurational dimensions of narrative, a competition that makes narrative a successive whole or whole succession. And even more fundamentally, the rift between the contract and the struggle, underlying this dialectic, reveals that aspect of time that Augustine, following Plotinus, characterized as a distension of the mind. We ought not therefore to continue to speak of time but of temporalization. This distension is, in fact, a temporal process that is expressed through the delays, the detours, the suspense, and every strategy of procrastination in the quest. This temporal distension is expressed even more by means of the alternatives, the bifurcations, the contingent connections, and finally by the unforeseeable outcome of the quest as a success or a failure. In fact, the quest is the active principle of the story inasmuch as it both separates and reunites the lack and the overcoming of the lack, just as the test is the core of the process without which nothing would happen. In this way, the actantial syntax refers back to the plot in Aristotle's *Poetics* and, through it, to Augustine's *Confessions*.

The narrative semiotics of *Du Sens* and *Maupassant* does not really constitute a new model so much as the radicalization and at the same time the enriching of the actantial model we have just been discussing. It is a radicalization in the sense that Greimas attempts to trace the constraints on narrativity back to their ultimate source, the constraints attached to the most elementary functioning of any semiotic system. Narrativity will then be justified as an activity from which chance has been removed. It is an enrichment in the sense that the movement of reduction to the most elementary level is compensated for by a movement of deployment that goes toward the complex forms. His ambition, therefore, is to return along the regressive path to the semiotic level that is even more basic than the discursive level itself and to find narrativity there already in place and organized prior to its manifestation. Conversely, along the progressive path, the importance of Greimas's narrative grammar lies in its effort to put together, step by step, the conditions of narrativity beginning from a logical model that is as simple as possible and that initially includes no chronological aspect.

The question is whether, in rejoining the structure of narratives actually produced by oral and written traditions, the successive additions Greimas makes in order to enrich his initial model get their specifically narrative capacity from the initial model or from assumptions extrinsic to it. His wager is that, in spite of these additions, an equivalence can be maintained from beginning to end between the initial model and the final matrix. It is this wager that we must consider, both theoretically and practically.

Let us follow the order suggested in "The Interaction of Semiotic Constraints": first, the *deep structures* that define the conditions of intelligibility of semiotic objects; next the *intermediate* structures, termed "superficial" in relation to the former structures, where narrativization finds its actual articulation, and finally the structures of *manifestation*, particular to this or that language and this or that expressive material.

The first stage, that of the "deep structures," is the stage of the "constitutional model." [37] The problem Greimas seeks to resolve here is to obtain a model that immediately presents a complex character, yet without being instantiated in some linguistic or nonlinguistic substance or medium. It has to be somehow articulated, however, if it is to be narrativized. His stroke of genius, we may say, is to have sought for this already articulated character in the simplest logical structure possible, the "elementary structure of meaning" (ibid.). This structure refers to the conditions for grasping a meaning, any meaning whatsoever. If something—no matter what—"means something" [*signifie*], it is not because we can have some intuition of its sense but because we can state an elementary system of relations as follows. "White" means something because we can articulate it in terms of three relations, one of contradiction (white vs. not-white), one of contrariety (white vs. black), and one of presupposition (not-white vs. black). We have then Greimas's well-known "semiotic square," whose logical force is said to preside over every subsequent enrichment of the model.[38]

How will this constitutional model be narrativized, at least in a virtual sense? By giving a dynamic representation of the taxonomic model—that is, of the system of unoriented relations constitutive of the semiotic square—or, in short, by treating these *relations* as *operations*. Here we rediscover the very important concept of a transformation, already introduced by the actantial model in the form of conjunction and disjunction. Reformulated in terms of operations, the three relations of contradiction, contrariety, and presupposition appear as transformations by means of which one content is negated and another one is affirmed. The very first condition of narrativity is nothing else than this setting into motion of the taxonomic model by means of such oriented operations. This first reference to narrativity already bears witness to the attraction that the goal to be attained exercises over this analysis. This goal is to account for the unstable character of the narrative process at the level of manifestation. This is why it is so important to put the structure into motion. We may ask, however, whether it is not the competence gained through a long acquaintance with traditional narratives that allows us, through anticipation, to call "narrativization" the simple reformulating of the taxonomy in terms of operations, and that also requires us to proceed from stable relations to unstable operations.

The second stage—that of the "superficial" though not yet "figurative" structures—takes place through instantiating the constitutional model in the order of "doing something." To speak of the figurative level, we would have to consider real actors accomplishing tasks, undergoing tests, and attaining goals. But at the level we are considering now, we can confine ourselves to the grammar of doing something in general. This is what introduces the second constitutional stage. Its basic statement is the simple narrative statement of the type "someone is doing something." To turn this into a "program statement," we must add to it various modalities that give it different potentialities: wanting to do something, wanting to have (something), wanting to be (a value), wanting to know (something), wanting to be able (to do something).[39]

We attain the narrative level by next introducing a *polemical* relation between two programs, and therefore between a subject and an antisubject. It then suffices to apply the transformation rules stemming from the constitutional model to a syntagmatic series of narrative statements to obtain confrontation (through disjunction), wanting to dominate and domination (through modalization), and, at last, the attribution of an object/value to the subject of the domination (through conjunction). A syntagmatic series of the form confrontation, domination, attribution (to which we may if we wish, apply all the modalities of doing something, wanting to do something, knowing how to do something, and being able to do something) is called a "performance." In speaking of a performance as such a unified syntagmatic series, Greimas writes, "it is probably the most characteristic unit in narrative syntax" (*Du Sens*, p. 173). Hence it is to this complex constitution of the performance that the principle of equivalence between the deep grammar and the superficial grammar applies. This equivalence rests entirely upon the relation of implication between confrontation, domination, and attribution.[40]

The constituting of the narrative model ends with the addition to the polemical category of a category of *transference*, borrowed from the structure of exchange. Reformulated in terms of an exchange, the attribution of an object/value, the last of the three narrative statements constitutive of the performance, signifies that one subject acquires something which another subject is deprived of. Attribution can thus be decomposed into two operations: a privation, equivalent to a disjunction, and an attribution properly speaking, equivalent to a conjunction. Together they constitute the transfer expressed by two "translative" statements.

This reformulation leads to the concept of a "performative series." And it is in such a series that we are to see the formal skeleton of every narrative.

The advantage of this reformulation is that it allows us to represent all the prior operations as changes in "places," the initial and final places of the transferences; in other words, to satisfy the conditions for a topological syntax of translative statements. In this way, the four corners of the semiotic square become the points from which and toward which the transferences take place. In turn, the fecundity of this topological syntax can be spelled out in greater detail inasmuch as the topological analysis can be deployed on the two planes of "doing something" and "wanting to do something."

If we first consider just the value/objects, acquired or transferred by doing something, the topological syntax can represent the ordered series of operations on the semiotic square along the lines of contradiction, contrariety, and presupposition as a *circular transmitting of values*. We may even say without hesitation that this topological syntax of transferences is the true active principle of the narration "insofar as it is a process that creates values" (p. 178).

If we next consider not just the operations but the operators,[41] that is, within the schema of exchange, the senders and the receivers of the transferences, the topological syntax governs the transformations affecting the capacity to do something, hence the bringing about of the transferences of values considered above. In other words, it governs the very *instituting* of the syntactic operators by creating subjects endowed with the virtual capacity of doing something.

This splitting of the topological syntax corresponds therefore to the splitting of doing and wanting (being able to, knowing how to), that is, the splitting of narrative statements into descriptive statements and modal statements, hence also the splitting into two series of performances. For example, acquisition is the transference bearing either on value-objects or on modal values (acquiring the ability, the knowledge, the wanting to do something).

The second series of performances is the more important one from the point of view of unleashing the syntactic course of action. The operators have to be instituted as capable of, then as knowing how to and wanting to do something, if the transferences of objects of value are to be connected together in their turn. If therefore we ask where the first actant comes from, it is necessary to refer to the *contract* that institutes the subject of the desire by attributing to him, her, or it the modality of wanting. The particular narrative unit in which this wanting by a "knowing" or a "capable" subject is posited constitutes the initial performance of the narrative.

The "completed narrative" (p. 180) combines the series of transferences of objective values with the series of transferences instituting a knowing or a capable subject.

Greimas's topological emphases thus represent the most extreme attempt to push an extension of the paradigmatic as far as possible into the heart of the syntagmatic. Nowhere does he feel closer to realizing the old dream of making linguistics into an algebra of language.[42]

The fact is that semiotics, at the end of its own passage from the level of immanence to the surface level, makes the narrative itself appear as such a passage [*parcours*]. But it takes this passage as the strict homology of the operations implied by the elementary structure of meaning on the level of the basic grammar. It is the "linguistic manifestation of the narrativized meaning" (*Du Sens*, p. 183).

In fact, the passage through the semiotic levels is not so much ended as interrupted. The reader will have noted that nothing is said here of the third level, that of manifestation, where the places formally defined on the plane of the surface grammar are filled in some figurative way. The figurative level has remained up to now the poor cousin of the semiotic analysis. The reason for this, it seems, is that the figuration (whether axiological, thematic, or actantial) is not taken to be the product of an autonomous *configurational* activity. Whence the name "manifestation" given to this level—as though nothing interesting happened there, except for the displaying of the underlying structures. In this sense, this model offers figurations without configuration. All the dynamism of emplotment finds itself referred to the logical-semantical operations and to the syntagmatization of the narrative statements into programs, performances, and performance series. It is not by chance, therefore, that the term "plot" does not appear in the technical vocabulary of narrative semiotics. In truth, it could not find a place there, since it stems from the narrative understanding which semiotic rationality tries to provide an equivalent for or, better, a simulation of. It is necessary therefore to wait for narrative semiotics to develop a specific interest in "figurativity" before we can pass judgment on the fate reserved for the "interplay of semiotic constraints" on the figurative level.

Before proposing some critical reflections concerning this semiotic model, I would like to underscore the intensity of the inquiry that animates the work of Greimas and his school. We have already noted how the semiotic model radicalizes and enriches the initial actantial model. We ought therefore to consider *Du Sens* as one step in an inquiry that is still under way.

Maupassant adds to it and makes some important shifts in direction. I would like to point out three of them.

On the level of the deep structures, Greimas has begun to transform the achronic character of the transformation operations applied to the semiotic square by adding to them aspectual structures: "durativity" which results from the temporalizing of a state and which characterizes every continuous process; next, the two point-like aspects that delimit the process: "inchoativity" and "terminativity" (for example, the terms "dying" and "being born" in Maupassant's short story "Deux Amis");[43] "iterativity," which we may join to "durativity"; and finally, "tensitivity," the relation of tension established between a durative "seme" and a pointlike one, which is expressed in such phrases as "rather close," "too much," and "far away."

The place of these aspectual structures is not easy to define in relation to the deep structures, on the one hand, and in relation to the discursive structures coextensive with doing something, on the other. On the one side, in fact, these aspectual structures are homologized to logical operations. For example, the opposition permanence/occurrence governs the opposition durativity/pointlike. Similarly, the temporal positions before/during/after are taken as "temporalized positings" (*Maupassant*, p. 71) of the logical relations prior/concomitant/posterior. As for the articulation permanence/occurrence, it is only "the adaptation to time" of the pair continuous vs. discontinuous. Yet, with these expressions, we only make the relationship to time more distant. On the other side, we may ask whether such aspectual considerations can be introduced before any syntagmatic interconnections, any discursive traversal. This is why, in the detailed analyses of the sequences of Maupassant's short story, they are introduced on the occasion of their discursive instantiations. One hardly sees how, in fact, the logical relations could be temporalized if some process did not unfold that requires a syntagmatic structure of discourse based on some temporal linearity. So the introduction of the aspectual structures into the model does not take place without a certain difficulty.

A second important addition—also at the turning point between the logical-semantic level and its discursive instantiation—contributes to *dynamizing* the model even further without weakening its paradigmatic basis. It has to do with the highly axiological character of the contents put at the top of the semiotic square. Thus the whole story in "Deux Amis" unfolds in terms of one dominant "isotopy," where life and death constitute the axis of the contraries along with their intersecting contradictories: not-life and not-death. These are not actants—otherwise we would have to talk about them using the categories of doing something—but rather "euphoric" and "dysphoric" connotations capable of underlying every narrative. Much of the remaining semiotic treatment consists of assigning characters and also slightly anthropomorphized entities (the sun, the sky, the water, Mount Valérien) to these places. Everything indicates that these underlying axiological values represent more than cultural stereotypes or ideologies. The respective values of life and death are assumed by every human being. What belongs to any culture, any school of thought, any storyteller is the instantiation of these key values in some determined figures, just as "Deux Amis" puts the sky on the side of not-life and water on the side of not-death. What is interesting about this placing of the euphoric and dysphoric values on the deepest level possible is not just that it assures the stability of the narrative as it unfolds, but that, by joining the axiological and the logical, it favors the narrativization of the basic model. Have we not learned from Aristotle that the changes a drama deals with most of all are those that change good luck into bad and vice versa? But, once again, the place of these axiological determinations in the general scheme is not easy to establish. First of all, it is difficult once more not to refer to the thematic roles these connotations affect, that is, to the discursive subjects that are unfolded by a narrative passage. Next, the polemical character is already hinted at by the opposition between values. Nevertheless, these oppositions are supposed to precede the roles and the subjects in their polemical relations.

A third addition to the elementary model is even more difficult to distinguish from its discursive instantiations. Yet, its logical priority in relation to doing something and to the actants, and its frankly paradigmatic character, assure it a place as close as possible to the deep structures. It has to do with the "senders" for which the actants and the thematic roles are the delegated representatives, the incarnations, the figurations, depending on the varying hierarchical level of these senders or their narrativized representatives. Thus, to cite an example in the story "Deux Amis," life and death and their contradictories are senders, but so are Paris and Prussia. To this concept of a sender is attached the concept of a message, and hence of a sending, and along with it the concept of a setting in motion, of a dynamization. The first time Greimas mentions this concept in his text, he even emphasizes just this function: "to transform an axiology, given as a system of values, into an operative syntagmatization" (p. 62). Is is true that the semiotics of narrative only introduces this concept at the moment when it can make it correspond to an actantial distribution, but what is important, for the theory, is that this distribution covers the whole narrative. This is why Greimas can speak of the "proto-actantial status of the sender" (p. 63).[44] In this way, axiological predicates and senders are superimposed on the semiotic square of logical terms before any "figurative actors" are inscribed on it.

Even more important are the extensions *Maupassant* adds to the grammar of doing something, and therefore to the clearly discursive level. The modern story requires considering the processes that unfold on the *cognitive* level, whether it be a question of observation, information, persuasion or interpretation, trickery, illusion, lies, or secrets. Greimas takes up this requirement (which has its origin in the dramatic function of "recognition" in Aristotle and also in the well-known analyses of the trickster figure in anthropology) through a series of audacious methodological decisions. In the first place, he quite openly splits "doing something" into "doing something pragmatically" and "doing something cognitively," where the latter branch sets up the acting subject as a noological subject distinct from the bodily subject. Next, he apportions this cognitive doing something between two poles: *persuasive* doing something (exercised by the sender of the cognitive activity with respect to the receiver) and *interpretive* doing something (which is the receiver's corresponding response). The essential advantage of so treating the cognitive dimension in terms of doing something is that it allows him to submit the operations of knowing anything at all to the same transformation rules that govern action properly speaking (recall that Aristotle had already included the characters' "thoughts" in his muthos in terms of the category of *dianoia*). In this way, the inferences from appearance to reality, which interpretation consists of, are forms of doing something capable of being inscribed on a narrative traversal just as the other forms of doing something are. Similarly, the polemical relation may have to do with two persuasive forms of doing something as well as with two pragmatic ones, as, for example, in a discussion, or even with two interpretive forms, as, for example, in an accusation or a denial of guilt. Consequently, from now on when we speak of a polemical relationship, we must keep in mind the whole palette of "doing something." [45]

However, the break introduced into the theory of doing something, which had been relatively homogeneous to this point, is a considerable one. To take account of persuasion and interpretation, we must in fact make recourse to new categories for semiotics but old ones for philosophy—the categories of being and appearing. To persuade is to make someone believe that what appears to be so is so, and to interpret is to infer reality from appearances. Yet Greimas insists that we limit these terms to "the sense of semiotic existence" (p. 107). And he calls the passage from one level to another a "fiduciary" relation which sets up such values as certitude, conviction, doubt, hypothesis, even while he claims not yet to possess the categorization warranted by such fiduciary values (cf. p. 108). In this way he believes he can preserve a logical character for the narrative transformations in which a subject, for example, by camouflaging himself, intends that another subject interpret this not-appearing as a form of nonbeing. This process is put under the category of the secret, where the first subject conjoins being and not appearing. This situation, set within the cognitive dimension of a narrative, then conserves both its narrative inscription and its logical features through the introduction of a new semiotic square, the square of "veridiction," constituted beginning from the opposition being vs. appearing, and completed with the respective contradictories: nonbeing and not-appearing. Truth indicates the conjunction of being and appearing, falsity that of not-appearing and nonbeing, the lie that of appearing and nonbeing, and the secret that of being and not-appearing. Trickery is the persuasive form of doing something that consists of transforming the lie into truth—making something pass for something else; that is, in presenting what appears, but is really not so, as what appears to be so and is so—and getting it accepted as such. And illusion is the interpretive form of doing something that corresponds to the lie, by accepting it as a kind of contract with the deceptive sender. The deceiver, as an actantial role, the one who passes himself, herself, or itself off as someone or something else, can thus be given a precise definition on the level of veridiction.

This introduction of doing something cognitively, along with the distinction between cognitive and interpretive doing something, and the introduction of the structure of veridiction constitute the most important additions of *Maupassant* to the categorization of "doing something," particularly if we take into account the modal forms of "being able to do something" that are grafted to it. These latter include the most important one in the story "Deux Amis," refusal—that is, wanting to be able not to do something. And in this way, Greimas can account for a complex dramatic situation in Maupassant's story of an "illusory quest" transformed into a "secret victory." [46]

These are the most important improvements *Maupassant* adds to the semiotic model. I will say that they distend the model without bursting it, although it is probably the question of veridiction that most threatens such an explosion. To the extent, therefore, that they do not propose any significant rewriting of the model described ten years earlier in *Du Sens*, neither do they undercut the criticism we can level against the basic semiotic model with its three levels of deep, superficial, and figurative structures.

However, the fundamental question raised by the narrative grammar model is whether the so-called "surface" level is not richer in narrative potential than the deep grammar, and also whether the increasing enrichment of the model as it follows the semiotic traversal does not proceed from our ability to follow a story and our acquired familiarity with a narrative tradition.

The answer to this question is presupposed beginning with the initial designation of the deep grammar as the level of immanence and the surface grammar as the level of manifestation.

In other words, this question once again raises, although with regard to a considerably more refined model, the problem that has occupied us since the beginning of this chapter, the problem of the relationships between the rationality of narratology and narrative understanding, forged by the practice of emplotment. For this reason, our discussion must become even more close-knit.

My initial doubt, which the subsequent argument must put to the test, is whether, from its very first stage—that is, from the construction of the semiotic square—Greimas's analysis is not teleologically guided by an anticipation of the final stage, namely, the one where narration is a process that creates values (*Du Sens*, p. 178). This is where I see the equivalent on the level of semiotic rationality of what our narrative upbringing makes us understand as a plot. Let us be clear about what I am saying. This doubt in no way disqualifies Greimas's enterprise. It simply calls into question the alleged autonomy of such semiotic undertakings, just as the discussion of nomological models in history called into question the autonomy of historiographical rationality in relation to our narrative competence. This first part of my argument must stick to the level of the deep grammar.

I will set aside here the question of the logical consistency of the basic model and limit my discussion to two points.[47] The first one has to do with the conditions the model has to satisfy if it is to preserve its efficacity all along the semiotic traversal. As it is constituted on the plane of the elementary structure of signification, it is a strong model. But, as often happens in the interpretation of some given domain with a model constructed a priori, some of its requirements must be weakened if it is to function in this domain. We have already seen one example in the domain of historiography, where the covering law model had to be weakened to take into account the actual methodology implied by the historian's craft. The initial taxonomic model preserves a logical signification only if it remains a strong model. Yet it has its full force only on the level of a "semic" analysis, which, if not completed, at least brings us to the point where it allows a "limited inventory of semic categories" (p. 161). Under this condition, contrariety does constitute a strong form of contrariety, that is, a binary opposition between semes of the same category, as for example in the binary semic category white vs. black. Contradiction, too, is there a strong form of contradiction: white vs. not-white, black vs. not-black. And the presupposition of not-S_1 from S_2 is truly preceded by the two relations of contradiction and contrariety, in the rigorous sense just spoken of. Yet, we may doubt whether these three requirements are satisfied in all their rigor in the domain of narrativity. If they were, then all the subsequent operations would also be "foreseeable and calculable" (p. 166) as Greimas says. *But then nothing would happen.* There could be no event, no surprise. There would be nothing to tell. We may assume therefore that the surface grammar more often has to do with quasi-contradictions, quasi-contrarieties, and quasi-presuppositions.

The second point I would like to consider, still on the level of the deep grammar, has to do with the narrativization of the taxonomy assured by the passage from unoriented relationships in the taxonomic model to the oriented operations that give the model a syntactical interpretation.

In fact, the passage from the idea of a static relation to that of a dynamic operation implies an actual addition to the taxonomic model, which genuinely does chronologize it, at least in the sense that a transformation takes time. This addition is indicated in the text of "Elements . . ." by the notion of "a production of meaning by the subject" (p. 164). Hence there is more than a reformulation here. We have the introduction of a syntagmatic factor, on an equal basis, alongside the paradigmatic factor. The notion of equivalence then loses its sense of being a reciprocal relationship in the passage from morphology to syntax. After all, how are a stable relation and its transformation equivalent, if it is the orientation involved that is most pertinent in the latter? We may inquire therefore whether the construction of the model was not guided by the idea of oriented transformations which are made to appear in the inert terms.

This question can be posed on each of the levels of the model. The finality of one operation seems to lie in the following operation, and finally in the concluding idea of narrativity. In fact, this is what we observe in the passage from the deep grammar to the surface grammar.

The enriching of the initial model results from the massive aid provided by the various determinations of "doing something." Yet none of these new determinations stem directly from the taxonomic model but rather from a semantics of action.[48] We know, by a form of knowing immanent to "doing anything," that doing something is the object of statements whose structure differs essentially from the structure of predicative statements of the form "S is P," as well as from relation statements of the form "X is between Y and Z." This structure of sentences that describe action has been the object of much detailed work in analytic philosophy, which I have reviewed in my essay "Le Discours de l'action."[49] One noteworthy characteristic of these sentences is that they involve an open-ended structure running from "Socrates says . . ." to "Brutus killed Caesar, on the Ides of March, in the Roman Senate, with a knife. . . ." It is this semantics of action that, in fact, is presupposed in the theory of the narrative sentence. "To do" something can be substituted for any of the action verbs. This assistance from the semantics of action is nowhere more evident than in the passage, through mobilization, from statements concerning "doing something" to statements about "being able to do something." How else do we know that "wanting to do something" makes "doing something" contingent? Nothing about the semiotic square allows us to suspect this. Even so, the typology of wanting to do something, wanting to be something, wanting to have something, wanting to know something, and being able to want something is a good one. Yet it stems, from a linguistic pont of view, from a particular grammar, one that analytic philosophy has spelled out in the greatest detail in terms of what it calls intentional logic. If this original grammar is required to give a logical form to the relationship between the modal statements about "wanting to . . ." and descriptive statements about doing something, it is the implicit phenomenology of action involved that gives meaning to Greimas's statement that "the modal statements which have 'wanting' as their function set up the subject as a virtuality of doing something, while two other modal statements, characterized by the modalities of 'knowing' and 'being able,' determine this contingent doing of something in two different ways—either as a doing stemming from knowledge or as uniquely grounded on power" (*Du Sens*, p. 175). Even so, this implicit phenomenology is brought to light as soon as we interpret the modal statement as the "desire to realize" a program that is present in the form of a descriptive statement and, at the same time, serves as the object of a modal statement (cf. p. 169).

The result is that the relationship between the semiotic level and the level of actual praxis is one where each takes precedence over the other. The semiotic square brings its network of interdefined terms and its system of contradiction, contrariety, and presupposition. The semantics of action brings the major significations of "doing something" and the specific structure of those statements that refer to an action. In this sense, the surface grammar is a mixed grammar, a semiotic-praxic grammar.[50] In this mixed grammar, it seems as though it will be quite difficult to speak of an *equivalence* between the structures deployed by the semantics of action and the operations implied by the semiotic square.

We can take this objection one step further by observing that the simple narrative statement is an abstraction within the superficial grammar as long as we have not introduced the polemical relationship between programs and between opposed subjects. As we have already seen above, there is nothing specifically narrative about an isolated action sentence. Only a sequence of statements constitutes a narrative syntagm and allows us, retroactively, to speak of the action sentences that compose this chain as narrative. In this respect, the polemical relationship constitutes the first genuine threshold leading to narrativity in the superficial grammar, the second such threshold being constituted by the concept of a performance, and the third one being indicated by the syntagmatic sequence of performances and the transference of values that it brings about.

Let us consider each one of these thresholds in order, beginning with the first one, the polemical representation of logical relations.

Note, first of all, that the polemical representation brings with it new features that, before having the logical signification of contradiction or contrariety, do have an autonomous praxic signification. Confrontation and struggle are figures of the orientation of action toward others, as this has been dealt with, for example, in an interpretive sociology such as Max Weber's. Weber's sociology, in fact, introduces struggle (*Kampf*) at a well-defined place in the progressive constitution of the basic categories of his masterpiece, *Economy and Society*.[51] The introduction of the category of struggle, therefore, accentuates the mixed character of every narrative grammar, its half-logical, half-praxic character.

Observe, further, that the equivalence on the logical level between defiance and contradiction is highly contestable. The concept of defiance, it seems to me, brings into play a type of negativity which Kant, in his opuscule *Versuch, den Begriff der negativen Grössen in die Weltweisheit einzuführen* (1763), was the first to show is not reducible to contradiction. The opposition of a subject to an antisubject is not the opposition of two contradictory forms of doing something. And we may suspect that it is not a relationship of contrariety either.[52]

The addition of the categories of transference to the polemical categories poses an analogous problem. Again at this new stage, the implicit recourse to phenomenology is flagrant. If to transfer is to deprive someone of something and to give it to someone else, there is more to depriving and giving than disjoining and conjoining. The deprivation of a value/object a subject undergoes is a modification that affects this subject as a victim. What the final stage of the constitution of the model adds, therefore, is a phenomenology of suffering and acting in which concepts such as deprivation and donation get their meaning. The whole topological language of this final phase is a mixture of logical conjunctions and disjunctions and of modifications coming not just from the praxic realm but also from the realm of suffering.[53] This conclusion should not surprise us if it is true that the topological syntax of transferences, which repeats the traversal of the logical operations of the semiotic square, "organizes the narration inasmuch as it is a process creative of values" (*Du Sens*, p. 178). How does this doubling pass from the syntactic operations that, within the taxonomic framework, were "foreseeable and calculable" (p. 166), to "a process creative of values"? Somewhere the logic must be inadequate to the creativity proper to narrative. This gap opens up at the level of transference, inasmuch as correlation and presupposition become distanced from the strong logical model to express the dissymmetry of deprivation and attribution and the novelty belonging to the attribution. This aspect of novelty attached to attribution is even more manifest once it is power, knowledge, and wanting to do something—that is, the very virtuality of doing something—that befall the subject.

This gap between the initial schematism, where all the relationships balance one another out, and the final schematism, where new values are produced, is concealed in the particular case of Propp's Russian fairy tales where the circulation of the values ends with a restoration of the initial state. The king's daughter, enchanted by a villain who takes her off to hide her, is found by the hero and returned to her parents! Greimas himself, in his *Structural Semantics*, admits that the most general function of narrative has been to restore a threatened order of values. Yet we know, thanks to the schematism of plots produced by the cultures whose heirs we are, that this restoration characterizes only one category of narrative, and even no doubt one type of folktales. Plot articulates "crises" and "denouements" in so many different ways! And the hero (or antihero) is changed in the course of a plot in so many different ways. Is it even certain that every narrative can be projected onto Greimas's topological matrix made up of two programs, a polemical relation, and a transference of values? Our study of the metamorphoses of plot makes me tend to doubt this.

To conclude, Greimas's model seems to me to be under a double constraint, logical on the one hand, praxic and pathetic (that is, as having to do with acting and suffering) on the other. Yet it only satisfies the first of these, in continually pushing forward the inscription on the semiotic square of the components of narrativity introduced at each new level, if along with this the understanding we have of narrative and of plot gives rise to appropriate additions of a clearly syntagmatic order—without which the taxonomic model would remain sterile and inert.[54]

To recognize this mixed character of Greimas's model is not to refute it. On the contrary, it is to bring to light the conditions of its intelligibility, just as we have already done in Part II of volume 1 for the nomological models used in history.

3

Games with Time

The enrichment of the concept of emplotment and, correlatively, of narrative time—to which the following chapter is devoted—is most certainly a privilege belonging to fictional narrative, rather than to historical narrative, owing to the elimination of certain constraints characteristic of historical narrative. (These constraints will be the topic of a detailed study in Part IV in the next volume.) This privilege is due to the remarkable property narrative possesses of being split into utterance [*énociation*] and statement [*énoncé*]. To introduce this distinction, it suffices to recall that the configurating act presiding over emplotment is a judicative act, involving a "grasping together." More precisely, this act belongs to the family of reflective judgments.[1] We have been led to say therefore that to narrate a story is already to "reflect upon" the event narrated. For this reason, narrative "grasping together" carries with it the capacity for distancing itself from its own production and in this way dividing itself in two.

This power of teleological judgment to divide itself in two reappears today in a purely linguistic terminology as "utterance" and "statement," which under the influence of Gunther Müller, Gérard Genette, and the semioticians of Greimas's school has received the right to be used in narrative poetics. By means of such a shift in attention from the narrative statement to its utterance, the specifically fictive features of narrative time take on a distinctive outline. They are in a sense set free by the interplay between the various temporal levels stemming from the reflexivity of the configurating act itself. We shall consider several versions of this interplay, which already begins between the statement and the things that are narrated, but which is made possible by the split between utterance and statement.

UTTERANCE AND THE VERBAL TENSES

By way of a preface, I would like to consider the resources that the system of verbal tenses offers to utterance. This investigation seemed to me to belong at the head of my studies devoted to the games with time resulting from the split into utterance and statement inasmuch as the three authors I have chosen to examine have openly connected their theory of verb tenses to the function of utterance in discourse rather than to the structure of the resulting statements, which remain separated either from the speaker or the speech situation. In addition, the solution these authors have provided to the question of the organization of the verb tenses in natural languages gives rise to a paradox that directly concerns the status of time in fiction, hence of time at the level of mimesis$_2$.

On the one hand, the principal contribution of this inquiry is to demonstrate that the system of tenses, which varies from one language to another, cannot be derived from the phenomenological experience of time and from its intuitive distinction between present, past, and future. This independence of the system of tenses contributes to the independence of a narrative composition on two levels. On a strictly paradigmatic level (let us say, on the level of the table of verb tenses in a given language), the tense system provides a storehouse of distinctions, relations, and combinations from which fiction draws the resources for its own autonomy with respect to lived experience. In this regard, language, with its system of tenses, contains a ready-made means of modulating temporally all the action verbs throughout the narrative chain. What is more, at a level that may be called syntagmatic, these tenses contribute to the narrativization, not only by the interplay of their differences within the broad grammatical paradigm, but also by their successive arrangement along the chain of a narrative. The fact that French grammar contains within the same system an imperfect tense and a preterite or absolute past tense is already a great resource. But the fact that that succession of an imperfect tense followed by a preterite produces a new meaning-effect is an even more admirable one. In other words, the syntagmatization of tenses is just as essential as their paradigmatic constitution. However, the first point, just as much as the second one, expresses the autonomy of the system of tenses with respect to what, in an elementary semantics of everyday experience, we call time.

On the other hand, the question remains open to what extent the system of tenses can be free of all reference to the phenomenological experience of time. On this point, the hesitation of the three conceptions we are going to discuss is most instructive. It illustrates the complexity of the relation that I myself am acknowledging between the time of fiction and the time of phenomenological experience, whether we take this on the level of prefiguration (mimesis$_1$) or on the level of refiguration (mimesis$_3$). The necessity of disconnecting the system of tenses from our lived experience of time and the impossibility of separating them completely seem to me marvelously to illustrate the status of narrative configurations as at one and the same time being autonomous in relation to everyday experience and mediating between what precedes and what follows a narrative.

If I begin with the distinction introduced by Emile Benveniste between history and discourse and continue with the contributions of Käte Hamburger and Harald Weinrich to the problematic of verb tenses, this is for two reasons.[2]

On the one hand, we can in this way follow the progress from a study conducted within a purely paradigmatic framework to a conception that adds to the study of the static organization of tenses a study of their successive distribution within large textual units. On the other hand, we can observe, from one conception to the next, a progress in the dissociation of these tenses from the lived experience of time—and we can measure the obstacles that prevent us from carrying this effort through to its end. It is here that I shall seek the major contribution of these three conceptions to my own inquiry into the degree of autonomy belonging to narrative configurations in relation to the prefigured or refigured experience of time.

Let us recall briefly the basis of the distinction introduced by Benveniste between discourse and history. In historical utterance, the speaker is not implied: "no one speaks here; the events seem to narrate themselves" (p. 208). Discourse, however, designates "every utterance assuming a speaker and a hearer, and in the speaker, the intention of influencing the other in some way" (p. 209). Each mode of utterance has its own system of tenses: tenses that are included, others that are excluded. In this way, historical utterance includes three tenses: the aorist (or preterite), the imperfect, and the pluperfect (to which may be added the prospective—"he should have left" or "he was going to leave"). More particularly, historical utterance excludes the present and along with it the future, which is a present to come, and the perfect, which is a present in the past. Conversely, discourse excludes one tense, the aorist, and includes three basic tenses: the present, future, and perfect tenses. The present is the basic tense of discourse because it marks the contemporaneousness of what is stated with the "instance of discourse." It is thus bound up with the self-referential character of the instance of discourse. This is why the two levels of utterance are also distinguished by a second series of criteria: the categories of the persons. Historical utterance cannot exclude the present without excluding the relation between the persons "I" and "you." The aorist is the tense of events lying beyond the person of a narrator.

What about the relation between the system of tenses and lived temporal experience?

For one thing, the distribution of the personal forms of French tenses into two distinct systems must be held to be independent of the notion of time and its three categories of present, past, and future. The very duality of the two systems of tenses bears witness to this. Neither the notion of time nor the categories of present, past, and future time provide "the criterion that will determine the position or even the possibility of a given form within the verbal system" (p. 205). This statement is perfectly homogeneous with the shift brought about by the symbolic system as a whole on the level of mimesis$_2$ in relation to the empirical and praxic level of mimesis$_1$.

On the other hand, the distinction between the two systems of utterances is not entirely unrelated to time. The question arises mainly in connection with narrative. It has not perhaps been sufficiently remarked that the narrative Benveniste opposes to discourse is constantly termed "historical narrative" or "historical utterance." Historical utterance "characterizes the narrative of past events" (p. 206). In this definition the term "past" is just as important as the terms "narrative" and "events." These terms designate "events that took place at a certain moment of time . . . without any intervention of the speaker" (ibid.). If there is no formal contradiction between this definition and the attempt to dissociate the system of tenses from the intuitive distinction between past, present, and future, this is insofar as reference can be made either to the actual past, as in the case of the historian, or to the fictive past, as in the case the novelist (and this allows Benveniste to draw one of his examples from a passage by Balzac). Nevertheless, if narrative is characterized in relation to discourse as a series of events that seem to relate themselves without the intervention of a speaker, this is so to the extent that, according to Benveniste, it is part of the notion of past, whether real or fictive, not to imply the self-reference of the speaker in his utterance, as in discourse. What is not developed here is the relation between the fictive past and the real past. Does the fictive past assume the real past, hence memory and history, or is it the very structure of historical temporal expression that produces the characterization as past? But then it is not apparent why the fictive past is perceived as a quasi-past.[3]

As for the present of the instance of discourse, it is hard to say that it is without any relation to lived time, if we add that the perfect tense is the present in the past, and the future is the present to come. The grammatical criterion of the present, namely, the self-referential character of the instance of discourse, is one thing. The meaning of this self-reference itself, namely, the contemporaneity of what is recounted with the instance of discourse, is something else again. The mimetic relation of the grammatical categories with respect to lived experience is contained entirely within this relation, both of disjunction and conjunction, between the grammatical present of the instance of discourse and the lived present.[4]

This mimetic relation between the verb tenses and lived time cannot be confined to discourse if, following Benveniste's successors, we are more interested in the role of discourse *in* narrative than in the opposition between discourse and narrative. Can past events, whether real or imaginary, be presented without any intervention of the speaker in the narrative? Can the events simply appear on the horizon of the story without anyone speaking in any way? Does not the absence of a narrator from historical narrative result from a strategy by means of which the narrator makes himself absent from the narrative? This distinction, which we shall examine below for its own sake, cannot help but affect even at this early stage the question I am raising concerning the relation between verb tenses and lived time. If it is within narrative itself that we must distinguish between utterance (discourse in Benveniste's terms) and statement (narrative in his vocabulary), then the problem becomes double. It involves, first, the relation between the time of the utterance and the time of the statement and, second, the relation between these two times and the time of life or action.[5]

Before entering into this debate, let us widen even further, first with Käte Hamburger, the split between the basic time of fiction—the preterite—and that of assertions made about reality, the time of ordinary conversation, and then with Harald Weinrich, the dissociation of the entire system of tenses in natural languages from the categories of lived time: the past, present, and future.

We are in debt to Käte Hamburger for the clear distinction she makes between the grammatical form of verb tenses, in particular the past tenses, and their temporal signification in the realm of fiction. No one has stressed more than she has the break that literary fiction introduces into the functioning of discourse.[6] An insurmountable barrier separates assertive discourse (*Aussage*) that refers to reality from the fictional narrative. A different logic, the implications of which for time I shall speak of below, results from this break. Before ascertaining its consequences, we must grasp the reason for this difference. It results entirely from the fact that fiction replaces the I-Origo of assertive discourse, an origin that itself is real, with the I-Origines belonging to the characters in fiction. The entire weight of fiction rests on the invention of characters, characters who think, feel, and act, and who are the fictive I-Origines of the thoughts, feelings, and actions of the narrated story. These *Fiktive Ichpersonen* are the pivot for the logic of fiction. We could not be closer to Aristotle, for whom fiction is a mimesis of active characters. The criterion of fiction hence consists in the use of verbs designating internal processes, that is, psychic or mental processes. "Epic fiction," Hamburger states, "is the sole epistemological instance where the *Ich-Originität* (or subjectivity) of a third-person qua third person can be portrayed [*dargestellt*]" (p. 83).[7]

What upsets the system of tenses in the realm of fiction is the appearance in discourse of verbs designating internal processes belonging to a fictive subject. In the "assertive system" of language, the preterite designates the real past of a real subject who determines the zero point of the temporal system—origin here is taken in the sense in which geometers speak of the origin of a system of coordinates. There is a past only for a *Reale Ich-Origin*; the *ich* participates in the sphere of reality of this I-Origo. In the realm of fiction, the epic preterite loses its grammatical function of designating the past. The narrated action does not, properly speaking, occur. In this sense, we have the right to speak of the absence of temporality in fiction (cf. pp. 89–98). We cannot even speak of "presentification" (*Vergegenwärtigung*) in Schiller's sense, for this would indicate a relation to the real subject of assertion and would cancel out the purely fictive character of the I-Origines of the characters. It is rather a question of a present, in the sense of a time simultaneous with the narrated action, but a present that itself is unrelated to the real present of assertion.

If the introduction of verbs referring to mental states constitutes the criterion for the replacement of the I-Origo of the real subject of assertion by the I-Origines of fictive characters, the loss of the meaning of "past" in the epic preterite is a symptom of this. Other symptoms follow, for example, discordant combinations of temporal adverbs that would be impossible in assertions about reality. Thus we read in one fictional work: "Morgan war Weihnachten" ("Tomorrow was Christmas"). Or: "and, of course he was coming to her party tonight." Adding an adverb expressing the future to an imperfect proves that the imperfect has lost its grammatical function.

To say that its opposition to the assertion of reality constitutes a good definition of epic fiction and that the appearance of the fictive character can be taken as the principal sign of entry into narrative is uncontestably a strong way of marking out fiction. What remains debatable is that the loss of the meaning "past" is sufficient to characterize the system of verb tenses in fiction. Why is the grammatical form preserved, while its signification as past is abolished? Ought we not to look for a positive reason for maintaining the grammatical form, one as strong as the reason for the loss of its signification in real time? The key, it seems, is to be sought in the distinction made between the real author and the narrator, who is fictive.[8] In fiction two discourses are held together, the discourse of the narrator and that of the characters. Käte Hamburger, who is careful to sever all connections with the system of assertion, is willing to consider only a single center of consciousness, the fictive third person in third-person narratives.[9]

We must therefore set into the play the dialectic of the character and the narrator, the narrator being considered just as fictive a construction as the characters in the narrative.[10]

Harald Weinrich's attempt to dissociate the organization of tenses from the consideration of lived time and from the categories (past, present, and future) that grammar is supposed to have borrowed from the latter, starts from a different concern.

The first separation made between the verb tenses and the categories of lived time is contemporaneous with the very first effort to verbalize experience. (In this sense, the opposition between narrating and asserting falls inside a more inclusive grammar of tenses.)

This strong claim frees his project immediately from the assumption that some given tense is to be found in every language, and invites us to pay equal attention to all the tenses that make up the nomenclature of a particular language. The framework of this investigation is particularly favorable to our reflection on the relation between the organization of the tenses and the meaning of time in fiction, inasmuch as the dimension held to be most relevant is the text rather than the sentence. By breaking in this way with the exclusive privilege of the sentence, Weinrich intends to apply the structural perspective to a "textual linguistics." [11] In this way, Weinrich gives himself enough space to do equal justice to the positional value of a tense in the nomenclature and the distribution of tenses throughout a text. It is this passage from a paradigmatic point of view to a syntagmatic one that is richest in lessons for a study of time in fiction, to the extent that fiction too takes the text, not the sentence, as its unit of measurement.

If the principle of tense organization in a given language is not based on the experience of lived time, it must be sought elsewhere. Unlike Benveniste, Weinrich borrows his principle for the classification and distribution of tenses from communication theory. This choice implies that the syntax to which the study of tenses refers consists of the network of signals addressed by a speaker to a hearer or a reader that allows him or her to receive and decode a verbal message in a certain way. And it invites us to perform an initial distribution of the possible objects of communication in relation to certain axes of communication: "reflecting this schematic partitioning of the world is precisely the role of the syntactic categories" (p. 27). Let us put aside for later discussion the mimetic feature so obviously introduced by this reference to a world upon which syntax has already conferred an initial distribution, before semantics, or, let us say, before the lexicon.

Weinrich distributes the tenses of the natural languages he examines along three axes, all of which are axes of communication.

1. The "speech situation" (*Sprechsituation*) governs the first distinction between narrating (*erzählen*) and commenting or discussing (*besprechen*).[12] This is by far the most important distinction for our purposes, and it provides the subtitle for the original text: *Besprochene und erzählte Welt*. It corresponds to two different speech attitudes, commentary being characterized by tension or involvement (*gespannte Haltung*), narrative by relaxation, easing of tension, or detachment (*entspannte Haltung*).

Representative of the commented world are dramatic dialogues, political memoranda, editorials, testaments, scientific reports, scholarly essays, legal treatises, and all forms of ritual, codified, or performative discourse. This group is associated with an attitude of tension in that the interlocutors are concerned with or involved in the discourse. They are grappling with the reported content: "all commentary is a fragment of action" (p. 33). In this sense, only non-narrative speech is dangerous: *Tua res agitur*.

Representative of the narrated world are folktales, legends, short stories, novels, and historical narratives.[13] Here the interlocutors are not implied. They are not in question; they do not come on stage.[14] This why it may be said in reference to Aristotle's *Poetics* that even pitiful or terrifying events, when they are received with detachment, belong to the narrated world.

The division of tenses into two groups corresponding to each attitude is the signal that orients the communication situation toward tension or relaxation. "The 'obstination' of temporal morphemes in signaling commentary and narrative enable the speaker to influence the listener, to shape the reception the speaker wants to see reserved for his text" (p. 30). However, if the typology of communication situations on the basis of tension or relaxation is, in principle, accessible to common experience, it is marked on the linguistic level by the distribution of the syntactic signals that are the tenses. To two speech situations correspond two distinct groups of tenses. In French there are, for the commented world, the present, the compound past, and the future; for the narrated world, the preterite, imperfect, pluperfect, and conditional. (We shall see how these groups are subdivided in turn in relation to the two subsequent criteria that refine the basic distinction between commented world and narrated world.) Hence there is a relation of mutual dependence between the speech attitude and the tense distribution. On the one hand, these attitudes provide a motivation for the distribution of the tenses into two groups, inasmuch as the speaker employs commentary tenses in order "to make the partners feel the tension in the attitude of communication" (p. 32). On the other hand, the tenses themselves transmit a signal from the speaker to the listener indicating "this is a commentary, this a narrative." It is in this sense that they bring about an initial distribution among the possible objects of communication, an initial schematic division of the world into a commented world and a narrated world. And this distribution has its own criteria, since it rests on a systematic tabulation based on samplings from a number of texts. The preponderance of one group of tenses in one type of text and of another group of tenses in another type of text may thus be measured.

This initial distribution of tenses is not unrelated to the distinction between discourse and narrative in Benveniste, except that it no longer involves the relation of the speaker to the utterance but the relation of interlocution and, through it, the guidance of the reception of the message in order to allow an initial distribution of the possible objects of communication. The world common to the interlocutors is therefore also affected by a purely syntactic distinction. This is why, for Weinrich, it is a question of a narrated world and a commented world. As with Benveniste, this distinction has the advantage of freeing the distribution of tenses from the categories of lived time. This "neutrality" with respect to time (*Zeit*) (p. 44) is of the greatest importance for defining the tenses of the narrated world. What grammars call the past and the imperfect (which I shall oppose to one another below when I discuss the notion of "putting into relief") are narrative tenses, not because a narrative basically expresses past events, real or fictive, but because these tenses are oriented toward an attitude of relaxation, of uninvolvement. What is essential is that the narrated world is foreign to the immediate and directly preoccupying surroundings of the speaker and the listener. The model in this regard is still the fairy tale. "More than any other, it takes us out of our everyday life and distances us from it" (p. 45). The expressions "once upon a time," "il était une fois," "vor Zeiten," and "Érase que se era"—literally, "it was that it was"—(p. 47) serve to mark the entry into narrative. In other words, it is not the past as such that is expressed by the past tense but the attitude of relaxation, of uninvolvement.

This initial major bifurcation based upon the interlocutor's degree of vigilance has disconcerting consequences, from the very beginning, for the concept of narrativity. The act of configuration is in effect split in two, as soon as dialogical drama falls on the side of commentary, while the epic, the novel, and history fall on the side of the narrated world. In an unexpected way, we are brought back to the Aristotelian distinction between diegesis and drama, except that the criterion used by Aristotle was based on the direct or indirect relation of the poet to the action reported. Homer himself states the facts, although he effaces himself from his account as much as the diegetic genre allows, whereas Sophocles has the action produced by the characters themselves. The paradox that results for us is the same, however, insofar as the notion of plot has been borrowed from drama, which Weinrich also excludes from the narrated world. I do not think this difficulty should detain us for long inasmuch as the universe of discourse that I am placing under the title "narrative configuration" concerns the composition of statements and leaves intact the difference affecting utterances. Besides, the distinction between tension and relaxation is not as clear-cut as it may first appear. Weinrich himself mentions the example of exciting or thrilling (*spannend*) novels, and notes that "if the narrator gives a certain tension to his narrative, it is by way of compensation." By means of an appropriate technique, he "counterbalances in part the relaxation belonging to the initial attitude. . . . He narrates as if he were commenting" (p. 35). In Weinrich's mind this "as if" does not do away with the basic phenomenon of a withdrawal from the world of care. Instead it makes it more complex, matching up with it and overlapping it to the point of concealing it. Similarly, that the two groups of tenses do not mix confirms the persistence of the attitude of relaxation underlying that of the tension that compensates for it. But the concealment is so organically bound up with the attitude of withdrawal in all narratives that, like the novel, are related to exciting narratives, that relaxation and tension have to be superimposed rather than dissociated and a place has to be made for the composite genre born out of this sort of involvement-in-withdrawal.

With these remarks we rejoin the positions taken by Benveniste's successors, who, starting from a different division than Weinrich, have been more interested in including discourse *in* narrative than in severing the one from the other. One way of solving this problem will be to hierarchize the statement and the utterance. The entire range of speech attitudes, extending from withdrawal to involvement, will stem from the utterance.

2. With the "speech perspective" a second syntactic axis enters into play, one no less related to the communication process than the axis of the speech attitude. Here it is a question of the relation of anticipation, coincidence, or retrospection linking the time of the act with the time of the text. The possibility of a lag between the time of the act and the time of the text results from the linear character of the speech chain and hence from the unfolding of the text itself. On the one hand, every linguistic sign has something before it and something after it in the speech chain. As a result, the information already given and that anticipated contribute to determining each sign in the *Textzeit*. On the other hand, the orientation of the speaker in relation to the *Textzeit* is itself an action that has its own time, the *Aktzeit*. This time of action can coincide with the time of the text, fall behind it, or anticipate it.

Language has signals that warn us of the coincidence of, or the lag between, the *Aktzeit* and the *Textzeit*. Among the tenses of commentary, the compound past indicates retrospection, the future looking ahead, and the present itself is unmarked. Among the tenses of narrative, the pluperfect and the anterior past indicate retrospection, the conditional looking ahead, the preterite and imperfect the zero degree of the narrated world. The narrator is associated with the events whether engaged in them (as in first-person narrative) or whether only a witness to them (as in third-person narrative). In this way, the conditional is to narrative what the future is to commentary; both signal anticipated information. The notion of future time is thus eliminated. "'Anticipated information' only means that the information is given prematurely in relation to the moment of its realization" (p. 74). Nor are the retrospective tenses governed by the notion of the past. In commentary, I am concerned in the present with retrospective information. The retrospective tenses, therefore, open the past to our grasp while narrative makes it inaccessible to us. Debating the past is prolonging it into the present. The case of scientific history is noteworthy in this respect. Historians, in fact, both narrate and comment. They comment whenever they explain. This is why the tenses of historical representation are mixed. "In history, the basic structure of representation consists in setting narrative within commentary" (p. 79). The art of history lies in the mastery of such alternating tenses. The same manner of setting narrative within a framework of commentary can be observed in the judicial process and in certain interventions by the narrator in his story in the form of commentary. This disengagement of the syntactic function of signaling, which belongs to the tenses, in relation to the expression of time itself, is most noteworthy in the case of the French imperfect and preterite tenses that mark, not a distance back in time, but the zero degree of gap between *Aktzeit* and *Textzeit*. "The preterite (group II) indicates narrative. Its function is not to mark the past" (p. 100). In this way, past and narrative cannot be superimposed. For one thing, the past can be neutralized in other ways than simply by being narrated; for example, by being commented upon. I then hold it in the present instead of freeing myself from it or going beyond it (*aufheben*) through the language of narrative. For another, we can narrate other things than just the past: "the space in which fictional narrative unfolds is not the past" (p. 101). In order to put a narrative in the past we must add to the time of the narrated world other features that distinguish truth from fiction, such as the production and criticism of documents. The verb tenses no longer serve as the key to this process.[15]

3. "Putting into relief" constitutes the third axis of the analysis of tenses. This is still an axis of communication, without any reference to the properties of time. This putting into relief consists in projecting certain contours into the foreground and pushing others into the background. In this analysis Weinrich attempts to distance himself from the grammatical categories characterizing the aspect or mode of action, which in his opinion are too closely related to the primacy of the sentence and too dependent on the reference to time (whether we speak of a state, a process, or an event). Once again, the function of syntax is to guide the reader's attention and expectations. This is precisely what occurs in French in the tense that is particularly suited for putting-into-relief in the narrative domain, the preterite; whereas the imperfect signals the receding into the background of the narrated contents, as is frequently observed at the beginning and the end of folktales and legends. But this same observation can be extended to the narrative parts of a text such as the *Discourse on Method*. Descartes uses "the imperfect when he immobilizes his thought, the preterite when he progresses methodically" (p. 222). Here again, Weinrich makes no concessions: "Putting-into-relief is the *one and only function* of the opposition between the imperfect and the preterite in the narrated world" (p. 117, his emphasis).

Might it be objected that the notion of slow or rapid tempo designates a characteristic of time itself? No. The impression of rapidity is explained by the concentration of values in the foreground, as in the famous expression *Veni, vidi, vici* or in Voltaire's brisk style in his *Contes et Romans*. Conversely, the slowness of description in the realistic novel, underscored by the abundance of imperfects, is explained by the complacency with which the author lingers over the sociological background of the events he reports.[16]

We now see the architecture of the whole that in Weinrich's view governs the syntactic articulation of the tenses. The three relevant elements that provide the guideline for the analysis are not coordinated with one another but are subordinated one to the other and constitute a net of finer and finer mesh. First comes the broad division between narrative and commentary, with its two groups of tenses. Then, within each group, the threefold division of perspective/retrospective, zero degree, and anticipation. Finally, within each perspective, the bifurcation between the first and the second plane. If it is true that the syntactic articulations constitute in relation to the lexemes the first classification of possible objects of communications ("reflecting this schematic partitioning of the world is precisely the role of the syntactic categories" [p. 27]), then there exists between syntax and semantics, from the point of view of the classification of objects of communication, no more than a difference of degree in the fineness of the schematic division.[17]

Harald Weinrich's book is not limited, however, to this ever more detailed study of the paradigmatic division of the tenses. This mode of division finds an indispensable complement in the distribution of the same tenses throughout the course of a text, whether in commentary or in narrative. In this respect, the analyses devoted to temporal transitions, that is, to the "passage from one sign to the other in the course of the linear unfolding of the text" (p. 199), constitute a fundamental mediation between the resources offered by syntax and the utterance of some particular narrative configuration. This syntagmatic complement to the paradigmatic division of tenses in a natural language must not be overlooked if we recall that a text is composed of "signs arranged in a linear series, transmitted from speaker to listener in a chronological sequence" (p. 198).

These temporal transitions can be homogeneous, if they occur within the same group, or heterogeneous, if they are made from one group to another. The former are shown to be the most frequent. They guarantee, in effect, the consistency of the text, its textuality. The latter, however, are responsible for the richness of information. Thus we find the interruption of the narrative by direct discourse (dialogue), and the recourse to indirect discourse in the most varied and subtle forms, such as, for example, free indirect discourse (to which I shall return, below, in terms of the narrative voice). Other temporal transitions, concealed under the old name of the agreement of tenses, constitute but so many signals to guide the reading of texts.[18]

Of all the questions that can be raised by Weinrich's dense work, I shall retain only one: what is the relevance of resorting to the syntax of tenses for an investigation of time in the realm of fiction?

Let us return to the discussion at the point where Benveniste left us. Weinrich's work will enable us to make more precise the two theses I arrived at there. On the one hand, I maintained that the autonomy of tense systems in natural languages appears to be entirely compatible with the break made by fiction on the plane of mimesis $_2$. On the other hand, this autonomy of a tense system does not extend to a total independence in relation to lived time, inasmuch as this system articulates the time of fiction, which maintains a tie with lived time, on the two sides of fiction. Do Weinrich's analyses contradict this thesis?

The first part of the thesis poses no problem. The arrangement adopted by Weinrich is particularly well-suited for showing how the invention of plots is joined to the syntax of tenses.

First, by taking the text and not the sentence as his field of operation, Weinrich works on units of the same size as those with which narrative poetics is concerned. Next, by imposing finer and finer distinctions on the nomenclature of tenses and by combining this nomenclature with that of numerous other temporal signs, such as adverbs and adverbial phrases, without forgetting the person of the verb, textual linguistics shows the richness of the spectrum of differences available to the art of composition. The final differentiating factor, that of "putting into relief," has in this regard the greatest affinity with emplotment. The idea of putting into relief guides us effortlessly toward distinguishing just what constitutes an event in a narrated story. Does not Weinrich fervently quote Goethe's phrase for designating the foreground, namely, "the extraordinary event," which has as its equivalent Aristotle's peripeteia?[19] It is even clearer that the indications of tempo in a narrative resulting from the syntax of tenses and adverbs, whose rich fabric we glimpsed just above, take on their relief, precisely, as they contribute to the progress of the plot. The changes of tempo are scarcely definable outside of their use in narrative composition. Finally, by adding a table of temporal transitions to the tense groupings according to their paradigms, textual linguistics shows the meaningful sequences of tenses that are available to narrative composition for producing its meaning-effects. This syntagmatic complement constitutes the most appropriate transition between textual linguistics and narrative poetics. The transitions from one tense to another act as a guide for the transformations from an initial situation to a final situation, and this is what constitutes every plot. The idea that homogeneous transitions assure the consistency of the text, while heterogeneous transitions assure the wealth of its information-content, finds a direct parallel in the theory of emplotment. The plot, too, presents homogeneous features and heterogeneous features, a stability and a progression, recurrences and differences. In this sense, we can say that if syntax offers its range of paradigms and transitions to the narrator, these resources are actually realized in the work of composition.

This is the profound affinity that can be discerned between the theory of tenses and the theory of narrative composition.

On the other hand, I am not prepared to follow Weinrich in his attempt to dissociate the verb tenses (*Tempus*) from time (*Zeit*) in every respect. To the extent that the system of tenses can be considered as the linguistic apparatus allowing the structuring of the time appropriate for the activity of narrative configuration, we can both do justice to the analyses of *Tempus* and question the assertion that the tenses have nothing to do with time (*Zeit*). Fiction, I have said, continually makes the transition between the experience that precedes the text and the experience that follows it. In my opinion, the system of tenses, regardless of its autonomy in relation to time and its current designations, never makes a clean break in every respect with the experience of time. The system of tenses comes out of time and returns to it, and the signs of this descent and this destination are indelible in the distribution of tenses, both linearly and paradigmatically.

First of all, it is not without reason that in so many modern languages the same term designates time [*le temps*] and the verb tenses [*les temps verbaux*] or that the different designations attributed to the two orders retain a semantic kinship that is easily perceived by speakers. (This is the case in English between "tense" and "time," and in German the alternation between the German and Latin roots in *Zeit* and *Tempus* easily allows this kinship to be reestablished.)

Next, Weinrich himself has preserved a mimetic feature in his typology of tenses, since the function of signaling and guidance ascribed to the syntactic distinctions results in an "initial schematic partitioning of the world." And what is in question in the distinction made between the tenses in terms of the speech situation in a narrated world and a commented world. I am well aware that the term "world" here designates the sum of possible objects of communication, without any explicit ontological implication, if we are not to wipe out the initial distinction between *Tempus* and *Zeit*. However, a narrated world and a commented world remain worlds nonetheless, whose relations to the world of praxis are only held in suspension, following the law of mimesis$_2$.

The difficulty returns with each of the three axes of communication that govern the distribution of tenses. Weinrich justly asserts that the preterite of folktales and legends, of the novel and the short story, signals only the entry into narrative. He finds confirmation of this break with the expression of past time in the use of the preterite in the utopian narrative, in science fiction, and in novels dealing with the future. But can we conclude from this that the signal marking the entry into narrative has no connection whatsoever with the expression of the past as such? Weinrich does not, in fact, deny that in another communication situation these tenses express the past. Are these two linguistic facts completely unrelated? Can we not recognize, despite the caesura, a certain filiation that would be that of the *as if*? Does not the signal marking the entry into fiction make an oblique reference to the past through the process of neutralization, of suspension? Husserl discusses at great length this filiation by neutralization.[20] Following him, Eugen Fink defines *Bild* in terms of the neutralization of mere "presentification" (*Vergegenwärtigen*).[21] By this neutralization of the "realist" intention of memory, all absence becomes by analogy a *quasi-past*. Every narrative—even of the future—speaks of the irreal *as if* it were past. How could we explain that narrative tenses are also those of memory, if there were not between narrative and memory some metaphorical relation produced by neutralization?[22]

I am intentionally reinterpreting the criterion of relaxation proposed by Weinrich in terms of the neutralization of the presentification of the past to distinguish the narrated world from the commented world. The attitude of relaxation signaled by the narrative tenses is not limited, in my opinion, to suspending the reader's involvement in his or her real environment. It suspends even more fundamentally the belief in the past as having-been in order to transpose it to the level of fiction, as the opening phrases of fairy tales, referred to above, invite us to do. An indirect relation to lived time is thus preserved through the mediation of neutralization.[23]

The conservation of the temporal intention of the tenses, despite the break established when we enter into the realm of fiction, can also be observed along the other two axes that complete the division between narrative and commentary. As we have seen, in order to introduce the three perspectives—retrospection, anticipation, and zero degree—Weinrich is forced to distinguish between *Aktzeit* and *Textzeit*. The return of the term *Zeit* is not an accident. The textual unfolding, whether oral or written, is said to be "obviously an unfolding in time" (*Le Temps*, p. 67). This constraint results from the linear character of the speech chain. It follows that retrospection and anticipation are subjected to the same conditions of temporal linearity. Even if one tries to replace these two terms by those of reported or anticipated information, I do not see how the notions of future and past can be entirely eliminated from their definition. Retrospection and looking ahead express the most primitive structure of retention and protension of the living present. Without this oblique reference to the structure of time, we cannot understand what anticipation or retrospection means.

Similar remarks may be made concerning the third axis of communication, that of putting into relief. If it is in fact true that on the level of fiction the distinction between the imperfect and the past tense no longer owes anything to the usual tense designations, the primary sense of the distinction does seem to be tied to the capacity of discerning in the tense itself an aspect of permanence and an aspect of incidental occurrence.[24] It seems unlikely that no aspect of this characterization of time itself passes into the tenses involved in putting-into-relief. For if this were not the case, how could Weinrich write: "In the foreground of narrative, all that occurs, moves, changes"? (p. 176). Fictive time is never completely cut off from lived time, the time of memory and of action.[25]

I myself see in this twofold relation of filiation and breaking-off that is at work between the tenses of the lived past and the tenses of the narrative an exemplary illustration of the relations between mimesis₁ and mimesis₂. Past tenses first express the past; then by a metaphorical transition that preserves what it supersedes, they state the entry into fiction without a direct, though perhaps with an oblique, reference to the past as such.

There is an additional reason, and in my opinion the decisive one, for not burning all the bridges between the verb tenses and time. It has to do with the relation to what I have described as the second side of the text, the relation that defines the stage of mimesis₃. Fiction not only retains the trace of the world of praxis against which it stands out; it also redirects our gaze toward features of experience that it "invents," that is to say, both discovers and creates.[26] In this respect the tenses break with the designations of lived time, the time omitted by textual linguistics, so that they may rediscover this time with infinitely diversified grammatical resources.

It is this prospective relation with regard to an experience of time, as it is sketched out in literature, that explains that the great precursors, whose patronage Weinrich invokes, persistently tied the verb tenses to time. When Goethe and Schiller refer in their correspondence to the freedom and mobility of the omniscient narrator, who surveys a practically immobile epic action, when August Wilhelm Schlegel celebrates the "reflective serenity belonging to the narrator," they expect the emergence of a new quality of time itself from aesthetic experience. In particular, when Thomas Mann calls *Der Zauberberg* a *Zeitroman*, he never doubts that "its very object is time [*Zeit*] in its pure state" (p. 55).[27] The qualitative difference between the time of the "flat-lands" and the easy, carefree time of those who, up above, are devoted to the eternal snows (p. 56) is certainly a meaning-effect of the narrated world. In this sense it is as fictive as the rest of the universe of the novel. However, it does actually consist in a new consciousness of time, in the mode of the as-if. The verb tenses are in the service of this production of meaning.

I shall pursue this investigation no further here; it will be the topic of the next chapter. This investigation, in fact, involves a new notion, that of the fictive experience of time, such as this is undergone by the characters, themselves fictive, in the narrative. This fictive experience has to do with a different dimension of the literary work than the one we are considering here, namely, its power to project a world. It is in this projected world that the characters live who have an experience of time in it, an experience which is just as fictive as they are but which nonetheless has a world as its horizon. Does not Weinrich authorize this furtive insight into the notion of a world of the work when he himself speaks of a narrated world and a commented world? Does he not give this insight a more specific legitimation by taking syntax as an initial partitioning of the world of *possible* objects of communication? What indeed are these possible objects if not *fictions* capable of orienting us later in deciphering our own condition and its temporality?

These suggestions, which for the moment are no more than questions, allow us at least to glimpse some of the reasons why the study of tenses can no more cut its ties with the experience of time and with its customary designations than fiction can snap its moorings to the world of praxis, from which it proceeds and to which it returns.

THE TIME OF NARRATING (ERZÄHLZEIT) AND NARRATED TIME (ERZÄHLTE ZEIT)

With this distinction introduced by Günther Müller and taken up again by Gérard Genette, we enter into a problematic that, in contrast to the preceding one, does not seek in the utterance itself an internal principle of differentiation that would be apparent in the distribution of the tenses, but instead looks for a new key for interpreting time in fiction in the distinction *between* utterance and statement.

It is of the utmost importance to state, without further delay, that unlike the three authors discussed above, Müller introduces a distinction that is not confined to within discourse. It opens onto a *time of life* which is not unlike the reference to a narrated world in Weinrich. This feature does not carry over in Genette's structural narratology and can only be pursued in a meditation belonging to a hermeneutics of the world of the text, such as I shall sketch in the final chapter of this volume. For Genette, the distinction between the time of the utterance and the time of the statement is maintained within the bounds of the text, without any kind of mimetic implication.

My aim is to show that Genette is more rigorous than Müller in his distinction between two narrative times, but that Müller, at the cost perhaps of formal coherence, preserves an opening that is left to us to exploit. What we require is a three-tiered scheme: utterance-statement-world of the text, to which correspond a time of narrating, a narrated time, and a fictive experience of time projected by the conjunction/disjunction between the time it takes to narrate and narrated time. Neither of these two authors replies exactly to this need. Müller does not clearly distinguish the second from the third level, and Genette eliminates the third level in the name of the second one.

I am going to attempt to reorder these three levels by means of a critical examination of these two analyses, to which I am indebted for what are, at times, opposite reasons.

The philosophical context in which Müller introduces the distinction between *Erzählzeit* and *erzählte Zeit* is very different from that of French structuralism. This framework is that of a "morphological poetics," [28] directly inspired by Goethe's meditations on the morphology of plants and animals. [29] The reference of art to life, which constantly underlies this morphological poetics can only be understood within this context. [30] As a result, the distinction presented by Müller is condemned to oscillate between an overall opposition of narrative to life and a distinction internal to narrative itself. His definition of art allows both these interpretations: "narrating is presentifying [*vergegenwär-tigen*] events that are not perceptible to the listener's senses" (p. 247). It is in this act of presentification that the fact of "narrating" and the thing "narrated" are distinguished. This is therefore a phenomenological distinction by reason of which every narrating is narrating something (*erzählen von*), yet something which itself is not a narrative. From this basic distinction follows the possibility of distinguishing two times: the time taken to narrate and narrated time. But what is the correlate of presentification to which narrated time corresponds? Here we find two answers. On the one hand, what is narrated and is not narrative is not itself given in flesh and blood in the narrative but is simply "rendered or restored" (*Wiedergabe*). On the other hand, what is narrated is essentially the "temporality of life" (p. 251). However, "life does not narrate itself, it is lived" (p. 254). Both these interpretations are assumed by the following statement: "every narrating is narrating something that is not a narrative but a life process" (p. 261). Every narrative since the *Iliad* narrates this flowing (*Fliessen*): "je mehr Zeitlichkeit des Lebens, desto reinere Epik"—"the richer life is in temporality, the purer the epic" (p. 250).

Let us keep for later discussion this apparent ambiguity concerning the status of narrated time, and let us turn toward the aspects of the division into the time of narrating and narrated time that result from a morphological poetics.

Everything stems from the observation that narrating is, to use an expression borrowed from Thomas Mann, "setting aside" (*aussparen*), that is, both choosing and excluding.[31] We should thus be able to submit to scientific investigation the various modes of "folding" (*Raffung*) by means of which the time of narrating is separated from narrated time. More precisely, comparing the two times truly becomes the object of a science of literature once literature lends itself to measurement. Whence comes the idea of a metric comparison of the two times in question. This idea of a metric comparison of the two times seems to have come from a reflection on Fielding's narrative technique in *Tom Jones*. It is Fielding, the father of the novel that recounts the growth and development of a character, who concretely posed the technical question of *Erzählzeit*. As a master, conscious of playing with time, he devotes each of his eighteen books to temporal segments of varying lengths—from several years to several hours—slowing down or speeding up, as the case may be, omitting one thing or emphasizing another. If Thomas Mann raised the problem of *Aussparung*, Fielding preceded him by consciously modulating the *Zeitraffung*, the unequal distribution of narrated time in the time of narrating.

However, if we measure something, just what are we measuring? And is everything measurable here?

What we are measuring, under the name of *Erzählzeit*, is, as a matter of convention, a chronological time, equivalent to the number of pages and lines in the published work by reason of the prior equivalence posited between the time elapsed and the space covered on the face of a clock. It is by no means, therefore, a question of the time taken to compose the work. To what time is the number of pages and lines equivalent? To a conventional time of reading that is hard to distinguish from the variable time of actual reading. The latter is an interpretation of the time taken to tell the story which is comparable to the interpretation that a particular orchestra conductor gives to the theoretical time of performing a piece of music.[32] Once these conventions are admitted, we may say that narrating requires "a fixed lapse of physical time" that the clock measures. What is then compared are indeed "lengths" of time, both with respect to the now measurable *Erzählzeit* as well as to narrated time, which is also measured in terms of years, days, and hours.

Can everything now be measured by means of these "temporal compressions"? If the comparison of times were limited to the comparative measurement of two chronologies, the inquiry would be most disappointing—although, even reduced to these dimensions, it leads to surprising and frequently neglected conclusions (so great is the attention paid to thematics that the subtleties of this strategy of double chronology have been largely overlooked). These compressions do not consist only in abbreviations along a variable scale. They also consist in skipping over dead time, in precipitating the progress of the narrative by a staccato rhythm in the expression (*Veni, vidi, vici*), in condensing into a single exemplary event iterative or durative features ("every day," "unceasingly," "for weeks," "in the autumn," and so on). Tempo and rhythm thus enrich, in the course of the same work, the variations of the relative lengths of the time of narration and the time narrated. Taken together, all these notations contribute to outlining the narrative's *Gestalt*. And this notion of a *Gestalt* opens the way for investigations into structural aspects further and further removed from linearity, sequence, and chronology, even if the basis continues to be the relation between measurable time-lapses.

In this respect, the three examples used in Müller's essay "Erzählzeit und Erzählte Zeit," namely, Goethe's *Wilhelm Meisters Lehrejahre*, Virginia Woolf's *Mrs. Dalloway*, and Galsworthy's *Forsyte Saga*, are examined with an extraordinary minuteness which makes these analyses models worthy of imitation.

By the choice of method, this investigation is based in each instance on the most linear aspects of narrativity but is not confined to them. The initial narrative schema is that of sequence, and the art of narrating consists in restoring the succession of events (*die Wiedergabe des Nacheinanders*) (p. 270).[33] The remarks that shatter this linearism are therefore all the more precious. The narrative tempo, in particular, is affected by the way in which the narration stretches out in descriptions of scenes as if they were tableaux or speeds up through a series of strong, quick beats. Like Braudel the historian, we must not speak of time as being simply long or short, but as rapid or slow. The distinction between "scenes" and "transitions," or "intermediary episodes," is also not strictly quantitative. The effects of slowness or of rapidity, of briefness or of being long and drawn out are at the borderline of the quantitative and the qualitative. Scenes that are narrated at length and separated by brief transitions or iterative summaries—Müller calls them "monumental scenes"—carry the narrative process along, in contrast to those narratives in which "extraordinary events" form the narrative skeleton. In this way, nonquantifiable structural relations add complexity to the *Zusammenspiel* at play between two time-spans. The arrangement of scenes, intermediary episodes, important events, and transitions never ceases to modulate the quantities and extensions. To these features are added anticipations and flashbacks, the interlinkings that enable the memory of vast stretches of time to be included in brief narrative sequences, creating the effect of perspectival depth, while breaking up chronology. We move even further away from a strict comparison between lengths of time when, to flashbacks, are added the time of remembering, the time of dreaming, and the time of the reported dialogue, as in Virginia Woolf. Qualitative tensions are thus added to quantitative measurements.[34]

What is it, then, that inspires in this way the transition from the analysis of the measurement of time-spans to an evaluation of the more qualitative phenomenon of contraction? It is the relation of the time of narration to the time of life through narrated time. Here Goethe's meditation comes to the fore: life in itself does not represent a whole. Nature can produce living things but these are indifferent (*gleichgültig*). Art can produce only dead things, but they are meaningful. Yes, this is the horizon of thinking: drawing narrated time out of indifference by means of the narrative. By saving or sparing and compression, the narrator brings what is foreign to meaning (*sinnfremd*) into the sphere of meaning. Even when the narrative intends to render what is senseless (*sinnlos*), it places this in relation to the sphere of making sense (*Sinndeutung*).[35]

Therefore if we were to eliminate this reference to life, we would fail to understand that the tension between these two times stems from a morphology that at one and the same time resembles the work of formation/transformation (*Bildung-Umbildung*) active in living organisms and differs from it by elevating meaningless life to a meaningful work by the grace of art. It is in this sense that the comparison between organic nature and poetic work constitutes an irreducible component of poetic morphology.

If, following Genette, we may call the relation between the time of narrating and the narrated time in the narrative itself a "game with time," this game has as its stakes the temporal experience (*Zeiterlebnis*) intended by the narrative. The task of poetic morphology is to make apparent the way in which the quantitative relations of time agree with the qualities of time belonging to life itself. Conversely, these temporal qualities are brought to light only by the play of derivations and insertions, without any thematic meditation on time having to be grafted onto them, as in Laurence Sterne, Joseph Conrad, Thomas Mann, or Marcel Proust. A fundamental time is implied, without itself being considered as a theme. Nevertheless, this time of life is "codetermined" by the relation and the tension between the two times of the narrative and by the "laws of form" that result from them.[36] In this respect, we might be tempted to say that there are as many temporal "experiences" as poets, even as poems. This is indeed the case, and this is why this "experience" can only be intended obliquely through the "temporal armature," as what this armature is suited to, what it fits. It is clear that a discontinuous structure suits a time of dangers and adventures, that a more continuous, linear structure suits a *Bildungsroman* where the themes of growth and metamorphosis predominate, whereas a jagged chronology, interrupted by jumps, anticipations, and flashbacks, in short, a deliberately multidimensional configuration, is better suited to a view of time that has no possible overview, no overall internal cohesiveness. Contemporary experiments in the area of narrative techniques are thus aimed at shattering the very experience of time. It is true that in these experiments the game itself can become the stakes.[37] But the polarity of temporal experience (*Zeiterlebnis*) and temporal armature (*Zeitgerüst*) seems inescapable.

In every case, an actual temporal creation, a "poietic time" (p. 311) is uncovered on the horizon of each "meaningful composition" (p. 308). This temporal creation is what is at stake in the structuration of time at play between the time of narrating and narrated time.

Utterance, Statement, and Object in Genette's Narrative Discourse

Günther Müller's *Morphologische Poetik* has in the end left us with three times: the time of the act of narrating, the time that is narrated, and finally the time of life. The first is a chronological time; it is a time of reading rather than of writing. We can measure only its spatial equivalent, which is counted by the number of pages and lines. Narrated time, for its part, is counted in years, months, and days and may even be dated in the work itself. It is, in turn, the result of the "compression" of a time "spared" or "set aside," which is not narrative but life. The nomenclature Gérard Genette proposes is also ternary.[38] But it cannot, for all this, be superimposed upon Müller's. It results from the effort of structural narratology to derive all of its categories from features contained in the text itself, which is not the case for Müller with respect to the time of life.

Genette's three levels are determined starting from the middle level, the narrative statement. This is the narrative properly speaking. It consists in relating real or imaginary events. In written culture this narrative is identical with the narrative text. The narrative statement, in its turn, stands in a twofold relation. In the first place, the statement is related to the object of the narrative, namely, the events recounted, whether they be fictitious or real. This is what is ordinarily called the "told" story. (In a similar sense, the universe in which the story takes place can be termed "diegetic.")[39] Secondly, the statement is related to the act of narrating taken in itself, to the narrative "utterance." (For Ulysses, recounting his adventures is just as much an action as is massacring the pretenders.) A narrative, we shall therefore say, tells a story, otherwise it would not be a narrative. And it is proferred by someone, otherwise it would not be discourse. "As narrative, it lives by its relationship to the story that it recounts; as discourse, it lives by its relationship to the narrating that utters it" (*Narrative Discourse*, p. 29).[40]

How do these categories compare with those of Benveniste and Günther Müller (leaving aside Harald Weinrich, who is not in question here)? As the very title of this work indicates, it is quite clear that the division into discourse and narrative, received from Benveniste, is retained only as something to be challenged. Every narrative includes discourse inasmuch as any narrative is no less something uttered than, let us say, lyric song, confession, or autobiography. If the narrator is absent from the text, this is still a fact of utterance.[41] In this sense, utterance derives from the instance of discourse, in the broad sense Benveniste ascribes to this term elsewhere in order to oppose it to the virtual system of language [*langue*] rather than to discourse in the more limited sense, in which it is opposed to narrative. It may be admitted, however, that his distinction between discourse and narrative has made us aware of a dichotomy that we were subsequently obliged to situate within narrative, in the broad sense of the term. In this sense, the inclusive dichotomy, so to speak, of utterance and statement is heir to the more exclusive disjunction between discourse and narrative, according to Benveniste.[42]

The relation to Günther Müller is even more complex. The distinction between *Erzählzeit* and *erzählte Zeit* is retained by Genette but is entirely made over. This reworking results from the difference in status of the levels to which temporal features are ascribed. In Genette's terminology the diegetic and the utterance designate nothing external to the text. The relation between the statement and what is recounted is assimilated to the relation between signifier and signified in Saussurean linguistics. What Müller calls life is therefore set out of bounds. Utterance, for its part, does indeed come out of the self-referential character of discourse and refers to the person who is narrating. Narratology, however, strives to record only the marks of narration found in the text.

A complete redistribution of temporal features results from this reorganization of the levels of analysis. First, the *Zeiterlebnis* is set out-of-bounds. All that remain are the relations internal to the text between utterance, statement, and story (or diegetic universe). It is to these relations that the analyses of a model text are devoted, Proust's *Remembrance of Things Past*.

The main emphasis of the analysis bears on the relation between the time of the narrative and the time of the diegesis, somewhat at the expense of the time of utterance, for reasons I shall state below. What is the time of the narrative, if it is neither that of the utterance nor that of the diegesis? Like Müller, Genette holds it to be the equivalent of and the substitute for the time of reading, that is, the time it takes to cover or traverse the space of the text: "the narrative text, like every other text, has no other temporality than what it borrows, metonymically, from its own reading" (*Narrative Discourse*, p. 34). We must, therefore, take "for granted and accept literally the quasi-fiction of the *Erzählzeit*, this false time standing in for a true time and to be treated—with the combination of reservation and approval that this involves—as a *pseudo-time*" (p. 79, his emphasis).[43]

I shall not take up in detail Genette's analysis of the three essential determinations—order, duration, frequency—in terms of which the relations between the time of the story and the pseudo-time of narrative can be studied. In these three registers, what is meaningful are the discordances between the temporal features of the events in the diegesis and the corresponding features in the narrative.

With respect to order, these discordances may be placed under the general heading of anachrony.[44] The epic narrative, since the *Iliad*, is noted in this regard for the way it begins *in media res* and then moves backward in order to explain events. In Proust, this procedure is used to oppose the future, become present, to the idea one had of it in the past. The art of narrating is for Proust in part that of playing with prolepsis (narrating ahead of events) and analepsis (narrating by moving back in time), and inserting prolepses within analepses. This initial game with time gives rise to a very detailed typology, which I shall not attempt to give an account of here. For subsequent discussion, I shall retain only what concerns the ultimate *end* [*finalité*] of these anachronic variations. Whether it is a question of completing the narration of an event by bringing it into the light of a preceding event, of filling in an earlier lacuna, or provoking involuntary memory by the repeated recalling of similar events, or of correcting an earlier interpretation by means of a series of reinterpretations—Proustian analepsis is not a gratuitous game. It is governed by the meaning of the work as a whole.[45] This recourse to the opposition between meaningful and unmeaningful opens a perspective on narrative time that goes beyond the literary technique of anachrony.[46]

The uses of prolepsis within a globally retrospective narrative seems to me to illustrate even better than analepsis this relation to overall meaning opened by narrative understanding. Some prolepses take a particular line of action to its logical conclusion, to the point of rejoining the narrator's present. Others are used to authenticate the narrative of the past through testimony to its persistence in current memory ("today, I can still see . . ."). In order to account for this game with time, we have to borrow from Auerbach the notion of the "symbolic omnitemporality" of the "remembering consciousness."[47] But then the theoretical framework chosen for the analysis proves inadequate: "A perfect example," Genette states, "of fusion, of quasi-miraculous fusion, between the event recounted and the narrating instance, which is both late (final) and 'omni-temporal'" (p. 70).[48]

Taking an overall view of the anachronies in Proust's *Recherche*, Genette declares that "the importance of the 'anachronic' narrative in *Recherche du temps perdu* is obviously connected to the retrospectively synthetic character of Proustian narrative, which is totally present in the narrator's mind at every moment. Ever since the day when the narrator in a trance perceived the unifying significance of his story, he never ceases to hold all of its places and all of its moments, to be capable of establishing a multitude of 'telescopic' relations amongst them" (p. 78). But must we not then say that what narratology takes as the pseudo-time of a narrative is composed of the set of temporal strategies placed at the service of a conception of time that, first articulated in fiction, can also constitute a paradigm for redescribing lived and lost time?

Genette's study of the distortions of duration leads me to the same reflections. I shall not go back over the impossibility of measuring the duration of the narrative, if by this is meant the time of reading (p. 86). Let us admit with Genette that we can only compare the respective speeds of the narrative and of the story, the speed always being defined by a relation between a temporal measure and a spatial one. In this way, in order to characterize the speeding up or slowing down of the narrative in relation to the events recounted, we end up comparing, just as Müller did, the duration of the text, measured by pages and lines, with the duration of the story measured by clock time. As in Müller, the variations—here called "anisochronies"—have to do with large narrative articulations and their internal chronology, whether expressly given or inferred. We may then apportion the distortions in speed between the drastic slowing down of "pauses" and the dramatic acceleration of ellipses by situating the classical notion of a "scene" or "description" alongside of that of a pause, and that of a "summary" alongside of that of an ellipsis.[49] A highly detailed typology of the comparative dimensions of the length of the text and the duration of the narrated events can then be sketched out. However, what seems to me to be important is that narratology's mastery of the strategies of acceleration and slowing down serves to enhance our understanding of procedures of emplotment that we have acquired through our familiarity with the procedures of emplotment and the function of such emplotment procedures. For example, Genette notes that in Proust the fullness (and hence the slow pace of the narrative, which establishes a sort of coincidence between the length of the text and the time taken by the hero to be absorbed by a spectacle) is closely related to the "contemplative halts" (p. 102) in the hero's experience.[50] Likewise, the absence of a summary narrative, the absence of descriptive pauses, the tendency of the narrative to constitute itself as a scene in the narrative sense of this term, the inaugural character of the five major scenes—morning, dinner, evening—which by themselves take up some six hundred pages, the repetition that transforms them into typical scenes; all these structural features of *Remembrance of Things Past*—features that leave intact none of the traditional narrative movements (p. 112), features that can be discerned, analyzed, and classified by an exact narratological science—receive their meaning from the sort of temporal immobility created by the narrative on the level of fiction.

However, the modification that gives the narrative temporality of *Remembrance* "a completely new cadence—perfectly unprecedented" (ibid.) is certainly the iterative character of the narrative, which narratology places under the third temporal category, that of frequency (recounting once or *n* times an event that occurs once or *n* times) and that it sets in opposition to the "singulative" narrative.[51] How is this "intoxication with the iterative" (p. 123) to be interpreted? The strong tendency of instants in Proust to merge together and become confused with one another is, Genette grants, "the very condition for experiencing 'involuntary memory'" (p. 124).[52] And yet in this exercise of narratology, it is never once a question of this experience. Why?

If the memory experience of the narrator-hero is so easily reduced to a mere "factor in (I should say rather a means of) the emancipation of the narrative with respect to temporality" (p. 156), this is in part because the inquiry concerning time has been until this point artificially contained within the limits of the relation between the stated narrative and the diegesis, at the expense of the temporal aspects of the relationship between statement and utterance, described in terms of the grammatical category of "voice."[53]

Postponing any discussion of the time of the narration is not without its drawbacks. For example, we cannot understand the meaning of the reversal by which, at the turning point in Proust's work, the story, with its steady chronology and the predominance of the singulative, takes control over the narrative, with its anachronisms and its iterations, if we do not attribute the distortions of duration, which then take over, to the narrator himself, "who in his impatience and growing anguish is desirous both of *loading* his final scenes . . . and of jumping to the denouement . . . that will finally give him being and legitimate his discourse" (p. 157, his emphasis). Within the time of the narrative must therefore be integrated "another temporality, no longer the temporality of the narrative but in the final instance governing it: the temporality of the narrating itself" (ibid.)[54]

What, then, may be said about the relation between utterance and statement? Does it possess no temporal character at all? The basic phenomenon whose textual status can be preserved here is that of the "voice," a notion borrowed from grammarians[55] and one that characterizes the implication of the narration itself in the narrative, that is, of the narrative instance (in the sense in which Benveniste speaks of the instance of discourse) with its two protagonists: the narrator and the real or virtual receiver. If a question about time arises at this level of relation, it is insofar as the narrative instance, represented in the text by the voice, itself presents temporal features.

If the time of utterance is examined so briefly and so late in *Narrative Discourse*, this has in part to do with the difficulties involved in establishing the proper order of the relations between utterance, statement, and story,[56] but more importantly, it has to do with the difficulty that, in *Remembrance*, is connected to the relation between the real author and the fictive narrator, who here happens to be the same as the hero, the time of narration displaying the same fictive quality as the role of the narrator-hero's "I" calls for an analysis that is, precisely, an analysis of voice. Indeed, if the act of narration does not carry within itself any mark of duration, the variations in its distance from the events recounted is important for "the narrative's significance" (p. 216). In particular, the changes referred to above concerning the temporal dimension of the narrative find a certain justification in these variations. They make us feel the gradual shortening of the very fabric of the narrative discourse, as if, Genette adds, "the story time tended to dilate and make itself conspicuous while drawing near to its end, *which is also its origin*" (p. 226, his emphasis). The fact that the time of the hero's story approaches its own source, the narrator's present, without being able to catch up with it, is part of the meaning of the narrative, namely, that it is ended or at least broken off when the hero becomes a writer.[57]

Its recourse to the notion of the narrative voice allows narratology to make a place for subjectivity, without confusing this with the subjectivity of the real author. If *Remembrance* is not to be read as a disguised autobiography, this is because the "I" uttered by the narrator-hero is itself fictive. However, for lack of a notion like that of a world of the text (a notion I shall justify in the next chapter), this recourse to the notion of narrative voice is not sufficient to do justice to the fictive experience the narrator-hero has of time in its psychological and metaphysical dimensions.

Without this experience, which is just as fictive as the "I" who unfolds it and recounts it, and yet which is worthy of being called "experience" by virtue of its relation to the world projected by the work, it is difficult to give a meaning to the notions of time lost and time regained, which constitute what is at stake in *Remembrance of Things Past*.[58]

It is this tacit rejection of fictive experience that makes me uneasy when I read and reread the pages entitled "The Game with Time" (pp. 155–60), which give, if not the key to the work, at least its tone. (These pages are at the very least premature, when we consider that the study of the time of narration is postponed.) The narrator-hero's fictive experience of time, because it cannot to be connected to the meaning of the narrative, is referred back to the extrinsic justification of the work that the author, Proust, gives for his narrative technique, with its interpolations, its distortions, and above all its iterative condensations. This justification is assimilated to the "realist motivation" that Proust shares with other writers of the same tradition. Gérard Genette wants to stress with respect to this tradition only its "contradictions" and "compliancies" (p. 158): the contradiction between the concern with remembering things as they were lived in the instant and the concern with recounting them as they are remembered later. Hence, the contradiction between attributing at times to life and at time to memory the overlappings reflected in the anachronisms of the narrative. The contradiction, above all, inherent in a search committed both to the "extra-temporal" and to "time in its pure state." But are not these contradictions the very heart of the fictive experience of the narrator-hero? As for the compliancies, they are ascribed to "those retrospective rationalizations that great artists are never niggardly with, and this in direct proportion to their *genius*, in other words, to the lead their practice has over any theory—including their own" (ibid., his emphasis). Narrative practice, however, is not the only thing that keeps ahead of aesthetic theory. The fictive experience that gives a meaning to this practice is also in quest of a theory that always falls short of it, as witnessed by the commentaries with which the narrator overloads his narrative. It is precisely for a theoretical view foreign to the poiesis at work in the narrative itself that the experience of time in *Remembrance of Things Past* is reduced to "the contradictory aim" of an "ontological mystery" (p. 160).

It is perhaps the function of narratology to invert the relations between reminiscence and narrative technique, to see in the motivation referred to simply an aesthetic medium; in short, to reduce vision to style. The novel of time lost and regained then becomes, for narratology, a "novel of Time ruled, captured, bewitched, surreptitiously subverted, or better, *perverted*" (ibid., his emphasis).

But must not this reversal itself ultimately be reversed, and must not the formal study of narrative techniques be held to make time appear as perverted in order to gain by a long detour a sharpened comprehension of the experience of time lost *and* regained? It is this experience that, in *Remembrance of Things Past*, gives meaning and intention to the narrative techniques. If not, how may we speak about the novel as a whole, as its narrator does about dreams, in terms of the "formidable game it creates with Time" (ibid.)? Could a game be "formidable," that is, frightening as well, if nothing was at stake in it?

Over and above the discussion of the interpretation of *Remembrance* proposed by Genette, the question remains whether, in order to preserve the *meaning* of the work, it is not necessary to subordinate the narrative technique to the *intention* that carries the text beyond itself, toward an experience, no doubt feigned but nonetheless irreducible to a simple game with time. To pose this question is to ask whether we must not do justice to the dimension that Müller, recalling Goethe, named *Zeiterlebnis*, and that narratology, by decree and as a result of its strict methodology, sets out of bounds. The major difficulty is then to preserve the fictive quality of this *Zeiterlebnis*, while resisting its reduction to narrative technique alone. It is to this difficulty that my own study of Proust's *Remembrance* in the next chapter is devoted.

POINT OF VIEW AND NARRATIVE VOICE

Our investigation of "games with time" calls for a final complement that takes into account the notions of point of view and narrative voice, notions we encountered above, without seeing how they were connected to the major structures of narrative.[59] The notion of a fictive experience of time, toward which all our analyses of the configuration of time by fictional narrative converge, cannot do without these concepts of point of view and narrative voice (categories I am temporarily considering to be identical), inasmuch as point of view is a point of view directed toward the sphere of experience to which the character belongs and the narrative voice is that which, by addressing itself to readers, presents the narrated world (to use Weinrich's phrase) to them.

How can the notions of point of view and narrative voice be incorporated into the problem of narrative composition?[60] Essentially, by tying them to the categories of "narrator" and "character." The narrated world is the world of the characters and it is narrated by the narrator. The notion of a character is solidly anchored in narrative theory to the extent that a narrative cannot be a mimesis of action without being at the same time a mimesis of acting beings. And acting beings are, in the broad sense that the semantics of action confers on the notion of an agent, beings who think and feel—better, beings capable of talking about their thoughts, their feelings, and their actions. It is thus possible to shift the notion of mimesis from the action toward the character, and from the character toward the character's discourse.[61] There is more. When the discourse spoken by one of the characters concerning their experience is incorporated in the diegesis, the pair utterance/statement (around which this chapter is constructed) can be reformulated in a vocabulary that personalizes the two terms. The utterance becomes the discourse of the narrator, while the statement becomes the discourse of a character. The question will then be to determine by which special narrative means the narrative is constituted as *the discourse of a narrator recounting the discourse of the characters*. The notions of point of view and of narrative voice designate two of these means.

It is important, first, to take the measure of the shift from the mimesis of action toward the mimesis of the character, which initiates the entire chain of notions that leads to those of point of view and narrative voice.

Having given consideration first to drama, Aristotle was led to accord an eminent place to the character and to his or her thoughts, although they are always subordinated to the inclusive category of muthos in his theory of mimesis. The character truly belongs to the "what" of mimesis. And as the distinction between drama and diegesis depends solely on the "how"—that is, on the poet's manner of presenting the characters—the category of character has the same status in diegesis as in drama. For us, in the modern world, it is, on the contrary, through the diegesis as it is opposed to drama that we enter most directly into the problematic of the characters, with their thoughts, their feelings, and their discourse. Indeed no mimetic art has gone as far in the representation of thoughts, feelings, and discourse as has the novel. And it is the immense diversity and the seemingly unlimited flexibility of its means that have made the novel the privileged instrument for the investigation of the human psyche, to the point that Käte Hamburger was able to take the invention of centers of fictive consciousness, distinct from the real subjects of assertions about reality, as the criterion for determining the break between fiction and assertion.[62] Contrary to the prejudice that the power to describe the subjects of action, thought, and feeling from inside is derived from a subject's self-confession and examination of conscience, she goes so far as to suggest that it is the third-person novel, that is, the novel that recounts the thoughts, feelings, and words of a fictive other, that has gone furthest in the inspection of what goes on inside minds.[63]

Following this direction indicated by Hamburger, to whom she pays homage, Dorrit Cohn does not hesitate to place the study of third-person narration at the head of a magnificent study of the "narrative modes for presenting consciousness in fiction" (the subtitle of her work that I am considering here).[64] The first "mimesis of consciousness," she states, is the "mimesis of other minds" (p. 7). The study of consciousness in "first-person texts," that is, fictions that simulate a confession or an autobiography,[65] is put in second place and is conducted following the same principles as for the study of third-person narration. This is a remarkable strategy, if we consider that, among first-person texts, there are many in which the first-person is just as fictive as the third-person narratives using "he" or "she," so much so that this fictive first-person can, without any major damage, be permutated into a no less fictive third-person, as this was experimented with by Kafka and Proust.[66]

An excellent touchstone as regards the narrative techniques available to fiction for expressing this "inner transparency" is provided by the analysis of the ways of conveying the words and thoughts of fictive subjects in third- and first-person narratives. This is the path followed by Dorrit Cohn. It has the advantage of respecting the parallelism between third-person and first-person narrative and at the same time allowing for the extraordinary flexibility and inventiveness of the modern novel in this area.

The major technique employed on either side of the dividing line between the two great classes of narrative fiction is the direct narration of thoughts and feelings, whether the narrator attributes them to a fictive other or to him/herself. If "self-narration" in the first-person novel is mistakenly held to be self-evident, under the pretext that it simulates a memory, which is in truth fictitious, the same thing cannot be said about "psycho-narration," narration applied to other minds. This affords a privileged means of access to the well-known problem of the omniscient narrator, to which we shall return below in my discussion of point of view and voice. This privilege no longer appears scandalous if we are willing to admit with Jean Pouillon that it is in any case by means of the imagination that we understand all other minds.[67] The novelist does this, if not effortlessly, at least without any qualms, because it is part of the writer's art to supply expressions appropriate to thoughts, which he or she is able to read directly, because the novelist invents them, rather than deciphering these thoughts on the basis of their expression, as we do in daily life. All the magic of the third-person novel lies in this short circuit.[68]

In addition to the direct narration of thoughts and feelings, there are two other techniques available to the novel. The first consists in quoting the internal monologue of a fictional other ("quoted monologue") or of having the character quote himself or herself in the course of a monologue ("self-quoted monologue").[69] My purpose is not to explicate the licenses, conventions, even the unlikelihoods, of this technique, which presupposes, no less than the preceding one, the transparency of the mind, since the narrator is the one who adjusts the reported words to thoughts that are apprehended directly, without having to move from words back to thoughts as in daily life. To this "magic" stemming from the direct reading of thoughts, this procedure adds the major difficulty of lending to a solitary subject the use of speech intended, in practical life, for communication—what in fact does talking to oneself mean? Leading the dialogic dimension of speech off its customary path for the benefit of soliloquy poses immense technical and theoretical problems that are not within my province here, but concern a study of the fate of subjectivity in literature. However, I shall return to the relation between the narrator's discourse and the character's quoted discourse within the framework of my discussion of point of view and voice below.

The third technique, initiated by Flaubert and Jane Austen, the famous *style indirect libre*, or the narrated monologue, or the *erlebte Rede* of German stylistics, does not consist in quoting the monologue but in recounting it. So we should speak here of a "narrated" rather than a "quoted monologue." The words, as concerns their contents, are indeed those of the characters, but they are reported by the narrator, in the past tense and in the third person. The major difficulties of the quoted monologue or the self-quoted monologue are not so much resolved as they are covered over. For them to reappear, we have only to translate the narrated monologue into a quoted monologue, putting in the appropriate persons and tenses. Other difficulties, well known to readers of Joyce, arise in texts in which no boundary remains to separate the narrator's discourse from that of the characters. At any rate, this marvelous combination of psycho-narration and narrated monologue constitutes the most complete integration within the narrative fabric of others' thoughts and words. The narrator's discourse takes in hand the character's discourse by lending this discourse its voice, while it conforms to the tone of what the character said or is saying. The "miracle" of the well-known *erlebte Rede* thus adds the crowning touch to the "magic" of internal transparency.

In what way are the notions of point of view and voice called for by the preceding remarks on the representation of thoughts, feelings, and words in fiction?[70] The intermediary link is constituted by the search for a typology capable of accounting for the two great dichotomies, which I have employed spontaneously before elucidating them for themselves. The first posits two kinds of fiction. On the one hand, there is fiction that recounts the lives of characters taken as third parties (Dorrit Cohn's "mimesis of other minds"). Here we speak of a third-person narrative. On the other hand, we also find fictional narratives that attribute the grammatical person of the narrator to their characters. These are termed first-person narratives. However, another dichotomy runs through this first one, depending on whether the narrator's discourse predominates over that of the character. This dichotomy is easier to identify in third-person narratives, inasmuch as the distinction between narrating discourse and narrated discourse is maintained by grammatical distinctions concerning the persons and the verb tenses. It is more concealed in first-person fiction, inasmuch as the difference between the narrator and the character is not marked by the distinction of personal pronouns. The task of distinguishing between the narrator and the character under the identity of the grammatical "I" therefore devolves on other signals. The distance from one to the other can vary, as can the degree to which the narrator's discourse predominates in relation to the character's discourse. It is this double system of variations that has given rise to the construction of typologies that are intended to cover all possible narrative situations.

One of the more ambitious of these efforts is the theory of typical narrative situations presented by Franz K. Stanzel.[71] Stanzel does not directly employ the categories of perspective and voice. He prefers instead to distinguish between the types of narrative situations (*Erzählungsituationen*, abbreviated to *ES*) in terms of the feature that seems to him universally to characterize novelistic fictions, namely, that they "transmit" (mediate) thoughts, feelings, and words.[72] Either the mediation/transmission privileges the narrator, who imposes his or her perspective from on high (*auktoriale ES*),[73] or else the mediation is performed by a reflector (a term borrowed from Henry James), that is, by a character who thinks, feels, perceives, yet speaks not as the narrator but as one of the characters. The reader then sees the other characters through the eyes of this character (*personale* or *figurale ES*). Or the narrator identifies himself/herself as one of the characters, speaking in the first person and living in the same world as the other characters (*Ich ES*).

Actually, Stanzel's typology, despite its remarkable power of clarification, shares with many other typologies the double drawback of being too abstract to be discriminating and too poorly articulated to cover all narrative situations. A second work of Stanzel's attempts to remedy the first drawback by taking each of the three situation-types as the marked term of a pair of opposites placed at the poles of three heterogeneous axes. The *auktoriale ES* thus becomes the marked pole along the axis of "perspective," depending on whether the narrator has an external, hence broad, view of the characters, or an internal, hence limited, view of them. The notion of perspective thus receives a determined place in the taxonomy. The *personale* or *figurale ES* is the marked pole along the axis of "mode," depending on whether the character does or does not define the vision of the novel in the name of the narrator, who then becomes the unmarked pole of the opposition. As for the *Ich ES*, it becomes the marked pole along the axis of the "person," depending on whether the narrator belongs to the same ontic domain as the other characters. In this way, Stanzel avoids reference to the purely grammatical criterion of the use of personal pronouns.

With regard to the second shortcoming, Stanzel mitigates it by inserting between each of his three situation-types, now considered axial poles, a number of intermediary situations that he places in a circle (*Typenkreis*). A wide variety of narrative situations can thus be accounted for, depending on whether they come closer to or move away from each of these poles. The problem of perspective and of voice thus becomes the object of a more and more detailed attention. The perspective of the narrator-author cannot be effaced without the narrative situation moving closer to the *personale ES*, where the figure of the reflector comes to occupy the place left vacant by the narrator. Following the circular movement, we move away from the *personale ES* and move closer to the *Ich ES*. Here we see the character, who in the narrated monologue (*erlebte Rede*) still spoke through the voice of the narrator while imposing his or her own voice, share the same region of being as the other characters. It is this character who now says "I." The narrator, as a consequence, has only to borrow this voice.

Despite his effort to provide his typology with greater dynamism, Stanzel does not reply in a completely satisfactory way to the two objections raised above. We could reply adequately to the shortcoming of abstraction only if, by giving up the attempt to take as a starting point for our analysis metalanguages that present a certain logical coherence and using models such as these to describe texts, we were to search for theories that account for our literary competence, that is, the aptitude readers have for recognizing and summing up plots, and for grouping similar plots together.[74] If we were thus to adopt the rule of following closely the experience of the reader in the process of organizing step-by-step the elements of the told story in order to put a plot together, we would encounter the notions of perspective and voice less as categories defined by their place in a taxonomy than as a distinctive feature, taken from an unlimited constellation of other features and defined by its role in the composition of the literary work.[75]

As for the objection of incompleteness, it remains without a thoroughly satisfactory answer in a system that multiplies the forms of transition without ever moving outside the circle that is imperiously governed by the three narrative situation-types. For example, it does not seem that enough weight is given to the major feature of narrative fiction exemplified by its ability to present a third person as a third person, in a system in which the three narrative situation-types continue to be variations of the narrator's discourse, depending on whether it simulates the authority of the real author, the perspicacity of a reflector, or the reflexivity of a subject endowed with a fabulous memory. Hence it seems that what the reader can identify as point of view or as voice has to do with the way the bipolar relation between the narrator and the character is treated when the appropriate narrative techniques are used.

These two series of critical remarks applied to the typology of narrative situations suggest that the notions of perspective and voice can be approached, on the one hand, without an excessively taxonomical concern, as autonomous features characteristic of the composition of narrative fictions and, on the other hand, in direct relation to that major property of narrative fiction, which is the fact that it produces the discourse of a narrator recounting the discourse of fictional characters.[76]

Point of view, I will say, designates in a third- or first-person narrative the orientation of the narrator's attitude toward the characters and the characters' atitudes toward one another. This affects the composition of the work and is the object of a "poetics of composition," once the possibility of adopting variable points of view—a property inherent in the very notion of point of view—gives the artist the systematically exploited opportunity of varying points of view within the same work, of multiplying them, and of incorporating these combinations into the configuration of the work.

The typology offered by Boris Uspensky bears exclusively on these resources of composition provided by point of view.[77] In this way, the study of the notion of point of view can be incorporated into that of narrative configuration. Point of view lends itself to a typology to the extent that, as Lotman has also stressed, the work of art can and must be read on several levels.[78] In this fact lies the essential plurivocity of the work of art. Each of these levels also constitutes a possible place for manifesting a point of view, a space allowing for the possibilities of composition between points of view.

It is first of all on the plane of ideology, that is, of evaluations, that the notion of point of view takes shape, insofar as an ideology is the system that governs the conceptual vision of the world in all or part of a work. It may be the vision of the author or that of the characters. What is termed the "authorial point of view" is not the conception of the world of the real author but that which presides over the organization of the narrative of a particular work. At this level, point of view and voice are mere synonyms. The work can make voices other than the author's heard and can mark several ordered shifts in point of view, accessible to formal study (for example, a study of the use of fixed epithets in folklore).

It is on the level of phraseology, that is, on the level of the characteristics of discourse, that the study of the marks of the primacy of the narrator's discourse (authorial speech) or of that of the discourse of a particular character (figural speech) in third-person or first-person fiction occurs. This study belongs to a poetics of composition insofar as the shifts in point of view become the bearers of the structuration (as is shown in the variations in the names of characters, variations so characteristic of the Russian novel). It is on this plane that all the complexities of composition resulting from the correlation between the discourse of the author and that of the character are revealed. (Here we return to my remark, made earlier, about the numerous ways of reporting the discourse of a character, as well as to a system of classification similar to that which I borrowed from Dorrit Cohn.) [79]

The spatial and temporal planes of expressing point of view are of prime interest to us. It is first of all the spatial perspective, taken literally, that serves as a metaphor for all the other expressions of point of view. The development of a narrative always involves a combination of purely perceptual perspectives, implying position, angle of aperture, and depth of field (as is the case for film). The same thing is true with respect to temporal position, that of the narrator in relation to the characters as much as among the characters themselves. What is important once again is the degree of complexity resulting from the composition involving multiple temporal perspectives. The narrator may walk in step with the characters, making the present of narration coincide with his or her own present, and thereby accepting the limits and lack of knowledge imposed by this perspective. Or, on the contrary, the narrator may move forward or backward, considering the present from the point of view of the anticipation of a remembered past or as the past memory of an anticipated future, etc. [80]

The plane of verb tenses and aspects constitutes a distinct plane, inasmuch as what is considered here are purely grammatical resources and not temporal significations properly speaking. As in Weinrich, what is important for a poetics of composition are the modulations that occur throughout the text. Uspensky is especially interested in the alternation between the present tense, when it is applied to scenes that mark a pause in the narrative, scenes in which the narrator synchronizes his or her present with the present of the halted narrative, and the past tense, when it expresses the jumps in the narrative as if they were discrete quanta. [81]

Uspensky does not want to confuse the psychological plane with the planes just referred to. He reserves for this plane the opposition between the objective and subjective points of view, depending on whether the states described are treated as facts assumed to impose themselves on every attitude or as impressions experienced by a particular individual. It is on this plane that an external point of view (conduct seen by an observer) can legitimately be opposed to an internal point of view (that is, internal to the character described), without the localization of the speaker being necessarily determined in time and space. What is too hastily termed an omniscient observer is the person for whom psychic as well as physical phenomena are stated as observations unrelated to an interpreting subjectivity: "he thought," "he felt," and so on. A small number of formal marks suffice: "apparently," "obviously," "it seemed that," "as if," etc. These marks of a "foreign" point of view are generally combined with the presence of a narrator placed in a synchronic relation with the scene of action. The two senses of the word "internal" must therefore not be confused. The first characterizes phenomena of consciousness that can be those of a third person, while the second—the only one in question here—characterizes the position of the narrator (or of the character who is speaking) in relation to the perspective described. The narrator can be placed inside or outside by means of a process said to be internal, that is, mental.

Correlations are thereby established with the earlier distinctions, without being term-by-term correspondences; for example, between a retrospective point of view on the plane of time and objective point of view on the psychological plane, and between the synchronic point of view and the subjective point of view. However, it is important not to confuse these levels, for it is precisely out of the interconnection of these points of view, which are not necessarily congruent, that a work's dominant style of composition results. Known typologies (first- or third-person narratives, narrative situations in Stanzel's sense, etc.) in fact characterize these dominant styles, while implicitly privileging one plane or another.

One cannot help but admire the balance attained here between the spirit of analysis and the spirit of synthesis. But what is to be praised above all else is the art with which the notion of point of view is incorporated into a poetics of *composition* and thus placed within the gravitational field of narrative *configuration*. In this sense, *the notion of point of view marks the culminating point of a study centered around the relation between utterance and statement.*

If the privileged status of point of view in a problematic of composition is such as I have described, what are we to say about narrative voice?[82] This literary category cannot be eliminated by that of point of view, inasmuch as it is inseparable from the inexpungable category of the narrator, considered as the fictive projection of the real author in the text itself. If the point of view can be defined without the use of a personalizing metaphor, as a place of origin, an orientation, or as the aperture of a light source, which at one and the same time illuminates its subject and captures its features,[83] the narrator—the speaker of the narrative voice—cannot to the same extent be freed of all personalizing metaphor inasmuch as the narrator is the fictive author of the discourse.[84]

The impossibility of eliminating the notion of narrative voice is vividly confirmed by the category of novels constructed out of a polyphony of voices, where each remains perfectly distinct and yet every voice is posited in relation to every other. According to Mikhail Bakhtin, Dostoevsky is the creator of this sort of novel, which this inspired critic calls the "polyphonic novel." [85] The import of this innovation has to be understood correctly. If this type of novel does in fact mark the culminating point of my investigation into configuration in fictional narrative, it also designates a limit placed on composition in terms of levels, a limit beyond which my starting point in the notion of plot becomes unrecognizable. The final stage of our investigation is thus to be, also, our point of exit from the field of structural analysis.

By polyphonic novel, Bakhtin means a novelistic structure that breaks with what he calls the monologic (or homophonic) principle of the European novel, including the novels of Tolstoy. In the monological novel the voice of the narrator-author establishes itself as a single voice at the summit of the pyramid of voices, even if they are harmonized in the complex and subtle way spoken of above, by treating the point of view as the principle of composition. The same novel may be rich not only in monologues of all sorts but also in dialogues by which the novel raises itself to the level of drama. It nevertheless constitutes, as an ordered whole, the great monologue of the narrator. At first sight it seems hard to imagine that things could be otherwise as soon as the narrator is held to speak with a single voice, as will be confirmed by the rhetoric of fiction in Wayne Booth's sense. It is therefore a revolution in the conception of the narrator and the voice of the narrator, as much as in that of the character, that constitutes the strange originality of the polyphonic novel. The dialogical relation between the characters is, in effect, developed to the point of including the relation between the narrator and his/her characters. The "single and unified authorial consciousness" disappears (*Dostoevsky's Poetics*, p. 6). In its place appears a narrator who "converses" with his/her characters and who becomes a plurality of centers of consciousness irreducible to a common denominator. It is this "dialogization" of the narrator's own voice that constitutes the difference between the monologic novel and the dialogical novel. "The important thing is the final dialogicality, i.e. the dialogical nature of the total work" (p. 14). It is therefore the very relation between the narrator's discourse and the character's discourse that is entirely subverted.

My first reaction is to rejoice to see the very principle of the dialogical structure of discourse, of thinking, of self-consciousness, raised to the level of a structural principle of the novel.[86] My second reaction is to ask if the dialogical principle, which appears to crown the pyramid of the principles of composition governing narrative fiction, does not at the same time undermine the base of the edifice, namely, the organizing role of emplotment, even when it is extended to include all the forms of the synthesis of the heterogeneous by means of which narrative fiction remains a mimesis of action. By sliding from the mimesis of action to the mimesis of characters, then to that of their thoughts, feelings, and language, and by crossing the final threshold, that from monologue to dialogue, on the plane of the narrator's as much as the characters' discourse, have we not surreptitiously substituted for emplotment a radically different structuring principle, which is dialogue itself?

Observations to this effect abound in *Dostoevsky's Poetics*. The retreat of plot in the face of a principle of coexistence and of interaction bears witness to the emergence of a dramatic form in which space tends to supplant time.[87] Another image imposes itself, that of "counterpoint," which makes all the voices simultaneous. The very notion of "polyphony," identified with that of dialogical organization, already indicated this. The coexistence of voices seems to have been substituted for the temporal configuration of action, which has served as the starting point of all my analyses. In addition, with dialogue comes a factor of incompleteness, of remaining unfinished, that affects not only the characters and their worldview but the composition itself, condemned, it seems, to remain "open-ended," if not "endless." Must we then conclude that the monologic novel alone continues to conform to the principle of composition based on emplotment?

I do not think this conclusion is called for. In the chapter devoted to "Characteristics of Genre and Plot Composition in Dostoevsky's Works" (pp. 83–149), Bakhtin seeks in the perenniality and the reemergence of forms of composition inherited from the adventure novel, from confessions, from the lives of the saints, and especially from the forms of serious comedy, which themselves combine Socratic dialogue and Menippean satire, the resources for a genre, which without itself being a type of plot, constitutes a matrix of plots. Termed "carnivalistic" by Bakhtin, this genre is perfectly identifiable, despite the variety of its incarnations.[88] The carnivalistic genre thus becomes the limitlessly flexible principle of a composition that can never be said to be formless.

If we are allowed to draw a conclusion from this comparison between the polyphonic novel and the carnivalistic genre, it would be as follows. It is incontestible that the polyphonic novel stretches to the breaking point the capacity of extension belonging to the mimesis of action. At the limit, a pure novel of multiple voices—Virginia Woolf's *The Waves*—is no longer a novel at all but a sort of oratorio offered for reading. If the polyphonic novel does not cross this threshold, it is due to the organizing principle it receives from the long tradition marked out by the carnivalistic genre. In short, the polyphonic novel invites us to dissociate the principle of emplotment from the monologic principle and to extend it to the point where narrative fiction is transformed into a new genre. But who ever said that narrative fiction was the first and last word in the presentation of consciousnesses and their world? Its privilege begins and ends at the point where narration can be identified as a "tale of time," or better yet, as a "tale about time."

The notion of voice is especially significant to me precisely because of its important temporal connotations. As the author of some discourse, the narrator in fact determines a present—the present of narration—which is just as fictive as the instance of discourse constituting the narrative utterance. This present of narration may be considered atemporal if, as Käte Hamburger does, we allow only one sort of time, the "real" time of "real" subjects of assertions bearing on "reality." But there is no reason to exclude the notion of a fictive present, once we admit that the characters are themselves the fictive subjects of thoughts, feelings, and discourse. These characters unfold their own time in the fiction, a time that includes a past, present, and future—even quasi-presents—as they shift their temporal axis in the course of the fiction. It is this fictive present that we attribute to the fictive author of the discourse, to the narrator.

This category imposes itself for two reasons. First, the study of verb tenses in narrative fiction, in particular that of the monologue recounted in *erlebte Rede*, has placed us several times in the midst of an interplay of interferences between the time of the narrator and the times of the characters. This is a "game with time" that is added to those I analyzed above, for now the split between utterance and statement is extended to the split between the discourse of the speaker (narrator, fictive author) and the discourse of the character.

Moreover, attributing a present of narration to the narrative voice allows us to solve a problem I have left in abeyance until now, namely, the position of the preterite as the basic tense of narration. If I agreed with Käte Hamburger and Harald Weinrich in severing the preterite of narration from its reference to lived time, hence to the "real" past of a "real" subject who remembers or reconstructs a "real" historical past, it finally seems to me insufficient to say, with the first author, that the preterite preserves its grammatical form while casting off its signification of the past, and, with the second author, that the preterite is only the signal of the entry into narrative. For why would the preterite preserve its grammatical form if it had lost *all* temporal signification? And why should it be the privileged signal of the entry into narrative? One answer comes to mind. Could we not say that the preterite preserves its grammatical form and its privilege because the present of narration is understood by the reader as *posterior* to the narrated story, hence that the told story is the *past of the narrative voice*? Is not every told story in the past for the voice that tells it? Whence the artifices employed by writers of other ages, who pretended to have found the diary of their hero in a chest or in an attic, or to have heard the story from a traveler. Such an artifice was intended to simulate, in the latter case, the signification of the past for memory, and in the former, its signification for historiography. When the novelist casts these artifices aside, there still remains the past of the narrative voice, which is neither that of memory nor that of historiography but that which results from the relation of the posteriority of the narrative voice in relation to the story it tells.[89]

On the whole, the two notions of point of view and voice are so inseparable that they become indistinguishable. In Lotman, Bakhtin, and Uspensky, we find no lack of analyses that pass without transition from one to the other. It is rather a matter of a single function considered from the perspective of two different questions. Point of view answers the question, "From where do we perceive what is shown to us by the fact of being narrated?" Hence, from where is one speaking? Voice answers the question, "Who is speaking here?" If we do not want to be misled by the metaphor of vision when we consider a narrative in which everything is recounted, and in which making something visible through the eyes of a character is, according to Aristotle's analysis of *lexis* (elocution, diction), "placing before our eyes," that is, extending understanding to quasi-intuition, then vision must be held to be a concretization of understanding, hence, paradoxically, an appendix to hearing.[90]

Given this, only a single difference remains between point of view and voice—point of view is still related to a problem of composition (as we saw in Uspensky), and so remains within the field of investigation of narrative configuration. Voice, however, is already involved in the problems of communication, inasmuch as it addresses itself to a reader. It is therefore situated at the point of transition between configuration and refiguration, inasmuch as reading marks the point of intersection between the world of the text and the world of the reader. It is precisely these two functions that are interchangeable. Every point of view is the invitation addressed to readers to direct their gaze in the same direction as the author or the characters. In turn, the narrative voice is the silent speech that presents the world of the text to the reader. Like the voice that spoke to Augustine at the hour of his conversion, it says, *Tolle! Lege!* "Take and Read!"[91]

4

The Fictive Experience of Time

The distinction between utterance and statement within narrative provided an appropriate framework in the last chapter for studying the games with time that result from the division into the time taken to narrate and the time of the things narrated, which itself parallels this distinction. Our analysis of this reflexive temporal structure has shown the necessity for assigning these games with time the aim [*finalité*] of articulating *an experience of time* that would be what was at stake in these games. In doing this we open the field for an investigation in which the problems of narrative configuration border on those of the refiguration of time by narrative. However, this investigation will not for the moment cross the threshold leading from the first problematic to the second, inasmuch as the experience of time at issue here is a fictive experience that has an imaginary world for its horizon, one that remains the world of the text. Only the confrontation between the world of the text and the life-world of the reader will make the problematic of narrative configuration tip over into that of the refiguration of time by narrative.

Despite this restriction, posed as a matter of principle, the notion of the world of the text requires us to "open up"—to return to the expression employed earlier[1]—the literary work to an "outside" that it projects before itself and offers to critical appropriation by a reader. This notion of an opening does not contradict that of closure implied by the formal principle of configuration. A work can be at one and the same time closed upon itself with respect to its structure and open onto a world, like a "window" that cuts out a fleeting perspective of a landscape beyond.[2] This opening consists in the pro-position of a world capable of being inhabited. And in this regard, an inhospitable world, such as that many modern works project, is so only within the same problematic of an inhabitable space. What I am calling here the fictive experience of time is the temporal aspect of this virtual experience of being-in-the-world proposed by the text. It is in this respect that the literary work, escaping its own closure, "relates to . . . ," "is directed toward . . . ," in short, "is about. . . ." Short of the reception of the text by the reader and the intersection between this fictive experience and the reader's actual experience, the world of the work constitutes what I shall term a transcendence immanent in the text.[3]

The, at first sight, paradoxical expression "fictive experience" therefore has no function other than designating a projection of the work, capable of intersecting the ordinary experience of action—an experience certainly, but a fictive one, since the work alone projects it.

To illustrate what I am saying, I have chosen three works, *Mrs. Dalloway* by Virginia Woolf, *Der Zauberberg* by Thomas Mann, and *A la recherche du temps perdu* by Marcel Proust. Why this choice?

First, because these three works illustrate the distinction proposed by Mendilow between "tales of time" and "tales about time."[4] All fictional narratives are "tales of time" inasmuch as the structural transformations that affect the situations and characters take time. However only a few are "tales about time" inasmuch as in them it is the very experience of time that is at stake in these structural transformations. The three works I shall discuss are such tales about time.

Moreover, each of these works explores, in its own way, uncharted modes of discordant concordance, which no longer affect just the narrative composition but also the lived experience of the characters in the narrative. I shall speak of "imaginative variations" to designate these varied figures of discordant concordance, which go far beyond the temporal aspects of everyday experience, whether in the sphere of praxis or of pathos, as I described them in volume 1 under the title of mimesis $_1$. These are varieties of temporal experience that only fiction can explore and they are offered to reading in order to refigure ordinary temporality.[5]

Finally, these three works have in common their exploration, within the limits of the fundamental experience of discordant concordance, of the relation of time to eternity, which already in Augustine offered a wide variety of aspects. Literature, here again, proceeds by way of imaginative variations. Each of the three works under consideration, freeing itself in this way from the most linear aspects of time, can, in return, explore the hierarchical levels that form the depth of temporal experience. Fictional narrative thus detects temporalities that are more or less extended, offering in each instance a different figure of recollection, of eternity in or out of time, and, I will add, of the secret relation between eternity and death.

Let us now allow ourselves to be instructed by these three tales about time.

BETWEEN MORTAL TIME AND MONUMENTAL TIME: Mrs. Dalloway

Before beginning my interpretation, I must stress once again the difference between two levels of critical reading with respect to the same work. On the first level, our interest is concentrated on the work's configuration. On the second level, our interest lies in the worldview and the temporal experience that this configuration projects outside of itself. In the case of *Mrs. Dalloway*, the first type of reading, while not impoverished, is clearly truncated.[6] If the narrative is configured in the subtle manner I shall describe, this is to allow the narrator—I do not say the author but the narrative voice that makes the work speak and address itself to a reader—to offer the reader an armful of temporal experiences to share. On the other hand, I do not hesitate to admit that it is the narrative configuration of *Mrs. Dalloway*—a quite unique configuration, although one that can easily be situated in the family of "stream of consciousness" novels—that serves as the basis for the experience that its characters have of time, and that the narrative voice of the novel wants to communicate to the reader.

The fictive narrator limits all of the events of the story being told to the span of time between the morning and the evening of a splendid June day in 1923, hence a few years after the end of what was called the Great War. The subtlety of the narrative technique is matched by the simplicity of the story-line. Clarissa Dalloway, a woman of around fifty belonging to upperclass London society, is giving a party that very evening, and the vicissitudes of this gathering will mark the culmination and the closure of the narrative. The emplotment functions to form an ellipse, whose second focal point is the young Septimus Warren Smith, a veteran of the Great War, whose madness leads to suicide a few hours before Clarissa's party. The knot holding these elements of the plot together consists in having the news of Septimus's death announced by Dr. Bradshaw, a medical celebrity who belongs to Clarissa's circle of social acquaintances. The story begins with Clarissa in the morning when she is getting ready to go out to buy flowers for her party and it will leave her at the most critical moment of the evening. Thirty years before, Clarissa had almost married Peter Walsh, a childhood friend whom she expects to see soon, as he is returning from India, where his life has floundered in subordinate occupations and unsuccessful love affairs. Richard, whom Clarissa preferred to Peter in those days and who, since then, has become her husband, is an important man in parliamentary committees, without being a brilliant politician. Other characters frequenting the London social world gravitate around this core of childhood friends. It is important that Septimus not belong to this circle and that the relationship between the fates of Septimus and Clarissa is reached (by narative techniques I shall speak of below) at a deeper level than the *coup de théâtre*—the unexpected news, midway through the party, of Septimus's suicide—that allows the plot to reach its culmination.

The narrative technique displayed in *Mrs. Dalloway* is highly subtle. The first procedure I might mention, and the easiest to detect, consists in marking out the passing of the day as it progresses by means of numerous small events. Except for Septimus's suicide, of course, these sometimes minor events draw the narrative toward its expected end—the party given by Mrs. Dalloway. The list of comings and goings, of incidents and meetings, is long indeed: in the morning, the Prince of Wales or some other royal figure crosses her path; an airplane skywrites its advertising, tracing out capital letters that are spelled out by the crowd; Clarissa goes home to get her dress ready for the party; Peter Walsh, just back from India, surprises her while she is sewing; after having stirred the ashes of the past, Clarissa kisses him; Peter leaves in tears; he passes through the same places as Clarissa had and comes across the couple, Septimus and Rezia (she is the little Milanese milliner who has become Septimus's wife); Rezia takes her husband to a first psychiatrist, Dr. Holmes; Richard considers buying a pearl necklace for his wife but chooses roses instead (roses that circulate from one end of the narrative to the other, roses fixed for a moment on the wallpaper of Septimus's room, after he has been sentenced to a rest home by the medical profession); Richard, too bashful, cannot pronounce the message of love that the roses signify; Miss Kilman, the pious and ugly tutor of Elizabeth, the Dalloway's daughter, goes shopping with Elizabeth, who leaves her governess in the middle of her chocolate eclair; Septimus, told by Dr. Bradshaw to leave his wife for a clinic in the country, throws himself out of the window; Peter decides to go to the party given by Clarissa; then comes the big scene of Mrs. Dalloway's party, with Dr. Bradshaw's news of Septimus's suicide; Mrs. Dalloway takes the news of the suicide of this young man whom she does not know in a way that determines the tone she herself will give to the termination of the evening, which is also the death of the day. These events, large or small, are punctuated by the tolling of the powerful strokes of Big Ben and other bells in London. I shall show below that the most important meaning of this remainder of the hour is not to be sought at the level of the configuration of the narrative, as if the narrator were limited to helping the readers situate themselves in the narrated time. The strokes of Big Ben have their true place in the experience that the various characters have of time. They belong to the fictive refiguration of time that this work opens out to.

To this first procedure of progressive accumulation is grafted another, even more widely recognized one. As the narrative is pulled ahead by everything that happens—however small it may be—in the narrated time, it is at the same time pulled backward, delayed so to speak, by ample excursions into the past, which constitute so many events in thought, interpolated in long sequences, between the brief spurts of action. For the Dalloway's circle, these reported thoughts—"he thought," "thought she"—are in the main a return to their childhood at Bourton and especially to everything that may be related to a lost love, to the refusal of a marriage between Clarissa and Peter. For Septimus and Rezia, similar plunges into the past are a desperate rumination on the series of events that led to a disastrous marriage and to utter misfortune. These long sequences of silent thoughts—or what amounts to the same thing, of internal discourse—not only constitute flashbacks that, paradoxically, make the narrated time advance by delaying it, they hollow out from within the instant of the event in thought, they amplify from within the moments of narrated time, so that the total interval of the narrative, despite its relative brevity, seems rich with an implied immensity.[7] Along the line of this day, whose advance is punctuated by the strokes of Big Ben, the fits of memory, the calculations by which each character attempts to guess the conjectures the others are making about his or her appearance, thoughts, secrets—these form a series of loops that gives its specific distension to the narrated time's exten- sion.[8] So the art of fiction here consists in weaving together the world of ac- tion and that of introspection, of mixing together the sense of everydayness and that of the inner self.

For a literary criticism more attentive to the depiction of character than to the exploration of narrated time and, through this, the time lived by the char- acters in the narrative, there is no doubt that this plunge into the past along with the incessant weighing of souls that the characters practice on one an- other, contribute along with the actions described from the outside to recon- struct from within the characters in their present state. By giving a temporal depth to the narrative, the entanglement of the narrated present with the re- membered past confers a psychological depth on the characters without, how- ever, giving them a stable identity, so discordant are the glimpses the charac- ters have of one another and of themselves. The reader is left holding the scattered pieces to a great game of character identification, but the solution to it escapes the reader as much as it does the characters in the narrative. The attempt to identify the characters certainly corresponds to the promptings of the fictive narrator, when this voice leaves the characters to their interminable quest.[9]

Another procedure that belongs to the narrative technique used in *Mrs. Dalloway*—a procedure not quite so obvious as the preceding one—also de- serves our attention. The narrator—to whom the reader readily grants the ex- orbitant privilege of knowing the thoughts of all the characters from the in- side—is provided with the ability *to move* from one stream of consciousness to another, by having the characters meet in the same places (London streets, a public park), perceive the same sounds, be present at the same incidents (the Prince of Wales's car passing by, the airplane flying overhead, etc.). It is in this way that the story of Septimus, completely foreign to the Dalloway's circle, is incorporated for the first time into the narrative field. Septimus, like Clarissa, heard the rumors stemming from the royal incident (we shall see later the im- portance this takes on in the view the various protagonists have of time itself). By resorting to this same process the narrator jumps from Peter's ruminations on his lost love of yesteryear to the fatal exchange of thoughts between Rezia and Septimus, going over the disaster of their own union. The unity of place, the face-to-face discussion on the bench in the same park, is equivalent to the unity of a single instant onto which the narrator grafts the extension of a span of memory.[10] The procedure is made believable by the resonance-effect that compensates for the rupture-effect created by the jump from one stream of consciousness to another: over and done with, leaving no possibility of return, is Peter's love of yesteryear; over, and without any possible future, is also the marriage of Rezia and Septimus. We later move from Peter to Rezia through a similar transition, by way of the harpings of the old invalid woman, singing of faded loves. A bridge is built between these souls both through the continuity of place and the reverberation of an internal discourse in another person. On another occasion, the description of lovely clouds in the June sky allows the narrative to bridge the gap that separates the thoughts of young Elizabeth, returning from her escapade after escaping Miss Kilman, and Septimus's stream of consciousness as he lies on his bed under the order of the psychiatrists. A point in space, a pause in time form the footbridges between two temporalities foreign to each other.

That these procedures, characteristic of the temporal configuration, serve to bring about the sharing of a temporal experience by the narrator and the reader, or rather of a whole range of temporal experiences, therefore serves *to refigure time itself in our reading*—this is what it is now important to show by penetrating into the tale about time that runs through *Mrs. Dalloway*.

Chronological time is, quite clearly, represented in the fiction by the striking of Big Ben and the other bells and clocks, as they ring out the hours. What is important is not this reminder of the hour, striking at the same time for everyone, however, but the relation that the various protagonists establish with these marks of time. The variations in this relation, depending on the character and the occasion, themselves constitute the fictive temporal experience that the narrative constructs with such extreme care in order to be convincing to the reader.

Big Ben strikes for the first time when Clarissa, on her way to the deluxe shops of Westminster, goes over in her mind the breakup of her idyll with Peter, without realizing yet that he is back. The important thing is what Big Ben's striking signifies for her at this moment: "There! Out it boomed. First a warning, musical; then the hour irrevocable. The leaden circles dissolved in the air" (p. 5). This sentence, which is repeated three times in the course of the narrative, will of itself recall the sameness of clock time for everyone. The hour irrevocable? And yet in this June morning, the irrevocable is not burdensome; it gives new impetus to the joy of being alive, in the freshness of each moment and the expectation of the brilliant evening to come. But a shadow passes. If Peter were to come back, would he not call her again, with his tender irony, "The perfect hostess"? Thus passes internal time, pulled back by memory and thrust ahead by expectation. *Distentio animi*: "she always had the feeling that it was very, very dangerous to live even one day" (p. 11). Strange Clarissa, symbol of the preoccupation forged by the world's vanity, concerned about the image of herself that she displays for the interpretation of others, on the watch for her own changing moods and, above all, *coura-geously* taken with life despite its precariousness and its duplicity. For her the refrain of Shakespeare's *Cymbeline* sings and will sing again in the course of the narrative:

> Fear no more the heat o' the sun
> Nor the furious winter's rages.[11]

But before we look at the other occasions when Big Ben strikes, it is impor-tant to note that the official time with which the characters are confronted is not only this time of clocks but all that is in complicity with it. In agreement with it is everything that, in the narrative, evokes monumental history, to use Nietzsche's expression, and to begin with, the admirable marble decor of the imperial capital (the "real" place, in this fiction, of all the events and their internal reverberations). This monumental history, in its turn, secretes what I will venture to call a "monumental time," of which chronological time is but the audible expression. To this monumental time belong the figures of au-thority and power that form the counterweight to the living times experienced by Clarissa and Septimus; of the time that, because of his severity, will lead Septimus to suicide, and that, because of her pride, will push Clarissa to con-front life head-on.[12] However the highest authority-figures are the horrible doctors who torment poor Septimus, lost in his suicidal thoughts, to the point of pushing him to his death. For what indeed is madness for Sir William Bradshaw, that eminent medical personage elevated even higher by his knight-hood, other than "not having a sense of proportion"? (p. 146). "Proportion, divine proportion, Sir William's goddess" (p. 150). It is this sense of propor-tion that sets his entire professional and social life within monumental time. The narrator is not afraid to add to these authority figures, so consonant with official time, religion as it is embodied by Miss Kilman, the ugly, hateful, pious tutor who has stolen the affection of Elizabeth away from her mother, before the young girl escapes and acquires a time of her own, with its prom-ises and its dangers. "But Proportion has a sister, less smiling, more formid-able. . . . Conversion is her name" (p. 151).

Clock time, the time of monumental history, the time of authority-figures—the same time! Dominated by this monumental time, more complex than simple chronological time, the hours are heard to ring out—or better, to strike—throughout the course of the narrative.

Big Ben sounds a second time, just when Clarissa has presented her daugh-ter to Peter.[13] "The sound of Big Ben striking the half-hour struck out between them with extraordinary vigour, as if a young man, strong, indifferent, incon-siderate, were swinging dumb-bells this way and that" (p. 71). It is not, like the first time, a reminder of the inexorable but of the introduction—"between them"—of the incongruous. "The leaden circles dissolved in the air," the nar-rator repeats. For whom, then, has the half-hour sounded? "Remember my party tonight," Mrs. Dalloway calls after Peter as he goes away rhythmically modulating these words to the striking of Big Ben. Only half past eleven, he thinks. Then the bells of St. Margaret's join in, friendly, hospitable, like Clarissa. Joyous, then? Only until the sound as it dies away brings to mind Clarissa's old illness, and until the strength of the final stroke becomes the death knoll tolling her imagined death. What resources fiction has for following the subtle variations between the time of consciousness and chronological time!

Big Ben rings out a third time (p. 142). The narrator has noon strike once for Septimus and Rezia on their way to give themselves up to Dr. Holmes, whose hidden relation to official time has already been stated, and for Clarissa spreading out her green dress on her bed. For each one, for no one, "the leaden circles dissolved in the air" (ibid.). Shall we say once again that the hour is the same for all? Yes, from outside; no, from inside. Only fiction, precisely, can explore and bring to language this divorce between worldviews and their irreconcilable perspectives on time, a divorce that undermines public time.

The clock strikes again, half past one; this time we hear the clocks in the wealthy business district. To Rezia in tears, they "counselled submission, upheld authority, and pointed out in chorus the supreme advantages of a sense of proportion" (pp. 154–55).

Big Ben strikes three o'clock for Richard and Clarissa. For the former, full of gratitude for the miracle that his marriage with Clarissa seems to mean to him, "Big Ben was beginning to strike, first the warning, musical, then the hour, irrevocable" (p. 177). An ambiguous message—a punctuation of happiness or of time lost in vain preoccupations. As for Clarissa in her drawing room, absorbed in the problems of her invitations, "the sound of the bell flooded the room with its melancholy wave" (p. 178). But here is Richard, before her, holding out flowers. Roses, yet again roses. "Happiness is this, is this, he thought" (p. 180).

When Big Ben strikes the next half hour, it is to punctuate the solemnity, the miracle, the miracle of the old woman glimpsed by Clarissa across the way, framed in her window, then withdrawing back into her room; it is as if the blows struck by the huge bell were reimmersing Clarissa in a domain of peacefulness where neither the vain regret of the love Peter once sought, nor the overbearing religiousness professed by Miss Kilman are able to penetrate. But two minutes after Big Ben, another bell rings, and its light sounds, messengers of futility, are mixed with the final majestic echoes of the bells of Big Ben, pronouncing the Law.

When the clock strikes six it is to inscribe within public time the supremely private act of Septimus's suicide. "The clock was striking—one, two, three: how sensible the sound was; compared with all this thumping and whispering; like Septimus himself. She [Rezia] was falling asleep. But the clock went on striking, four, five, six" (p. 227). The first three bells, like something concrete, solid, in the tumult of whispers—the last three, like a flag raised in honor of the dead on the battlefield.

The day advances, pulled ahead by the arrow of desire and expectation shot off at the beginning of the narrative (this evening's party to be given by Mrs. Dalloway) and pulled back by the incessant retreat into memory that, paradoxically, punctuates the inexorable advance of the dying day.

The narrator has Big Ben strike the hour one last time when the announcement of Septimus's suicide throws Clarissa into the contradictory thoughts I shall speak of below. And again the same phrase returns: "the leaden circles dissolved in the air." For everyone, for every sort of mood, the noise is the same, but the hour is not simply the noise that inexorable time makes in passing. . . .

We must not stop with a simplistic opposition between clock time and internal time, therefore, but must consider the variety of relations between the concrete temporal experience of the various characters and monumental time. The variations on the theme of this relation lead fiction well beyond the abstract opposition we have just referred to and make of it, for the reader, a powerful means of detecting the infinitely varied way of combining the perspectives of time that speculation by itself fails to mediate.

These variations constitute a whole range of "solutions" here, the two extremes of which are depicted by the deep agreement between monumental time and the figures of authority epitomized by Dr. Bradshaw, and by the "terror of history"—to use Mircea Eliade's expression—represented through Septimus. Other temporal experiences, that of Clarissa first and foremost, and that of Peter Walsh to a lesser degree, are ordered in relation to these poles, following their greater or lesser kinship with the primary experience that the narrator sets up as a standard for the entire exploration of temporal experience: the experience of the mortal discordance between personal time and monumental time, of which Septimus is both the hero and the victim. We must therefore start from this pole of radical discordance.

Septimus's "lived experience" abundantly confirms that no gulf would have opened up for him between the time "struck" by Big Ben and the horror of history that leads to his death, if monumental history, everywhere present in London, and the various figures of authority, epitomized in the medical profession, did not give to clock time the train of power that transforms time into a radical threat. Septimus, too, saw the royal car pass by; he heard the murmurs of respect from the crowd, just as he perceived the airplane flying overhead with its trail of advertising—all of which only makes him cry, the beauty of the places making everything seem terrible. Horror! Terror! These two words sum up for him the antagonism existing between the two temporal perspectives, just as it exists between himself and others—"That eternal loneliness" (p. 37)—and between himself and life. If these experiences, inexpressible at their limit, do nevertheless attain internal language, it is because they have encountered a verbal complicity in the reading of Aeschylus, Dante, and Shakespeare, a reading that has transmitted to Septimus only a message of universal meaninglessness. At least these books are on his side, protesting against monumental time and all the oppressive and repressive powers of medical science. Precisely because they are on his side, these books create an additional screen between himself, others, and life. One passage in *Mrs. Dalloway* says it all. This is when Rezia, the little milliner from Milan, lost in London where she has followed her husband, utters, "It is time." "The word 'time' split its husk; poured its riches over him; and from his lips fell like shells, like shavings from a plane, without his making them, hard, white, imperishable words, and flew to attach themselves to their places in an ode to Time; an immortal ode to Time" (p. 105). Time has recovered its mythical grandeur, its somber reputation of destroying rather than generating. The horror of time, bringing back from the dead the ghost of his war comrade, Evans, rising up from the depths of monumental history—the Great War—at the heart of the imperial city. Note the narrator's grating humor: " 'I will tell you the time,' said Septimus, very slowly, very drowsily, smiling mysteriously.[14] As he sat smiling at the dead man in the grey suit the quarter struck—the quarter to twelve. And that is being young, Peter Walsh thought as he passed them" (p. 106).

The two extremes of temporal experience confront each other in the scene of Septimus's suicide. Dr. Bradshaw—Sir William!—has decided that Rezia and Septimus must be separated for the good of the patient. "Holmes and Bradshaw were on him!" (p. 223). What is worse, "human nature" has pronounced a guilty verdict on him, a death sentence. In the papers that Septimus asks be burned and that Rezia tries to save are his "Odes to Time" (p. 224). His time, henceforth, has no common measure with that of the holders of medical knowledge, their sense of proportion, their verdicts, their power to inflict suffering. Septimus throws himself out the window.

The question arises whether, beyond the horror of history that it expresses, Septimus's death is not charged by the narrator with another meaning that would make time the negative side of eternity. In his madness, Septimus is the bearer of a revelation that grasps in time the obstacle to a vision of cosmic unity and in death the way of reaching this salvific meaning. In any event, the narrator did not want to make this revelation the "message" of the narrative. By connecting revelation and madness, the narrator leaves the reader uncertain with respect to the very sense of Septimus's death.[15] Moreover, it is to Clarissa, as I shall state below, that the narrator gives the task of legitimizing, although only up to a certain point, this redemptive sense of Septimus's death. We must therefore never lose sight of the fact that what makes sense is the juxtaposition of Septimus's and Clarissa's experience of time.[16] Considered separately, Septimus's worldview expresses the agony of a soul for whom monumental time is unbearable. The relation that death can have with eternity, in addition to this, intensifies this agony (in accordance with the interpretation of the relation of eternity to time that I proposed in my reading of Augustine's *Confessions*).[17] It is therefore in relation to this insurmountable fissure [*faille*] opened up between the monumental time of the world and the mortal time of the soul that the temporal experiences of each of the other characters are ordered and, with this, their way of handling the relation between the two sides of this opening. I shall limit myself to Peter Walsh and Clarissa, although there is much that could be said about other imaginative variations carried out by the narrator.

Peter, his former love lost forever—"it was over!"—his present life in ruins, is made to mutter: "the death of the soul" (p. 88). If he does not have Clarissa's lively self-confidence to help him spring back, he does possess, to help him survive, a certain levity. "It was awful, he cried, awful, awful! Still, the sun was hot. Still, one got over things. Still, life had a way of adding day to day. Still. . . . still. . . . Peter Walsh laughed out" (pp. 97–98). For if age does not weaken passions, "one has gained—at last!—the power which adds the supreme flavour to existence,—the power of taking hold of experience, of turning it round, slowly, in the light" (p. 119).

Clarissa is, quite clearly, the heroine of the novel. It is the narrative of her actions and internal discourses that sets the boundaries for the narrated time, but, even more, it is her temporal experience contrasted with that of Septimus, of Peter, and of the figures of authority that constitutes what is at stake in the game with time, as it is set out by the narrative techniques characteristic of *Mrs. Dalloway*.

Her social life, her acquaintance with authority-figures make part of her belong to the side of monumental time. Will she not, this very evening, take her place at the top of her staircase, like the queen welcoming her guests to Buckingham Palace? Is she not a figure of authority in other people's eyes, by the way she holds herself straight and erect? Seen by Peter, is she not a fragment of the British empire (p. 116)? Does not Peter's tender and cruel expression define her through and through, "The perfect hostess"?[18] And yet the narrator wants to communicate to the reader the sense of a deep kinship between Clarissa and Septimus, whom she has never seen, whose name she does not even know. The same horror dwells in her, but unlike Septimus she will confront it, sustained by an indestructible love for life. The same terror: just evoking the draining of life from Mrs. Bruton's face—the woman who did not invite her to lunch with her husband!—is enough to remind her how much "she feared the time itself" (p. 44). What maintains her fragile equilibrium between mortal time and the time of resolution in the face of death—if we may dare to apply to her this major existential category of *Being and Time*—is her love of life, of perishable beauty, of changing light, her passion for "the falling drop"

(p. 54). Whence her astonishing power to rebound from memory, to plunge "into the very heart of the moment" (ibid.).

The way in which Clarissa receives the news of the suicide of this unknown young man is the occasion for the narrator to situate Clarissa on a crest between the two extremes spanned by the narrative's range of imaginative variations on temporal experience. This we guessed long ago: Septimus is Clarissa's "double"; in a certain way, he dies in her place.[19] As for Clarissa, she redeems his death by continuing to live.[20] The news of the suicide, thrown out for conversation right in the middle of the evening, first provokes in Clarissa this thought, at once frivolous and in complicity: "Oh! thought Clarissa, in the middle of my party, here's death," (p. 279). But deeper within herself is the unsurpassable certainty that by losing life this young man saved the highest sense of death. "Death was defiance. Death was an attempt to communicate; people feeling the impossibility of reaching the centre which, mystically, evaded them; closeness drew apart, rapture faded, one was alone. There was an embrace in death" (p. 281). Here the narrator joins together in a single narrative voice, the narrator's own, Septimus's voice, and Clarissa's. It is clearly Septimus's voice that says, as an echo through Clarissa's, "Life is made intolerable; they make life intolerable, men like that" (ibid.). It is through the eyes of Septimus that she sees Dr. Bradshaw as "obscurely evil, without sex or lust, extremely polite to women, but capable of some indescribable outrage—forcing your soul, that was it" (ibid.). But Clarissa's time is not Septimus's time. Her party will not end in disaster. A "sign" placed once again by the narrator will help Clarissa to link terror and love of life in the pride of facing up. This sign is the gesture of the old woman across the way, opening her curtains, moving away from the window, and going to bed "quite quietly"—a figure of serenity, suddenly associated with the refrain of *Cymbeline*, "Fear no more the heat o' the sun." Earlier that same morning, we recall, Clarissa, stopping at a shop window, had seen the volume of Shakespeare open to these verses. She had asked herself, "What was she trying to recover? What image of white dawn in the open country" (p. 12)? Later in the day, in a moment of peaceful return to the reality of time, Septimus was to find some words of consolation in these same verses: "Fear no more, says the heart in the body; fear no more. He was not afraid. At every moment Nature signified some laughing hint like that gold spot which went round the wall—there, there, there—her determination to show, by . . . standing close up to breathe through her hollowed hands Shakespeare's words, her meaning" (pp. 211–12). When Clarissa repeats the verse, toward the end of the book, she repeats it as Septimus did, "with a sense of peace and reassurance."[21]

Thus the book ends. Septimus's death, understood and in some way shared, gives to the instinctive love that Clarissa holds for life a tone of defiance and of resolution. "He made her feel the beauty; made her feel the fun. But she

111

must go back. She must assemble" (p. 284). Vanity? Arrogance? The perfect hostess? Perhaps. At this point, the voice of the narrator merges with that of Peter, who, at this final moment of the narrative, becomes for the reader the most trustworthy voice; "What is this terror? What is this ecstasy? he thought to himself. What is it that fills me with extraordinary excitment? It is Clarissa, he said. For there she was" (p. 296).

The voice says simply, "For there she was." The force of this presence is the gift of the dead man to Clarissa.[22]

Overall, may we speak of a single experience of time in *Mrs. Dalloway*? No, insofar as the destinies of the characters and their worldviews remain juxtaposed; yes, insofar as the proximity between the "caves" visited constitutes a sort of underground network that *is* the experience of time in *Mrs. Dalloway*. This experience of time is neither that of Clarissa nor that of Septimus; it is neither that of Peter nor that of any other character. Instead, it is suggested to the reader by the reverberation—an expression Bachelard liked to borrow from E. Minkowski—of one solitary experience in another solitary experience. It is this network, taken as a whole, that is the experience of time in *Mrs. Dalloway*. This experience, in turn, confronts, in a complex and unstable relationship, monumental time, itself resulting from all the complicities between clock time and the figures of authority.[23]

Der Zauberberg

That *The Magic Mountain* is a novel about time is too obvious for me to have to insist upon the fact.[24] It is much more difficult to say in what sense it is one. To begin, let us limit ourselves to the most evident features that give *The Magic Mountain* the overall definition of *Zeitroman*.

First of all, abolishing the sense of measurement of time is the major feature of the way the guests at the Berghof, the Davos sanatorium, exist and live. From the beginning to the end of the novel, this effacing of chronological time is clearly underscored by the contrast between "those up here," acclimatized to this beyond-time, and "those down below"—those of the flatland—whose occupations follow the rhythm of the calendar and of clocks. The spatial opposition reduplicates and reinforces the temporal opposition.

Next, the story-line, which is relatively simple, is punctuated by several comings and goings between those down below and those up above, and this dramatizes the bewitchment of the place. Hans Castorp's arrival constitutes the first event of this sort. This young engineer in his early thirties from Hamburg—a flat-land if ever there was one—comes to visit his cousin, Joachim, who has been in treatment for more than six months at the Berghof. His initial intention is to stay only three weeks in this strange place. Found to be ill by Dr. Behrens, the sinister and clownish director of the institution, Hans Castorp becomes, in his turn, one of the guests at the Berghof. The departure of

Joachim, who returns to military life, his subsequent return to the sanatorium to die there, in his turn, the abrupt departure of Madame Chauchat—the central character in the amorous adventure that is interwoven with the tale about time—after the decisive episode of "Walpurgis-night," her sudden return in the company of Mynheer Peeperkorn—all these arrivals and departures constitute so many points of rupture, trials, and questioning in an adventure that, for the most part, takes place in the spatial and temporal seclusion of the Berghof. Hans Castorp himself will stay there seven years, until the "thunderbolt" of the declaration of war in 1914 tears him away from the bewitchment of the magic mountain. But the irruption of great history will return him to the time of those down below only to hand him over to the "feast of death" that is war. The unfolding of the narrative in its episodic aspect, therefore, makes us tend to see in Hans Castorp's confrontation with abolished time the main thread of the narrative in *The Magic Mountain*.

The narrative technique employed in the work confirms, in turn, the characterization of the novel as a *Zeitroman*. The most visible procedure concerns the accent placed on the relation between the time of narration and the narrated time.[25]

The division into seven chapters covers a chronological span of seven years. But the relation between the length of time narrated by each chapter, and the time taken to narrate it, measured by the number of pages, is not proportional. Chapter 1 devotes 15 pages to "the arrival." Chapter 2 constitutes a return through past time up to the moment when the decision is made to undertake the fatal journey; I shall discuss its meaning below. Chapter 3 devotes 54 pages to the first complete day there (the day following Hans's arrival). After this, the 89 pages of Chapter 4 suffice to cover the first three weeks, the exact interval of time that Hans Castorp intended to stay at the Berghof. The first seven months require the 160 pages of Chapter 5. The 196 pages of Chapter 6 cover one year and nine months. The remaining four and a half years take up the 175 pages of Chapter 7. These numerical relations are more complex than they appear. On the one hand, the *Erzählzeit* continually diminishes in relation to the *erzählte Zeit*. On the other hand, the stretching out of the chapters, combined with this abbreviation of the narrative, creates a perspectival effect, essential to the communication of the major experience, the hero's internal debate over his loss of the sense of time. To be perceived, this perspectival effect requires a cumulative reading that allows the totality of the work to remain present in each of its developments. In fact, due to the length of the work, only by rereading can we reconstitute this perspective.

These considerations on the length of the narrative lead us to a final argument in favor of interpreting *The Magic Mountain* as a *Zeitroman*. This argument is in a sense the most decisive. But, at the same time, it throws us into the very heart of the confusion that the reader experiences when he or she wonders in what sense and at what price this novel is indeed a *Zeitroman*. We must, in fact, draw support here from the statements of the author himself, who has accorded himself the privilege—indisputable as such, and frequently assumed by novelists of the past—of intervening in his narrative. It is impossible not to take account of this, inasmuch as these intrusions help, in a written work, to put into relief and to stage the narrative voice within the work. (Moreover, it is solely in this sense that I draw any argument from the author's interventions, determined as I am to ignore biographic and psychographic information relating to Thomas Mann, which these interruptions encourage. Not that I deny that the narrator encountered in the narrative is the author himself, that is, Thomas Mann. For us it is enough that the author, external to the work and now dead, has been transformed into a narrative voice that today is still audible in his work.) The narrative voice that, from place to place, calls upon the reader and expounds on his hero is indeed part and parcel of the writing of the text. In the same stroke, this voice, distinct from the narrative properly speaking and superimposed upon the narrated story, has an indisputable right to be heard—with the reservations I shall state below—when it characterizes the narrative as a *Zeitroman*.

Its first intervention can be heard in the *Vorsatz* or Foreword (literally, "design") placed at the start of the narrative. This *Vorsatz* is not exactly an introduction. It imposes the authority of the narrative voice within the text itself. The problem posed by the *Vorsatz* is precisely that of the relation between the *Erzählzeit* and the *erzählte Zeit*. This problem contains two aspects. I am beginning with the second of these, which takes up a debate that is familiar to us as a result of our study of games with time.[26] The question here is that of the duration (*Dauer*) of reading. And the answer to this question immediately takes us out of the realm of chronological time: "for when did a narrative seem too long or too short by reason of the actual time or space it took up?" (*The Magic Mountain*, p. x). The mere suggestion of boredom insinuates an analogy between the time of writing and the time of the experience projected by the narrative. Even the number seven—seven days, seven months, seven years—serves to strengthen this relation between the time of reading—considered as coextensive with the time of writing—and the narrated time, with the note of irony attached to the choice of the number seven, overcharged with hermetic symbolism: "Heaven forbid it should be seven years!" (ibid.), referring to the time that the storyteller and the reader will take to tell the story. Behind this dilatory reply is already apparent the question of the pertinence of measurements of time in the hero's experience.[27] However, more decisive for our purpose is the enigmatic remark that precedes these allusions. Speaking of the narrated time, the *Vorsatz* declares that the story we are about to read has to be told "out of the depth of the past" (*in der Zeitform der tiefsten vergangenheit*) (p. ix). The fact that stories are told in the past in itself constitutes a distinct problem that will occupy us in my concluding chapter in volume 3. The fact that, in addition, as regards the narrated past, "the more past the better" (ibid.), poses a specific enigma, age thereby losing its chronological character: "the degree of its [the story's] antiquity has noways to do with the passage of time" (ibid.). What, then, imposes it upon us? The ironic narrator gives an ambiguous reply. This antiquity under the circumstances splits up into a dated antiquity, which is over for us, that of the world before the Great War, and an ageless antiquity, that of the legend (*Märchen*).[28] This initial allusion is not without reverberation on the problem of the experience of time produced by the told story: "the author intentionally touches upon the strange and questionable double nature of that riddling element" (ibid.). What double nature? Precisely that which, throughout the entire novel, will confront the time of calendars and clocks with a time gradually divested of any measurable character and even of any interest in measurement.

At first sight, the problem posed by this double nature of time resembles that posed by *Mrs. Dalloway*. Schematically: the exploration of the conflicting relations between internal time and chronological time, enlarged to the dimensions of monumental time. There is actually a considerable difference between the two novels. In *The Magic Mountain*, the constellations that gravitate around the two poles are entirely different, to the point of making us doubt that *The Magic Mountain* is solely, or even principally, a *Zeitroman*. We must therefore now hear another side of this debate.

First, the line separating "those up there" from "those down below" separates at the same time the world of sickness and death from the everyday world—the world of life, health, and action. In fact, at the Berghof everyone is sick, including the doctors, the specialist in the treatment of tuberculosis as well as the charlatan psychiatrist. Hans Castorp penetrates a universe where the reign of sickness and death is already established. Whoever enters there is in turn condemned to death. If someone like Joachim leaves this world, he returns to die there. The magic, the bewitchment of the magic mountain is the bewitchment of death, of the death instinct. Love itself is a captive of this charm. At the Berghof, sensuality and putrefaction go hand-in-hand. A secret pact links love and death. This is also, and perhaps more than anything else, the magic of this place outside space and time. Hans Castorp's passion for Madame Chauchat is wholly dominated by this fusion between sensual attraction and the fascination with decomposition and death. Madame Chauchat is already there when he arrives. She is part, so to speak, of the institution of death. Her sudden departure and her unexpected return, accompanied by the flamboyant Mynheer Peeperkorn—who will commit suicide at the Berghof—constitute the major peripeteia in the Aristotelian sense of the term.

The Magic Mountain is therefore not simply a tale about time. The problem is rather how the same novel can be both a novel about time *and* a novel about a deadly sickness. Must the decomposition of time be interpreted as a prerogative of the world of sickness, or does this world constitute a sort of limit-situation for an unprecedented experience of time? Assuming the first hypothesis, *The Magic Mountain* is a novel about sickness; assuming the second, the novel about sickness is, first and foremost, a *Zeitroman*.

A second alternative can be added to this first one. The problem is fact complicated by the presence, in the development of the novel, of a third component alongside the effacement of time and the fascination with sickness. This third theme concerns the destiny of European culture. By giving such a large place to conversations, discussions, and controversies that take this destiny as their theme, by creating characters as clearly delineated as Settembrini, the Italian man of letters, spokesman for the philosophy of the Enlightenment, and Naphta, the Jesuit of Jewish origin, the perverse critic of bourgeois ideology, the author has made his novel a vast apologue of the decadence of European culture, where the fascination exerted by death within the walls of the Berghof sanatorium symbolizes—as Leibniz would have said—the temptation of nihilism. Love itself is transfigured by the debate on culture to such an extent that it surpasses individuals, making us wonder if this debate has not thereby exhausted love's redemptive capacity.

How then, we ask, can the same novel be a novel about time, a novel about illness, and a novel about culture? Does not the theme of the relation to time, which first seemed to predominate and then appeared to give way to the theme of the relation to death, recede one step further if the destiny of European culture becomes what is principally at stake?

Mann, it seems, has resolved the problem by incorporating these three dimensions—time, sickness, and culture—into the singular experience (in both senses of the French word: experience and experiment) of the central character, Hans Castorp. In doing this, he has composed a work related to the great German tradition of the *Bildungsroman*, illustrated a century earlier by Goethe in his famous *Wilhelm Meisters Lehrejahre*. The theme of the novel is consequently that of the instruction, development, and education of a young man who is "simple," yet "curious" and "enterprising" (all these expressions are those of the narrative voice). Consequently, when the novel is read as the story of a spiritual apprenticeship, centered around the person of Hans Castorp, the real question becomes: By what means has the narrative technique succeeded in integrating the experience of time, deadly sickness, and the great debate over the destiny of culture?

With regard to the first alternative mentioned above—is this a novel about time or a novel about sickness?—the narrative technique consists in raising the double confrontation with the effacement of time and the fascination with decomposition to the level of an intellectual experience, whose transformations we shall study below. Detemporalization and corruption become, through the art of the narrative, the indivisible object of the hero's fascination and speculation. Only fiction could create the unprecedented conditions required by this temporal experience, which itself is unprecedented, by instilling a complicity between the effacement of time and the attraction of death. In this way, even before we take into account the debate over the destiny of culture, the story of a spiritual apprenticeship joins the *Zeitroman* to the novel about sickness within the framework of a *Bildungsroman*.

The second alternative—the destiny of a hero, even an antihero, or the destiny of European culture—is resolved in the same way. By making Settembrini and Naphta Hans Castorp's "schoomasters," Mann has integrated the great European debate within the individual story of *une éducation sentimentale*. The interminable discussions with the spokesmen for optimistic humanism and for a nihilism tinged with communist-leaning Catholicism are raised to the level of objects of fascination and speculation in the same way as death and time are.

The *Bildungsroman*, within the framework of which the *Zeitroman* is placed, deserves this title not because what is at stake is the destiny of European culture, but because this trans-individual debate is in a sense miniaturized—if we may speak in this way about a novel of some seven hundred pages!—in the *Bildungsroman* centered around Hans Castorp. Thus between these three dimensions—time, death, and culture—exchanges occur. The destiny of culture becomes an aspect of the debate between love and death; in return, the deceptions of a love in which sensuality is accompanied by corruption become "schoolmasters" in the hero's spiritual quest, patterned after the teachers who use language.

Is this to say that in this complex architecture the *Zeitroman* becomes just one aspect of the *Bildungsroman*, on an equal footing with the novel about sickness and the novel about European decadence? The *Zeitroman* preserves, in my opinion, an indelible privilege that is apparent only if we ask the most difficult question of all, that of the true nature of the spiritual apprenticeship whose story is told in the novel. Thomas Mann chose to make the hero's investigation concerning time the touchstone of all of the other investigations into sickness and death, love, life, and culture. Time is compared, at a certain point in the story which I shall speak of below, to the thermometer without any marking that is given to the patients who cheat. It then carries the meaning—semi-mythical, semi-ironic—of a "silent sister." The "silent sister" of the attraction of death, of love mingled with corruption, of the concern with great history. The *Zeitroman*, we might say, is the "silent sister" of the epic of death and of the tragedy of culture.

Focused in this way on the experience of time, all the questions posed by the hero's apprenticeship in the various spheres into which the novel is divided are summed up in a single question: Has the hero learned anything at the Berghof? Is he a genius, as some have said, or an antihero? Or is his apprenticeship of a more subtle nature, breaking with the tradition of the *Bildungsroman*?

Here the doubts raised by the narrator's irony come back in force. I situated the privileged place of this irony in the distancing relation established between a narrative voice, put on stage with ostentation, insistence, and obstinacy, and the whole of the story told, throughout which this narrative voice intervenes unceasingly. The narrator is cast as the cunning observer of the story he is telling. As a first approximation, this critical distance appears to undermine the credibility of the narrator and render problematic any answer to the question of whether the hero has learned anything at the Berghof about time, life and death, love and culture. However, on further reflection, we begin to suspect that this distancing relation between the narrative voice and the narrative might constitute the hermeneutical key to the problem posed by the novel itself. *Might not the hero, in his debate with time, be in the same relation as the narrator with respect to the story he is telling—a relation of ironic distance?* Neither vanquished by the morbid universe, nor a Goethean victor in some triumph through action, might he not be a victim, who grows solely within the realm of lucidity, of reflective power?

This is the reading hypothesis that must be tested as we go over the seven chapters of *Der Zauberberg* a second time.[29]

The novel begins as follows. "An unassuming young man was travelling, in midsummer, from his native city of Hamburg to Davos-Platz in the Canton of Grisons, on a three weeks' visit" (p. 3). The *Zeitroman* is set into place by the mere mention of the three weeks.[30] But there is more. Upon rereading, the narrative voice is recognizable with the very first description of the hero as an "unassuming" (*einfach*) young man, which finds an echo in the final lines of the novel, in which the narrator unabashedly enjoins his hero: "Adventures of the flesh and in the spirit, while enhancing [*steigerten*] thy simplicity, granted thee to know in the spirit what in the flesh thou scarcely could have done" (p. 716). In addition, the irony of this voice is concealed by the apparent observation, "[He] was travelling . . . on a three weeks' visit." Upon rereading, these three weeks will present a contrast with the seven years spent at the Berghof. A question is thus implied in this innocent beginning: What will happen to the simplicity of this young man when his project is torn to pieces by the adventures that he himself has undertaken? We know that the length of his stay will provide the dramatic impetus for the entire narrative.

In this very brief first chapter, the narrator makes use for the first time of the spatial relation to signify the temporal relation: going away from his native city functions like forgetfulness. "Time, we say, is Lethe; but change of air is a similar draught, and, if it works less thoroughly, does so more quickly" (p. 4). Arriving at the Berghof, Hans Castorp carries with him the vision of time below. The first conversations between Hans and his cousin Joachim, who is already acclimatized to the time above, bring to the foreground the discordance between the two ways of existing, the two styles of living. Hans and Joachim do not speak the same language with regard to time. Joachim has already lost the preciseness of measurements. "Three weeks are just like a day to them. . . . One's ideas get changed" (p. 7). An expectation is thus created in the reader. Conversation will serve not only, as here, as a simple procedure for making apparent on the level of language the difference between ways of conceiving and experiencing time; it will be the privileged medium of the hero's apprenticeship.[31]

The second full day, recounted by Chapter 3, is made up of numerous minor events that follow one upon the other. Meal seems to follow meal without respite; a multifarious population is discovered in a brief lapse of time which appears at once to be abundantly filled and, in particular, to be precisely modulated by walks, sessions with the thermometer, and rest periods. Conversations with Joachim, then with the first schoolmaster, Settembrini, put on stage early on by the narrator, aggravate the discrepancies of language that were already intimated the day before, the day of his "arrival." Hans Castorp is astonished by Joachim's vague approximation.[32] At his first meeting with Settembrini, he defends his stay of "three weeks."[33] But the discussion with Settembrini has from the start a different case than the conversations with Joachim. The misunderstanding is from the outset the beginning of an investigation, a quest. Settembrini is right when he says, "Curiosity is another of the prescriptive rights of shadows" (p. 58). The section entitled *Gedankenscharfe*— "Mental Gymnastic" (or "Lucidity")—introduces the preamble to a speculation that the art of narrative will untiringly attempt to narrativize. In the thermometer scene, Han's assurance collapses but not his vigilance. Is it not at *fixed* hours and for *seven* (seven!) minutes that one's temperature is taken?[34] Hans holds fast to the ordering of what could be called "clinical time"; but this is precisely what throws time off. At least Hans takes the first step toward lucidity by disassociating time as it appears to "feeling" (*Gefühl*) from the time that is measured by the hands as they move around the dial of the clock (p. 66). Slim discoveries, no doubt, but ones that nevertheless must be ascribed to lucidity[35]—even if perplexity overrides all.[36] It is not without importance for the education of our hero that a first, sudden illumination concerning what time can truly be comes to him in a dream. How does time present itself? As "a 'silent sister,' a mercury column without degrees to be used by those who wanted to cheat" (p. 92). The thermometer scene is both repeated and abolished. The numbers have disappeared from the thermometer. Normal time has disappeared, as on a watch that no longer tells the hour. By their mood "of extravagant joy and suspense" (p. 90), the two dreams that are reported belong to the series of "happy moments"—in Proustian terms—that mark out his quest and to which our attention will be drawn in a second reading by the novel's final lines: "Moments there were, when out of death, and the rebellion of the flesh, there came to thee, as thou tookest stock of thyself [*ahnungsvoll und regierungsweise*], a dream of love" (p. 716). It is true that this dream is not yet one of those that the hero can be said to have "taken stock of." At least it indicates a curiosity that, although it is captive of the erotic attraction exerted by Clavdia Chauchat, is strong enough to make him resist Settembrini's advice that he leave: "He spoke with sudden insistence" (p. 87).

The erosion of the sense of time and of the language appropriate to it continues in the long Chapter 4 that covers the three weeks that Hans Castorp intended to spend as a simple visitor to the Berghof. The confusion of the seasons contributes to the blurring together of the common reference points of time, while the interminable political and cultural discussions with Settembrini get underway (Naphta has not yet been introduced). For an initial reading, these interminable discussions tend to make one lose sight of the hero's temporal experience and to force the *Bildungsroman* outside the boundaries of the *Zeitroman*. For a second reading, it appears that the role assigned to the *Exkurs über den Zeitsinn*—the "Excursus on the Sense of Time" (pp. 102–5)—is to reinsert the great debate on the destiny of European culture within the history of the hero's apprenticeship, and in this way to ensure the balance between *Zeitroman* and *Bildungsroman*. A single expression serves as the anchor point in this delicate adjustment that is the work of the narrator alone: "acclimatization," "habituating oneself" (*diesem Sicheinleben an fremden Ort*) (pp. 103–4), as a phenomenon that is at once cultural and temporal.[37] The digression moves on from here to become the rumination of the narrator himself on monotony and boredom. It is false, it is stated, that these impressions slow down the course of time. Far from it. "Vacuity, monotony, have, indeed, the property of lingering out the moment and the hour and of making them tiresome. But they are capable of contracting and dissipating the larger, the very large time-units, to the point of reducing them to nothing at all" (p. 104). This double effect of shortening and stretching out robs the idea of a length of time of its univocity and only allows one answer to the question, How long? "Very long" (p. 105).

The general tone of the *Exkurs* is instead that of a warning. "There is, after all, something peculiar about the process of habituating oneself in a new place, the often laborious fitting in and getting used, which one undertakes for its own sake, and of set purpose to break it all off as soon as it is complete, or not long thereafter, and to return to one's former state" (pp. 103–4). When it is a question of something quite different from an interruption, an intermission in the main course of life, a monotony that is too uninterrupted threatens to make us lose the very consciousness of duration, "the perception of time, so closely bound up with the consciousness of life that one may not be weakened without the other suffering a sensible impairment" (p. 104). The expression "consciousness of life" (*Lebensgefühl*) is obviously not without a hint of irony. However, by attributing analogous thoughts to his hero, the narrator indicates that he has simply a slight headstart over Castrop on the road to lucidity.[38] The hero's curiosity is never deadened, even if at times he experiences the desire "to escape awhile from the Berghof circle [*Bannkreis*], to breathe the air deep into his lungs" (p. 117).

Also contributing to the effacement of time, of which the hero is the partially lucid victim, is the episode of the apparition in a waking dream-state of

Pribislav Hippe, the schoolboy with the lead pencil, whose eyes and look become those of Clavdia Chauchat. Due to the emblematic character of the leitmotiv of the lead pencil that is borrowed and returned[39] (providing the narrator with an enigmatic ending to the *Walpurgisnacht* episode, which I shall discuss below), this episode, which Thieberger appropriately calls the *verträumte* Intermezzo, brings to the surface again the depth of accumulated time, already probed by the return into the past in Chapter 2—a depth that in its turn gives the present instant a sort of infinite duration (p. 122). Later, the series of dreams of eternity will be built upon this depth.

Even before the planned three weeks are up, for Hans, "the refreshment of his sense of time" has faded away, and yet the days that fly by continue to stretch out "long and longer to hold the crowded, secret hopes and fears that filled it to overflowing" (p. 141). His attraction to Clavdia and the prospect of leaving still give time movement and tension.[40] And yet when the end of the three weeks is in sight, Hans Castorp has already been won over by the ideas expressed by Joachim when they met. "Three weeks up here was as good as nothing at all; they had all told him so in the beginning. The smallest unit of time was the month" (p. 162). Was he not already regretting not having set aside more time for his visit? And by agreeing to take part in the "thermometer" sessions (an important subtitle in Chapter 4) (p. 161), has he not, like the other patients, fallen prey to the magic mountain?[41]

Once "habituated," Hans Castrop is nevertheless ready for the first experience of eternity, which opens Chapter 5, which is longer than the preceding chapter. The narrator has, from the start, taken things in hand in order to return to the question raised in the *Vorsatz* concerning the length of the novel. "We apprehend," states the narrative voice, "that these next three weeks will be over and done with in the twinkling of an eye" (p. 183). Here, the strangeness ascribed to the relation between the *Erzählzeit* and the *erzählte Zeit* contributes to putting into relief the strangeness belonging to the very experience of the hero of the fiction. It is said that the laws of narration call for the experience of time of writing and reading to expand or contract in accordance with the hero's adventure, but now that the law of those up above has won out, all that is left is to bury oneself deeper in the thickness of time. There are no more witnesses from down below. The time of feeling has eliminated clock time. Then, the mystery of time opens up, to our *surprise* (the word occurs twice on p. 183).

The episodes, *Ewigkeitssuppe und plötzliche Klarheit*, "Soup Everlasting" and "Sudden Enlightenment" (pp. 183–219), do not strictly speaking contain any of the announced "miracles" but rather the ground—even the underground—against which the decisive "miracles" will stand out. A strange eternity indeed is this selfsame eternity. It is once again the narrative voice that says of this series of days, all alike, spent in bed, "They bring you your midday broth, as they brought it yesterday and will bring it to-morrow . . . and what is being revealed to you as the true content of time is merely a dimensionless present in which they eternally bring you the broth. But in such a connexion it would be paradoxical to speak of time as passing slowly; and paradox, with reference to such a hero, we should avoid" (pp. 183–84). The ironical tone leaves no doubt. This indication is nonetheless of the greatest importance. The reader has to keep it in mind, in the cumulative time of re-reading that this type of novel particularly requires. The meaning of *Ewigkeitssuppe* must remain in suspense until a reply is given by the other two experiences of eternity, that of "Walpurgis-Night" at the end of the same chapter, and that of the "Snow" scene in Chapter 7.

The narrative element that permits this commentary by the narrator is Hans Castorp's new condition, under Dr. Behren's orders, flat on his back in the deathbed of the preceding patient. Three weeks of this eternity fly by at a gallop in ten pages. All that counts is the "abiding present of that midday hour" (p. 190), which is also expressed by an accumulation of remarks about time. One no longer knows what day it is; but one knows what time it is in the "day, artificially shortened, broken into small bits" (p. 192). Settembrini is given the opportunity to discourse—in the tone of a man of letters, a humanist politician—on the relation that everything, including religion and love, entertains with death. The X ray abruptly gives the fatal diagnosis: Hans Castorp is already the living victim of sickness and death. The sight of his own ghostly self on Dr. Behren's illuminated screen is a prefiguration of his own decomposition, a look into his own tomb. "With . . . penetrating, prophetic eyes, he gazed at this familiar part of his own body, and for the first time in his life he understood that he would die" (p. 219).

The last, precise account of time—again through the narrator's irony—stops at seven weeks, the seven weeks that Hans Castorp intended to spend at the Berghof; it is the narrator who gives this account (p. 219). It is not unimportant that this final count—six weeks are counted until Christmas and seven until the famous "night"—is placed under the title of the subchapter *Freiheit*, "Freedom" (p. 219). The progress of Hans Castorp's education is inseparable from this victory over a final pang of concern for dated time. Even more important is the fact that our hero learns to distance himself from his Italian teacher as he distances himself from time.[42] But he will not free himself from it until he has escaped the nihilism of the *Ewigkeitssuppe*, which, in turn, never ceases to leave its morbid imprint on love, intermingled with sickness and death.[43]

From here on Hans Castorp's education will take on the colors of an emancipation by way of empty time (pp. 287–88). Another subsection of this long chapter, in the course of which time steps outside of its points of reference as it extends beyond seven weeks, is entitled *Forschungen*, "Research" (pp. 267–86). It is burdened with apparent digressions on anatomy, organic life, matter, death, the mixture of voluptuousness and organic substance, of corruption and creation. Although he is infatuated with his reading on anatomy, it is nevertheless entirely by himself that Hans Castorp obtains his education on the theme of life in its relation with voluptuousness and death, under the emblem of the X-rayed hand's skeleton. Hans Castorp has already become an observer, just like the narrator. After "Research" follows *Totentanz*, "The Dance of Death" (pp. 286–322)—three days of festivity in honor of Christmas, where no light of the Nativity ever penetrates, but which is marked only by the contemplation of the "gentleman rider's" corpse. The sacred and indecent character of death, glimpsed before in the presence of his grandfather's earthly remains, imposes itself once more. However macabre the impulse that leads Hans Castorp from the bedside of one dying person to another, what animates him is the concern to pay homage to life, insofar as the honor paid to the dead seems to him to be the necessary path of this homage (p. 296). "Life's delicate child," in Settembrini's pretty phrase, cannot help but occupy himself with the "children of death" (p. 308). We are not able to say, at this stage, whether, in the experience that changes him, Hans Castorp is the prisoner of those up above or on the road to freedom.

It is in this undecided state, where the attraction of the macabre tends to occupy the place freed by the effacement of time that, a few days before the first seven months of his stay are up—to be precise on the eve of Mardi Gras, hence at carnival time—the hero is overcome by the extraordinary experience that the ironic narrator has placed under the title of *Walpurgisnacht*, "Walpurgis-Night" (pp. 322–43). It begins with the informal "thou" that Hans Castorp, half drunk, addresses to Settembrini, who does not miss seeing in this the freeing of his "pupil"—"That sounds like a parting" (p. 329)—and culminates in the conversation bordering on delirium with Clavdia Chauchat, in the midst of the "antics of the masked patients" (p. 335).[44] Following this witty but forced conversation centered upon the use of the familiar form "thou" which begins and ends with the pencil borrowed and returned—Hippe's pencil!—a dreamlike vision occurs, carrying with it the sense of eternity, an eternity quite different, surely, from the *Ewigkeitssuppe*, but a dreamed eternity nonetheless. "For it is like a dream to me, that we are sitting like this—*comme un rêve singulièrement profond, car il faut dormir très profondement pour rêver comme cela. Je veux dire—c'est un rêve bien connu, rêvé de tout temps, long, éternel, oui, être assis près de toi comme à présent, voilà l'éternité*" (p. 336, in French in the text). A dream of eternity which Clavdia's announcement of her impending departure, received like the news of a cataclysm, suffices to dissipate. But could Clavdia, preaching freedom through sin, danger, loss of self, have represented for Hans anything different than Ulysses' sirens, when he has himself tied to the mast of his ship to resist their songs? The body, love, and death are too closely bound together, sickness and voluptuousness, beauty and corruption still too thoroughly intermingled for the loss of the sense of counted time to be paid for, in its turn, by the courage to live, the price of which is this very loss.[45] The sequel to the *Ewigkeitssuppe* was no more than a dream of eternity, a carnival eternity— *Walpurgisnacht!*

The composition of Chapter 6, which by itself takes up more than half of the second part of *The Magic Mountain*, is a good illustration of the difference not only between *Erzählzeit* and *erzählte Zeit*, but between the narrated time and the experience of time projected by fiction.

On the level of the narrated time, the narrative framework is assured by the exchanges, increasingly infrequent and increasingly dramatic, between those up above and those down below, exchanges that at the same time provide a figure for the assaults of normal time on the detemporalized duration that is the common lot at the Berghof. Joachim, returning to his military vocation, escapes the sanatorium. Naphta, the second schoolmaster—the Jesuit of Jewish origin, at once anarchist and reactionary—is introduced into the story, breaking up the face-to-face conversation between Settembrini and Hans Castorp. The great uncle from Hamburg, as the representative of those down below, attempts in vain to tear his nephew away from the enchantment. Joachim returns to the Berghof to die there.

Out of all these events, there emerges one episode, *Schnee*, "Snow" (pp. 469–98), that alone deserves to be included within the series of moments and dreams of love referred to in the final lines of the book, "moments" (*Augenblicke*) that remain the discontinuous pinnacles, where the narrated time and the experience of time together find their culmination. The whole art of composition being to produce this conjunction at the peak between the narrated time and the experience of time.

Before this pinnacle is reached, Hans Castorp's ruminations on time—amplified by those of the narrator—stretch out the narrative framework we have just outlined to the point of bursting, as if the story of this spiritual apprenticeship never ceased to free itself from material contingencies. It is, moreover, the narrator who occupies the first scene, in a sense helping his hero to put his thoughts in order, to so great an extent does the experience of time, in evading chronology and in growing ever deeper, break up into irreconcilable perspectives. By losing measurable time, Hans Castorp has reached the same aporias that our discussion of the phenomenology of time in Augustine made apparent concerning the relationships between the time of the soul and physical change. "What is time? A mystery, a figment—and all-powerful. It conditions the external world, it is motion married to and mingled with the existence of bodies in space, and with the motion of these" (p. 344). It is therefore not, strictly speaking, internal time that poses a problem, once it is disconnected from measurement, but the impossibility of reconciling it with the cosmic aspects of time, which, far from having disappeared with the interest in the passage of time, are going progressively to be exalted. What preoccupies

Hans Castorp is precisely the equivocity of time—its eternal circularity and its capacity to produce change. "Time is functional, it can be referred to as action; we say a thing is 'brought about' by time. What sort of thing? Change!" (ibid.). Time is a mystery precisely in that the observations that are to be made regarding it cannot be unified. (This is exactly what, for me, constitutes an unsurpassable enigma. This is why I can readily forgive the narrator for seeming to whisper Hans Castorp's thoughts to him.) [46] How far the novel has moved away from the simple fiction of effacing measurable time! What has in a sense been freed by this effacement is the contrast between immobile eternity and the changes produced, whether it is a question of the visible changes of the seasons and the appearance of new vegetation (in which Hans Castorp take a new interest) or of more deeply hidden changes, which he experiences in himself—and this despite the *Ewigkeitssuppe*—thanks to his erotic attraction to Clavdia, then at the time of the plenitude of *Walpurgisnacht*, and now in awaiting her return. Hans Castorp's passions for astronomy, which now supplants his interest in anatomy, henceforth gives the monotonous experience of time cosmic proportions. The contemplation of the sky and the stars gives their very flight a paradoxical fixity, bordering on the Nietzschean experience of the eternal return. But what could bridge the dream-eternity of the *Walpurgisnacht* and the contemplated eternity of the fixity of the heavens? [47]

Hans Castorp's apprenticeship continues from here on by way of the discovery of the equivocity of thinking, in and through the confusion of feelings. [48] This discovery is more than a slight advance, compared to the stagnation of the Berghof guests in simple nontime. In what is incommensurable, Hans Castorp has discovered the immemorial—"for six long, incredible, though scurrying months" (p. 346).

This profound change in the experience of time is included by the narrator within the series of events that constitutes the narrated time of the novel. On the one hand, awaiting Clavdia's return provides the occasion for another apprenticeship, that of endurance with respect to absence. Hans Castorp is now strong enough to resist the temptation to leave the magic mountain with Joachim. No, he will not leave with him, he will not desert to return to the flat-land: "Alone I should never find my way back" (p. 416). The immobile eternity has at least accomplished its negative work; he has divested himself of life. This passage by way of the negative constitutes the central peripeteia of the *Bildungsroman* as well as of the *Zeitroman*. In its turn, the repulsed attack of great-uncle Tienappel, who has come from Hamburg to set a definite date for the fugitive's return, only transforms into obstinancy the endurance that remains the only available reply to the destructive action of eternal vanity. After this, is Hans the hostage of Dr. Behrens and his medical ideology, which merely repeats the cult of sickness and death that reigns at the Berghof? Or is he the new hero of a gnosis of eternity and of time? Both interpretations are carefully cultivated by the narrator. Hans Castorp has certainly divested himself of life, and this assuredly renders his experience suspect. In return, his resistance to the assaults from the flat-land "meant, for himself, the consummation of freedom—the thought of which had gradually ceased to make him shudder" (p. 440).[49]

Hans Castorp exercises this freedom mainly with respect to his mentors, Settembrini and Naphta. The narrator has most opportunely made the latter appear in the second half of his narrative, thus giving the hero the opportunity to keep at an equal distance from his two irreconcilable teachers and, in this way, to come little by little to the superior position that the narrator has ostensibly occupied since the *Vorsatz*. Naphta represents no less of a temptation than Settembrini and his optimistic humanism. Naphta's ramblings, in which Settembrini sees only a mysticism of death and murder, have a hidden connection to the lesson of the message left by Clavdia that famous *Walpurgisnacht*. If he does not speak of salvation through evil, he does teach that virtue and health are not "religious" states. This strange Christianity with a Nietzschean—or communist tinge,[50] according to which "to be man was to be ailing" (p. 465), plays in the novel of Hans Castorp's education the role of diabolical temptation, of slipping away into the negative as depicted by the *Ewigkeitssuppe*. But this temptation is no more successful than the emissary from the flat-land in interrupting the hero's intrepid experimentation.

The episode entitled *Schnee*, "Snow" (pp. 469–98), to which we now come, the most decisive one since *Walpurgisnacht*, owes its striking character to the fact that it directly follows the episode of Naptha's diabolical maneuvers (an episode significantly and ironically entitled *Operationes Spirituales*). It is also important that this episode has as its setting the phantasmagoria of snowy space which, curiously, corresponds with the seashore—"The monotony of the scene was in both cases profound" (p. 473). The mountain laid waste by the snow is in truth more than a setting for the decisive scene. It is the spatial equivalent of the temporal experience itself. "The primeval silence," *Das Urschweigen* (p. 476), unites space and time in a single symbolic system. In addition, the confrontation between human effort and nature and the obstacles it sets in the way exactly symbolizes the change of register in the relation between time and eternity, the spiritual stakes of the episode.[51] Everything is overturned when, courage transformed into defiance—"a repudiation of all caution whatsoever, in short . . . a challenge" (p. 481)—the fighter, drunk with fatigue (and port) is visited by a vision of foliage and blue sky, the song of birds, and sunlight: "So now with the scene before him, constantly transformed and transfigured as it was before his eyes [*sich öffnete in wachsender Verklärung*]" (p. 490). Certainly this remembering the Mediterranean, which he has never seen, yet "always" (*von je*) known (ibid.), is not free from terror—the two old women dismembering a child over a basin, between flaming braziers!—as if the ugly were irremediably bound up with the beautiful. As if irrationality and death were part of life—"it would not be life without it"

(p. 496)! Afterward, Hans has no more use for his schoolmasters. He *knows*. What does he know? "*For the sake of goodness and love, man shall let death have no sovereignty over his thoughts*" (pp. 496–97, emphasis in original).

Thus the dream of eternity of *Walpurgisnacht*, indistinguishable from the cult of sickness and death, finds a reply in another eternity, an "always" that is at once the recompense for and the origin of the courage to live.

Of lesser importance, then, is Joachim's return to the Berghof and the fact that this return apparently takes the form of the same temporal weightlessness as Hans' arrival in the past. Controversies may continue to rage between Settembrini and Naphta on the themes of alchemy and free masonry, but a new relation to the world of sickness and death is established, announcing a secret change in the relation to time itself. The episode of Joachim's death attests to this. Hans attends the dying man with neither repugnance nor attraction, and closes the dead man's eyes.[52] The lost feeling of the length of time passed, the mingling of the seasons, have brought about this disinterest for measurements of time—"for you are of time, and time is vanished" (p. 546)—and little by little life takes over from the fascination with sickness.

This new interest in life is put to the test in Chapter 7, marked essentially by Clavdia Chauchat's return to the Berghof, unexpectedly accompanied by Mynheer Peeperkorn. The extravagance of royal anger, the bacchic delirium of this Dutch giant inspire in Hans Castorp less the expected jealousy than a fearful reverence, gradually replaced by a sort of playful affability. In this way, despite his having to give up Clavdia after she arrives with her unexpected companion, the benefit drawn from this event is large indeed. First of all, the two "educators" of our "unassuming hero" have lost all influence over him, measured against the scale of this character upon whom the narrator confers—for a short time—an extraordinary presence and power. Above all, the strange triangular relationship that is established between Mynheer, Clavdia, and Hans demands of the latter a mastery of his emotions in which malice is joined to submission. Under the instigation of the Dutchman, decisions themselves take a wild and burlesque turn. The confrontation with Clavdia is much more difficult to evaluate, so much does the narrator's irony undermine the apparent meaning. The word "spirit" surfaces: "a highly spiritual dream," "these heights of the spirit," "death is the spiritual principle," "the spiritual way" (p. 596). Has our hero become, as Clavdia tells him, a quaint philosopher? A surprising victory over his teachers, if the *Bildungsroman* produces only a spiritual person, smitten with the hermetic and the occult.[53] The most unreasonable hypothesis, however, would be to expect from our hero a straight line of growth, in the way that Settembrini represents the "Progress of Humanity." The Dutchman's suicide, the confusion of the ensuing feelings, throws Hans into a state for which the narrator can only find one name, *Der grosse Stumpfsinn*, "The Great God Dumps" (pp. 624–35).[54] The great god "Dumps"—"An apocalyptic, evil name, calculated to give rise to mysterious fears. . . . He was frightened. It seemed to him 'all this' could come to no good, that a catastrophe was impending, that long-suffering nature would rebel, rise up in storm and whirlwind and break the great bond which held the world in thrall; snatch life beyond the 'dead point' and put an end to the 'small potatoes' in one terrible Last Day" (p. 634). Card games, replaced by the phonograph, do not take him out of this state. Behind an air by Gounod and the song of forbidden love, he sees the figure of Death. So enjoyment and corruption then have not been severed from one another? Or rather, renouncement and self-mastery take on the same colors as the morbid affections they are supposed to have conquered? The occult seance—intentionally placed under the subtitle *Fragwürdigstes*, "Highly Questionable" (pp. 653–81)— culminating in the ghostly apparition of cousin Joachim, carries the experimentation on time to the unmarked borderlines of equivocation and deception. The strangeness of the duel scene between Settembrini and Naphta (Settembrini shoots into the air and Naphta shoots himself in the head) is the height of confusion. "These were such singular times" (p. 703).

Then the thunderbolt strikes, *Der Donnerschlag*, with which we are all familiar, that deafening explosion of a deadly mixture of the cumulative effects of the "The Great God Dumps" and "*Hysterica Passio*," titles of the two preceding sections. A historic thunderbolt—"the shock that fired the mine beneath the magic mountain [so named for the first time], and set our sleeper ungently outside the gates" (p. 709). Thus speaks the voice of the narrator. In one fell swoop the distance and the very distinction between up here and down below in the flat-land is annihilated. But it is the irruption of *historical time* that breaks into the enchanted prison from outside. With this, all of our doubts about the reality of Hans Castorp's apprenticeship return: Was it possible for him to free himself from the bewitchment of those above without being torn out of the enchanted circle? Was the dominant, overwhelming experience of *Ewigkeitssuppe* ever overcome? Was the hero able to do anything more than let irreconcilable experiences pile up on top of one another, since he failed to put his capacity for integrating them to the test of action? Or must we say that the situation in which his experience unfolded was that most apt to reveal the irreducible plurality of the meanings of time? And that the confusion into which large-scale history throws him was the price to pay for exposing the very paradox of time?

The epilogue does not help to ease the reader's perplexity. In a final bout of irony the narrator mixes Hans Castorp's silhouette with the other shadows of the great killing: "and thus, in the tumult, in the rain, in the dusk, [he] vanishes out of our sight" (p. 715). In fact, his fate as a soldier belongs to another story, to world history. But the narrator suggests that between the story told— "it was neither short nor long, but hermetic" (p. 715)—and the history of the Western world as it is played out on the battlefield, there exists a tie of analogy that, in its turn, raises a question: "Out of this universal feast of death . . . may it be that Love one day shall mount?" (p. 716). The book ends with this question. But what is important is that it is preceded by a less ambiguous affirmation concerning the story just told. It is the self-assured tone of this other question that implies a note of hope in the final question. The judgment made by the narrator with respect to his story takes the rhetorical form of an address to the hero's "Adventures of the flesh and in the spirit, [which] while enhancing thy simplicity [*die deine Einfachheit steigerten*] granted thee to know in the spirit what in the flesh thou scarcely couldst have done. Moments there were, when out of death, and the rebellion of the flesh, there came to thee, as thou tookest stock of thyself, a dream of love" (ibid.). The *Steigerung* referred to here, has no doubt, allowed the hero only to "survive in the spirit" (*im Geiste überleben*) and has given him only a slight chance to "survive in the flesh" (*im Fleische*). He lacks the test of action, the ultimate criterion of the *Bildungsroman*. This is the irony of it, perhaps even the parody. But the failure of the *Bildungsroman* is the other side of the success of the *Zeitroman*. Hans Castorp's apprenticeship is limited to the presence of a few moments (*Augenblicke*) which, taken together, have no more consistency than "a dream of love." At least the dreams out of which this dream of love arose have been "taken stock of" by the hero. (In this respect the translation of the two key words *ahnungsvoll* and *regierungsweise* is too weak to bear the weight of the only positive message that the ironic narrator communicates to the reader, led to the very height of perplexity.)[55] As a result, are not the narrator's irony and the reader's perplexity at once the image and the model of those of the hero, at the moment of the abrupt interruption of his spiritual adventure?

If we now ask what resources *Der Zauberberg* is capable of bringing to the refiguration of time, it appears most clearly that it is not a speculative solution to the aporias of time that we are to expect from the novel but, in a certain way, their *Steigerung*, their "elevation to a higher level." The narrator has deliberately given himself an extreme situation where the effacement of measurable time has already been accomplished when his hero appears. The apprenticeship to which this experience condemns him constitutes in its turn a thought experiment that is not limited to a passive reflection of this condition of temporal weightlessness but one that goes on to explore the paradoxes of the extreme situation thus laid bare. The conjunction, through the narrative technique, of the novel about time, the novel about sickness, and the novel about culture is the medium that the poet's imagination produces to carry as far as possible the lucidity required by such an exploration.

Let us go further. The global opposition between the normal time of those down below and the loss of interest in measurements of time characteristic of those up above represents only the zero degree of the thought experiment undertaken by Hans Castorp. The major conflict between internal duration and the irrevocable exteriority of clock time cannot, therefore, be what is ultimately at stake in this experiment, as we could still say in a strict sense about *Mrs. Dalloway*. As the relations between those down below and those up above are weakened, a new space of exploration unfolds, one in which the paradoxes brought to light are precisely those that afflict the internal experience of time when it is freed from its relation to chronological time.

The most fruitful explorations in this regard concern the relation between time and eternity. And in this respect, the relations suggested by the novel are extraordinarily varied. Between the "Soup-everlasting" of Chapter 5, "le rêve bien connu, rêvé de tout temps, long, éternel," of *Walpurgisnacht*, which concludes Chapter 5, and the ecstatic experience with which the "Snow" episode culminates, the differences are considerable. Eternity unfolds its own paradoxes which the unsettling situation at the Berghof renders even more unsettling. The fascination with sickness and corruption reveals an eternity of death, whose imprint on time is the sempiternal repetition of the Same. For its part, the contemplation of the starry sky spreads a benediction of peace over an experience in which eternity is corrupted by the "bad infinity" of endless movement. The cosmic side of eternity, which would be better termed perpetuity, is not easily reconciled with the oneiric side of the two major experiences, *Walpurgisnacht* and "Snow," where eternity swings away from death and moves toward life, without for all that ever succeeding in uniting eternity, love, and life in the manner of Augustine. On the other hand, the ironic detachment, which is perhaps the most "elevated" state reached by the hero, marks a precarious victory over the eternity of death that borders on stoic ataraxy. But the insurmountable situation of bewitchment to which this ironic detachment replies does not allow it to be put to the test of action. Only the irruption of Great History—*Der Donnerschlag*—was able to break the charm.

At least ironic detachment, thanks to which Hans Castorp rejoins his narrator, will have permitted the hero to deploy a wide range of existentielle possibilities, even if he has not succeeded in making a synthesis out of them. In this sense, discordance finally wins out over concordance. But the consciousness of discordance has been "elevated" one step higher.

TIME TRAVERSED: Remembrance of Things Past

Are we justified in looking for a "tale about time" in *Remembrance of Things Past*?[56]

This has been contested, paradoxically, in a number of different ways. I shall not linger over the confusion, which contemporary criticism has dispelled, between what might be considered a dissimulated autobiography of Marcel Proust, the author, and the fictional autobiography of the character who says "I." We now know that if the experience of time can be what is at stake in a novel, this is not due to what the novel borrows from the experience of its real author but rather to literary fiction's power to create a narrator-hero who pursues a certain quest of him/herself, in which what is at stake is, precisely, the dimension of time. It remains to be determined in just what sense this is so. Regardless of the partial homonymy between "Marcel," the narrator-hero of *Remembrance*, and Marcel Proust, the author of the novel, the novel does not owe its fictional status to the events of Proust's life, which may have been transposed to the novel and have left their scar there, but to the narrative composition alone, which projects a world in which the narrator-hero tries to recapture the meaning of an earlier life, itself wholly fictive. Time lost and time regained are thus to be understood together as the features of a fictive experience unfolded within a fictive world.

My first reading hypothesis will therefore be to consider, uncompromisingly, the narrator-hero as a fictive entity supporting the tale about time that constitutes *Remembrance*.

A more forceful way of challenging the exemplary value of *Remembrance* as a tale about time is to say, with Gilles Deleuze in *Proust and Signs*, that what is principally at stake in *Remembrance* is not time but truth.[57] This challenge grows out of the very strong argument that "Proust's work is based not on the exposition of memory, but on the apprenticeship to signs" (p. 4)—signs of the social world, signs of love, sensuous signs, signs of art. If, nevertheless, "it is called a search for lost time, it is only to the degree that truth has an essential relation to time" (p. 15). To this I would reply that this mediation by means of the apprenticeship to signs and the search for truth is in no way damaging to the characterization of *Remembrance* as a tale about time. Deleuze's argument undercuts only those interpretations that have understood *Remembrance* solely in terms of the experiences of involuntary memory and that, for this reason, have overlooked the long apprenticeship to disillusionment that gives *Remembrance* the scope that is lacking in the brief and fortuitous experiences of involuntary memory. If the apprenticeship to signs imposes the long, circuitous path that *Remembrance* substitutes for the shortcut of involuntary memory, this interpretation does not, in its turn, exhaust the meaning of *Remembrance*. The discovery of the extratemporal dimension of the work of art constitutes an eccentric experience in relation to the entire apprenticeship to signs. As a result, if *Remembrance* is a tale about time, it is so to the extent that it is identified neither with involuntary memory nor with the apprenticeship to signs—which, indeed, does take time—but poses the problem of the *relation* between these two levels of experience and the incomparable experience that the narrator puts off and finally reveals only after almost three thousand pages.

The singular character of *Remembrance* is due to the fact that the apprenticeship to signs, as well as the irruption of involuntary memories, represents the form of an interminable wandering, interrupted rather than consummated, by the sudden illumination that retrospectively transforms the entire narrative into the invisible history of a vocation. Time becomes something that is at stake again as soon as it is a question of making the inordinately long apprenticeship to signs correspond to the suddenness of a belatedly recounted visitation, which retrospectively characterizes the entire quest as lost time.[58]

From this follows my second reading hypothesis. In order to avoid granting an exclusive privilege either to the apprenticeship to signs, which would deprive the final revelation of its role as a hermeneutical key for the entire work, or to the final revelation, which would divest the thousands of pages preceding the revelation of any signification and eliminate the very problem of the relation between the quest and the discovery, the cycle of *Remembrance* must be represented in the form of an ellipse, one focus being the search and the second the visitation. *The tale about time is then the tale that creates the relation between these two foci of the novel.* The originality of *Remembrance* lies in its having concealed both the problem and its solution up to the end of the hero's course, thus keeping for a second reading the intelligibility of the work as a whole.

A third, even more forceful way of undercutting the claim that *Remembrance* constitutes a tale about time is to attack, as Anne Henry does in *Proust romancier: le tombeau égyptien*, the primacy of the narrative itself in *Remembrance* and to see in the novel form the projection, on the plane of anecdote, of a philosophical knowledge forged elsewhere and therefore external to the narrative.[59] According to the author of this brilliant study, the "dogmatic corpus that was to support the anecdote at every point" (p. 6) is to be sought nowhere but in German Romanticism, in particular in the philosophy of art first proposed by Schelling in *The System of Transcendental Idealism*,[60] then continued by Schopenhauer in *The World as Will and Representation*,[61] and finally, reworked in psychological terms in France by Proust's philosophy teachers, Séailles, Darlu, and, especially, Tarde. Considered on its narrative level, the work therefore rests on a "theoretical and cultural base" (Henry, p. 19) that precedes it. The important thing to us here is that what is at stake for this philosophy that governs the narrative process from outside is not time but what Schelling called "Identity," that is, the suppression of the division between the mind and the material world, their reconciliation in art, and the necessity of establishing the metaphysical evidence of this in order to provide it with a lasting and concrete form in the work of art. *Remembrance* is as a result not only not a fictive autobiography—everyone agrees on this today—but a feigned novel, the "novel of *Genius*" (pp. 23ff., her emphasis). This is not all. Among the theoretical prescriptions governing the work is the psychological transposition undergone by the dialectic in order to become a novel—a transposition that also belongs to the epistemological base preceding the construction of the novel. What is more, in the opinion of Anne Henry, this transfer of the dialectic to the psychological plane indicates less a new conquest than the deterioration of the Romantic heritage. So if the passage from Schelling to Tarde by way of Schopenhauer explains that lost unity, according to Romanticism, could have become lost time, and that the double redemption of the world and the subject could have been transmuted into the rehabilitation of an individual past; in sort, if in a general manner memory could have become the privileged mediator for the birth of genius, the fact must not be concealed that this translation of the combat to within one consciousness expresses the collapse as much as the continuation of the great philosophy of art received from German Romanticism.

My recourse to Proust to illustrate the notion of the fictive experience of time is thus doubly contested. Not only does the theoretical core, with regard to which the novel is held to be a demonstration, subordinate the question of time to a higher question, that of identity lost and recovered, but the passage from lost identity to lost time presents the scars of a shattered belief. By tying the promotion of the psychological, of the self, of memory, to the deterioration of a great metaphysics, Anne Henry tends to disparage all that has to do with the novel as such. The fact that the hero of the quest is a bourgeois leading a life of leisure, dragging his boredom from one unhappy love to another, and from one silly salon to another, expresses an impoverishment corresponding to the "translation of the combat within a consciousness" (p. 46). "A life that is flat, bourgeois, never shaken by cataclysms . . . offers the ideal mediocrity for an experimental type of narrative" (p. 56).[62] A remarkably vigorous reading of *Remembrance* results from this suspicion that saps from within the prestige of the narrative genre as such. Once the major stake has been shifted from lost unity to lost time, all the prestige attaching to the novel of genius loses its luster.

Let us admit, provisionally, this thesis that *Remembrance* is generated out of the "transposition of the system into a novel." The problem of narrative *creation* thereby becomes, in my opinion, all the more enigmatic and its solution all the more difficult. Paradoxically, we return here to an explanation in terms of sources. We have, of course, done away with a naive theory of elements borrowed from Proust's life, but only to end up with a more subtle theory of elements borrowed from Proust's thought. The birth of *Remembrance* as an novel requires instead that we look in the narrative composition itself for the principle of the narrative's acquisition of "allogenic speculations," coming from Séailles and Tarde as well as from Schelling and Schopenhauer. The question is then no longer how the philosophy of lost unity could have degenerated into a quest for lost time but how the search for lost time, taken as the founding matrix of the work, accomplishes, through strictly narrative means, the recovery of the Romantic problematic of lost unity.[63]

What are these means? The only way to reintegrate the "allogenic speculations" of the author into the narrative work is to attribute to the narrator-hero not only a fictive experience but "thoughts" that form its sharpest reflexive moment.[64] Have we not recognized, since Aristotle's *Poetics*, that dianoia is a major component of poetic muthos? Moreover, narrative theory offers us irreplaceable assistance here, and this will become my third reading hypothesis, namely, the resource of distinguishing several narrative voices in the fiction of the narrator.

Remembrance makes us hear at least two narrative voices, that of the hero and that of the narrator.

The hero tells his worldly, amorous, sensuous, aesthetic adventures as they occur. Here, utterance takes the form of a march directed toward the future, even when the hero is reminiscing; hence the form of the "future in the past" that launches *Remembrance* toward its denouement. And it is the hero again who receives the revelation of the sense of his past life as the invisible history of a vocation. In this respect, it is of the greatest importance to distinguish between the hero's voice and that of the narrator, not only to place the hero's memories themselves back into the stream of a search that advances, but in order to preserve the event-like character of the visitation.

However, we must also be able to hear the voice of the narrator, who is ahead of the hero's progress because he surveys it from above. It is the narrator who, more than a hundred times, says, "as we shall see later." But, above all, the narrator gives the meaning to the experience recounted by the hero—time regained, time lost. Before the final revelation, his voice is so low that it can barely be distinguished from the hero's voice (which authorizes us to speak of the narrator-hero).[65] This is no longer the case in the course of and following the narrative of the great visitation. The narrator's voice takes over to such an extent that it ends up covering over that of the hero. The homonymy of the author and the narrator is then given free reign, at the risk of making the narrator the spokesman for the author in his great dissertation on art. But even then, it is the narrator's exposition of the author's conceptions as his own that is at issue for our reading. His conceptions are then incorporated into the narrator's thoughts. These thoughts of the narrator, in their turn, accompany the hero's lived experience and shed light on it. In this way, they participate in the event-like character of the birth of the writer's vocation as it is lived by the hero.

In order to put these reading hypotheses to the test, let us ask a series of three questions: (1) What would be the signs of time lost and time regained for the reader who is unaware of the conclusion to *Remembrance*, which we know was written during the same period as *Swann's Way*, in *Time Regained*? (2) By what precise narrative means are the speculations on art in *Time Regained* incorporated into the invisible history of a vocation? (3) What relation does the project of the work of art, stemming from the discovery of the writer's vocation, establish between time regained and time lost?

The first two questions place us in turn in each of the two foci of *Remembrance*, and the third allows us to bridge the gap separating them. It is on the basis of the third question that the interpretation I am proposing for *Remembrance of Things Past* will be decided.

Time Lost

The reader of *Swann's Way*—lacking the retrospective illumination projected by the end of the novel onto its beginning—has as yet no way to compare the bedroom in Combray, where between waking and sleeping a consciousness experiences the loss of its identity, its time, and its place, to the library in the Guermantes home, where an excessively vigilant consciousness receives a decisive illumination. On the other hand, this reader could not help but notice certain singular features of this opening section. From the very first sentence, the narrator's voice, speaking out of nowhere, evokes an earlier time that has no date, no place, a time that lacks an indication of distance in relation to the present of the utterance, an earlier time that is endlessly multiplied. (The uniting of the compound past with the adverb *longtemps* has been commented upon time and time again: "For a long time I used to go to bed early [*Longtemps, je me suis couché de bonne heure*]. Sometimes . . ." [I, p. 3].) In this way the beginning for the narrator refers back to an earlier time that has no boundaries (the only conceivable chronological beginning, the birth of the hero, cannot appear in this duo of voices). It is in this earlier time, in the zone between waking and sleeping, where childhood memories are set away, that the narrative moves two steps away from the absolute present of the narrator.[66]

These memories express themselves in reference to a unique episode, the experience of the madeleine, an episode which itself is characterized by a before and an after. Before it are only archipelagos of unrelated memories; the only thing that emerges is the memory of a certain goodnight kiss, itself placed against the backdrop of a daily ritual:[67] mother's kiss refused at the arrival of M. Swann; kiss awaited in anguish; kiss begged for still as the evening comes to an end; kiss obtained at last but immediately divested of the expected happiness.[68] For the first time, the narrator's voice is heard distinctly. Evoking the memory of his father, the narrator observes, "Many years have passed since that night. The wall of the staircase up which I had watched the light of his candle gradually climb was long ago demolished. . . . It is a long time, too, since my father has been able to say to Mama: 'Go along with the child.' Never again will such moments be possible for me" (I, pp. 39–40). The narrator thus speaks of time lost in the sense of time gone, abolished. But he also speaks of time regained. "But of late I have been increasingly able to catch, if I listen attentively, the sound of the sobs which I had the strength to control in my father's presence, and which broke out only when I found myself alone with Mamma. In reality their echo has never ceased; and it is only because life is now growing more and more quiet round about me that I hear them anew, like those convent bells which are so effectively drowned during the day by the noises of the street that one would suppose them to have stopped, until they ring out again through the silent evening air" (I, p. 40). Without the recovery of the same thoughts at the end of *Time Regained*, would we recognize the dialectic of time lost and time regained in the barely audible voice of the narrator?

Then comes the episode of the overture—told in the preterite—the experience of the madeleine (I, p. 48). The transition with its aftermath is made by means of a remark by the narrator on the incapacities of voluntary memory and on leaving to chance the task of rediscovering the lost object. For someone who is unaware of the final scene in the Guermantes library, which expressly connects the recovery of lost time to the creation of a work of art, the experience of the madeleine may misdirect readers and put them on the wrong track, if they do not set aside, within their own expectations, all of the reticences that go along with the evocation of this happy moment. "An exquisite pleasure had invaded my senses, something isolated, detached, with no suggestion of its origin" (ibid.). From this arises the question, "Whence could it have come to me, this all-powerful joy? I sensed that it was connected with the taste of the tea and the cake, but that it infinitely transcended those savours, could not, indeed, be of the same nature. Whence did it come? What did it mean? How could I seize and apprehend it?" (ibid.). Posed in this way, however, the question holds within it the trap of an overly brief reply, which would simply be that of involuntary memory.[69] If the answer given by this "unknown state" were fully accounted for by the sudden rush of memory of the first little madeleine offered long ago by Aunt Leonie, then *Remembrance* would already have reached its goal when it had only just got underway. It would be limited to the quest for similar reawakenings, of which the least we could say is that they do not require the labor of art. That this is not the case is conveyed by a single clue that speaks to the reader with a keen ear. It is a parenthesis and it says, "(although I did not yet know and must long postpone the discovery of why this memory made me so happy)" (I, p. 51). It is only a second reading, instructed by *Time Regained*, that these remarks, bracketed by the narrator, will take on meaning and force.[70] Nevertheless they are already perceptible on a first reading, even if they offer only a weak resistance to the hasty interpretation according to which the fictive experience of time in Proust would consist in equating time regained with involuntary memory, held to superimpose spontaneously two distinct but similar impressions owing to chance alone.[71]

If the ecstasy of the madeleine is no more than a premonitory sign of the final revelation, it at least already possesses certain of its qualities, opening up the door to memory and allowing the first sketch of *Time Regained*: the Combray narrative (I, pp. 52–204). For a reading not acquainted with *Time Regained* the transition to the Combray narrative seems to partake of the most naive of narrative conventions, even if it does not seem artificial and rhetorical. For a second, more educated reading, the ecstasy of the madeleine opens up the recaptured time of childhood, just as the meditation in the library will open up that of the time when the vocation, recognized at last, is put to the test. The symmetry between the beginning and the end is thus revealed to be the guiding principle of the entire composition. If Combray springs out of a cup of tea (I, p. 51), just as the narrative of the madeleine emerges out of the state between waking and sleeping experienced in a bedroom, it does so in the way that the meditation in the library will govern the chain of subsequent experiences. This series of insets that govern the narrative composition does not prevent consciousness from advancing. To the confused consciousness of the first pages—"I was more destitute than the cave-dweller" (I, p. 5)—replies the state of a consciousness that is awake, when the day dawns (I, p. 204).

I do not want to leave the section on "Combray" without having attempted to say what it is in the childhood memories that carries us away from speculation about involuntary memory and already directs our interpretation in the direction of an apprenticeship to signs, without for all that making this apprenticeship to disconnected aspects fit too easily within the history of a vocation.

Combray is first and foremost its church, "epitomising the town" (I, p. 52). On the one hand, it imposes on everything that surrounds it, owing to its enduring stability,[72] the dimension of a time that has not vanished but that has been traversed. On the other hand, through its stained glass and tapestry figures, through its gravestones, it imparts to all the living beings that the hero meets the general character of images to be deciphered. Along with this, the fact that the young hero is constantly absorbed in books tends to make the image the privileged access to reality (I, p. 91).

Combray is also the encounter with the writer Bergotte (the first of the three artists to be introduced in the narrative, in accordance with a carefully planned progression, long before Elstir, the painter, and Vinteuil, the musician). The encounter contributes to transforming surrounding objects into beings to be read.

In particular, however, the time of childhood continues to be made up of scattered islands, just as incommunicable among themselves as the two "ways," that of the Méséglise, which turns out to be that of Swann and Gilberte, and that of the Guermantes, that of the fabulous names of an out-of-reach aristocracy, especially that of Madame de Guermantes, the first object of an inaccessible love. Georges Poulet is correct to draw a sharp parallel here between the incommunicability of the islands of temporality and that of the sites, places, beings.[73] Distances that cannot be measured separate the instants evoked as much as the places traversed.

Combray is also, in contrast to the happy moments, the reminder of some events that foreshadow disillusionment, the meaning of which is postponed until a later inquiry.[74] Thus the Montjouvain scene, between Mlle de Vinteuil and her friend, where the hero, who is shown to be a voyeur, is introduced for the first time into the world of Gomorrah. It is not without importance for the subsequent understanding of the notion of lost time that this scene contains some abominable features: Mlle de Vinteuil spitting on her father's portrait, set on a small table in front of the sofa. A secret tie is thus established between this profanation and lost time, but it is too deeply hidden to be perceived. The reader's attention is directed instead to the reading of signs by the voyeur and his interpretation of the intimations of desire. More precisely, as a result of this strange episode, the art of deciphering is guided toward what Deleuze calls the second circle of signs, that of love.[75] The evocation of *The Guermantes Way* also acts as a springboard for a reflection on signs and their interpretation. Guermantes represents, first of all, fabulous names attaching to the tapestry and stained-glass figures. With an almost imperceptible touch, the narrator connects up this oneirism of names with the premonitory signs of the vocation that *Remembrance* is said to recount. Yet these dream thoughts, like his reading of Bergotte, create a sort of barrier, as if the artificial creations of dreams revealed the emptiness of his own talent.[76]

And if the impressions collected during walks also create an obstacle to the artist's vocation, this is so to the extent that material exteriority seems to govern them, maintaining "the illusion of a sort of fecundity" (I, p. 195) which spares one the effort of seeking what "lay hidden beneath them" (ibid.). The episode of the Martinville steeples, which corresponds to the experience of the madeleine, draws its meaning precisely from this contrast with the excessive richness of ordinary impressions, just as is the case with recurrent dreams. The promise of something hidden, something to be looked for and found, is closely associated with the "special pleasure" (I, p. 195) of the impression. These walks themselves guide the search. "I did not know the reason for the pleasure I had felt on seeing them upon the horizon, and the business of trying to discover that reason seemed to me irksome; I wanted to store away in my mind those shifting, sunlit planes and, for the time being, to think of them no more" (I, p. 197). This is, however, the first time that the search for meaning goes first by way of words and then by way of writing.[77]

Regardless of the remarks, still quite infrequent and entirely negative, relating to the history of a vocation, and, in particular, regardless of the hidden relation between this vocation and the two happy episodes connected to Combray, what seems to dominate the still inchoate experience of time in the section on Combray is the impossibility of coordinating the bundles of undated events,[78] which are compared to "the deepest layer of my mental soil" (I, p. 201). An indistinct mass of memories, which only something resembling "real fissures, real geological faults" (I, p. 201) can make distinct. In sum, the lost time of Combray is the lost paradise in which "the faith which creates" (I, p. 201) cannot yet be distinguished from the illusion of the bare and silent reality of external things.

It is doubtless in order to stress the character of autobiographical fiction of *Remembrance* as a whole that the author decided to intercalate "Swann in Love"—that is, a third-person narrative—between "Combray" and "Place-Names," which are both first-person narratives. At the same time, the illusion of immediacy that may have been produced by the childhood narratives, due to their classical charm, is broken by this emigration of the narrative into another character. In addition, "Swann in Love" constructs the diabolical mechanism of a love gnawed away by illusion, suspicion, disappointment; a love condemned to pass through the anguish of expectation, the bite of jealousy, the sorrow accompanying its decline, and the indifference that meets its death. This construction will serve as a model for the narration of other loves, in particular the hero's love for Albertine. It is due to this role of paradigm that "Swann in Love" says something about time.

There is no point in insisting on the fact that the narrative is not dated. It is loosely connected to the reveries, which are themselves relegated to an indeterminate past by the sleepy narrator who speaks in the opening pages of the book.[79] In this way, the narrative of "Swann in Love" is set within the hazy memories of childhood, as what occurred before birth. The artifice suffices to break the chronological line once and for all and to open the narrative up to other qualities of past time, indifferent to dates. More important is the distension of the tie between this narrative and the history of a vocation, held to govern *Remembrance* as a whole. This tie occurs on the level of the "association of memories," referred to at the end of the "Combray" section. The little phrase of Vinteuil's sonata appears to serve as a relay station between the experience of the madeleine (and the Martinville steeples) and the revelation of the final scene, due to its repeated appearances in the hero's story, reappearances that are reinforced in *The Captive* by the memory of Vinteuil's septet, the forceful homology to this little phrase.[80] This function of the musical phrase in the unity of the narrative may remain unperceived due to the close tie between the phrase and Swann's love for Odette. It is as someone who has fallen in love with the musical phrase (I, p. 231) that Swann clings to his memory. And this memory, henceforth, is too closely tied up with his love for Odette to provoke the interrogation contained in its promise of happiness. The entire field is occupied by a more pressing interrogation, pushed to the point of frenzy, one which is constantly generated by jealousy. The apprenticeship in the Verdurin salon to the signs of love, interwoven with that of the signs of society, is alone capable of making the search for lost time coincide with the search for truth, and lost time itself coincide with the defection that ravages love. Nothing, therefore, allows us to interpret lost time in terms of some time regained, the evocation of the phrase itself still being rooted in the soil of love. As for the "passion for truth" (I, p. 298) which is mobilized by jealousy, nothing allows it to be crowned with the prestige of time recaptured. Time is quite simply lost in the twofold sense of being over and done with and of having been scattered, dispersed.[81] At the very most, all that might suggest the idea of time regained would be either the weight accorded to a few rare moments when memory "joined the fragments together, abolished the intervals between them" (I, p. 342), characterizing a time in tatters, or the quietude of a secret vainly pursued at the time of jealousy and finally pinned down at the time when love has died (I, p. 346). The apprenticeship to signs would then come to an end in this context once a certain detachment is attained.

It is worthwhile to look at the way in which the third part of *Swann's Way*, entitled "Place Names: The Name" (I, pp. 416–62), links up with what precedes it concerning the interconnection of time spans.[82] For, indeed, the same "long nights of sleeplessness" (I, p. 416) that were recalled in order to serve as a setting for the childhood narratives associated with Combray are also used here in order to connect, in the dreamlike memory, the rooms at the Grand Hotel of Balbec beach with the rooms at Combray. It is therefore not surprising that a dream of Balbec precedes the real Balbec, at a period in the hero's adolescence when names foreshadow things and state reality before all perception. Thus are the names of Balbec, Venice, Florence, generators of images, and through images, of desire. At this stage of the narrative, what can readers make of this "imaginary time" in which several voyages are gathered together under a single name? (I, pp. 425–26). They can only keep it in the back of their minds, once the Champs-Elysées, quite real enough, and the games with Gilberte hide the dreams from sight: "in this public garden there was nothing that attached itself to my dreams" (I, p. 427). Is this hiatus between the "simulacrum" of an imaginary realm (ibid.) and reality another figure of lost time? Undoubtedly. The difficulty in joining this figure and all the others that follow to the general story-line is made even greater by the absence of any apparent identity between the earlier characters of Swann and, especially, of Odette—who could be thought to have "disappeared" at the end of the intermediary third-person narrative—and the Swann and Odette who turn out to be Gilberte's parents, at the period when the hero plays in the park near the Champs-Elysées.[83]

For the reader who breaks off the reading of *Remembrance* at the last page of *Swann's Way*, lost time would be summed up in "how paradoxical it is to seek in reality for pictures that are stored in one's memory, which must inevitably lose the charm that comes to them from memory itself and from their not being apprehended by the senses" (I, p. 462). *Remembrance* itself would seem to be limited to a hopeless struggle to combat the ever-increasing gap that generates forgetfulness. Even the happy moments at Combray, where the distance between the present impression and the past impression is magically transformed into a miraculous contemporaneousness, could appear to have been swallowed up in the same devastating oblivion. These moments of grace will never be brought up again—except in one instance—after the pages on "Combray." Only the savor of the phrase of Vinteuil's sonata—a savor we know only through a narrative within a narrative—carries with it another promise. But a promise of what? This enigma, just as the enigma of the happy moments at Combray, can be solved only by the reader of *Time Regained*.

In the long deciphering of the signs of the world, of love, and of sensory impressions, extending from *Within a Budding Grove* to *The Captive*, only the way of disillusionment remains open before this turnabout.

Time Regained

Let us now move in one fell swoop to *Time Regained*, the second focal point of the great ellipse of *Remembrance of Things Past*, saving for the third stage of our investigation the interval, enormously amplified, that separates these two foci.

What does the narrator mean by time regained? To attempt to reply to this question, we shall take advantage of the symmetry between the beginning and the end of the great narrative. Just as the experience of the madeleine in *Swann's Way* marks a before and an after, the before of the state between waking and sleeping and the after of the time regained with respect to Combray, the great scene in the Guermantes library demarcates, in its turn, a before to which the narrator has given significant amplitude and an after in which the ultimate signification of *Time Regained* is discovered.

It is not actually *ex abrupto* that the narrator relates the event marking the birth of a writer. He prepares for the illumination by passing through two initiatory stages. The first, which takes up by far the greatest number of pages, is made up of a mist of events that are poorly coordinated among themselves, at least in the state in which the unfinished manuscript of *Time Regained* was left to us, but which all bear the double sign of disillusionment and detachment.

It is significant that *Time Regained* begins with the narrative of a stay in Tansonville, not far from the Combray of childhood, the effect of which is not to rekindle memory but to extinguish desire.[84] In the moment, the hero is moved by this loss of curiosity, to such an extent it seems to confirm the feeling once experienced in the same place "that I would never be able to write" (III, p. 709). One must give up an attempt to relive the past if lost time is ever, in some as yet unknown way, to be found again. This death of the desire to see things again is accompanied by the death of the desire to possess the women he has loved. It is noteworthy that the narrator considers this "incuriosity" to be "brought by Time," the personified entity that will never be assigned wholly either to lost time or to eternity, and which to the end will be symbolized, as in the adages of ancient wisdom, by its power of destruction. I shall return to this at the end of our discussion.

All of the events recounted, all the encounters reported in what follows are placed under the same sign of decline, of death. Gilberte's narrative of the poverty of her relations with Saint-Loup, now her husband; the visit to the church in Combray, where the power of what endures accentuates the precariousness of mortal beings; and, especially, the sudden mention of the "long years" that the hero has spent in a sanatorium, contributing a realistic aspect to the feeling of separateness and of distanciation required by the final vision.[85] The description of Paris at war adds to the impression of erosion that affects everything.[86] The frivolity of Parisian drawing rooms has an air of decadence about it (III, pp. 746–47). The campaigns for and against Dreyfus have been forgotten. Saint-Loup's visit, home from the front lines, is that of a ghost; we learn of Cottard's death, then of the death of M. Verdurin. The chance encounter with M. de Charlus in a Paris street during the war places on this sinister initiation the seal of a deadly abjection. From the degradation of his body, of his loves, rises a strange poetry (III, p. 789) which the narrator ascribes to a complete detachment, something the hero is not yet able to attain (III, p. 799). The scene in Jupien's bordello, where the baron has himself whipped with a chain by soldiers on leave, reduces the painting of a society at war to its quintessence of abjection. The interconnection in the narrative between Saint-Loup's last visit, rapidly followed by the news of his death—evoking another death, that of Albertine[87]—and the narrative of Charlus's ultimate turpitudes, leading to his arrest, give these pages the tone of a funereal maelstrom, which will again prevail, although with an entirely different signification, in the symmetrical scene that follows the great revelation, the scene of the dinner surrounded by death's-heads, the first test of the hero converted to eternity.

To stress once again the sort of nothingness that surrounds the revelation, the narrator introduces a sharp break in his story. "The new sanatorium to which I withdrew was no more successful in curing me than the first one, and many years passed before I came away" (III, p. 885). One last time, during a return trip to Paris, the hero takes stock of his pitiful state: "the falsehood of literature," "the non-existence of the ideal in which I had believed," "an unattainable inspiration," "absence of emotion" (III, pp. 886–87).

This first stage of initiation by the shadows of reminiscence is followed by a much briefer second stage, marked by premonitory signs.[88] The tone of the narrative is indeed reversed the moment the hero allows himself to be seduced, as in the early days in Combray, by the name Guermantes, printed on the invitation to the afternoon party given by the prince. This time, however, the journey by car is experienced as an airplane flight. "And like an airman who hitherto has progressed laboriously along the ground, abruptly 'taking off' I soared slowly towards the silent heights of memory" (III, p. 890). The encounter with misfortune, in the personage of M. de Charlus, convalescent after an attack of apoplexy—"upon the old fallen prince this latest illness had conferred the Shakesperian majesty of a King Lear" (III, p. 891)—is not enough to foil this takeoff. Instead, the hero sees in his wasted figure "a sort of gentleness, an almost physical gentleness, and of detachment from the realities of life, phenomena so strikingly apparent in those whom death has already drawn within its shadow" (III, p. 892). It is then that the hero receives as a salvific "warning" a series of experiences that resemble entirely, through the happiness they give him, the experiences of Combray, "of which the last works of Vinteuil had seemed to me to combine the quintessential character" (III, p. 899): tripping against the uneven paving stones, the noise of a spoon knocking against a plate, the stiffness of a starched and folded napkin. But, whereas formerly the narrator had to postpone until later clarifying the reasons for this happiness, this time he has made up his mind to solve the enigma. It is not that, as early as the period of Combray, the narrator failed to perceive that the intense joy felt resulted from the fortuitous conjunction between two similar impressions despite their distance in time. This time, too, the hero is not long in recognizing Venice and the two uneven paving stones in the baptistry of Saint Mark's under the impression of the uneven stones in Paris. The enigma to be solved therefore is not that temporal distance can be abolished in this way "by chance," "as if by magic," in the identity of a single instant—it is that the joy experienced is "like a certainty and which sufficed, without any other proof, to make death a matter of indifference to me" (III, p. 900). In other words, the enigma to be solved is that of the *relation* between the happy moments, offered by chance and involuntary memory, and the invisible history of a vocation.

Between the considerable mass of narratives that extend over thousands of pages and the critical scene in the library, the narrator has thus worked in a narrative transition that shifts the sense of the *Bildungsroman* from the apprenticeship to signs to the visitation. Taken together, the two wings of this narrative transition serve at once to separate and to suture the two foci of *Remembrance*. Separation, through the signs of death, confirming the failure of an apprenticeship to signs that lacks the principle of their decipherment. Suture, through the premonitory signs of the great revelation.

We now find ourselves at the heart of the great visitation scene that determines the primary—but not the final—meaning to be ascribed to the very notion of time regained. The narrative status of what may be read as a grand dissertation on art—even as Marcel Proust's *ars poetica*, forcibly inserted into his narrative—is maintained by the subtle diegetic tie that the narrator establishes between this major scene and the earlier narrative of the events that function as transitional points in the hero's initiation. This tie involves two levels at once. First, on the anecdotal level, the narrator has been careful to situate his narrative of the final signs of warning in the same place as the narrative of the great revelation: "the little sitting-room used as a library" (III, p. 900). Next, on the thematic level, the narrator grafts his meditation on time onto the moments of happiness and the premonitory signs. The speculation on time thereby arises out of the thoughts of the narrator, reflecting on what had heretofore been provided by chance.[89] Finally, on a deeper level of reflection, the speculation on time is anchored in the narrative as a founding event in the vocation of the writer. The role of origin, assigned in this way to speculation in the history of a vocation, assures the irreducibly narrative character of this very speculation.

What may seem to place this speculation at a distance from the narrative is the fact that the time it brings to light is not, at first, time regained, in the sense of time lost that is found again, but the very suspension of time, *eternity*, or to speak as the narrator does, "extra-temporal" being (III, p. 904).[90] And this will continue to be the case as long as speculation has not been taken in hand by the decision to write, which restores to thought the intention of a work to be done. Several remarks by the narrator confirm to us that the extra-temporal is only the first threshold of time regained. First, there is the fugitive character of contemplation itself; then, there is the necessity to support the hero's discovery of an extratemporal being that constitutes him through the heavenly nourishment of the essences of things; finally, we find the immanent, and nontranscendent, character of an eternity that mysteriously circulates between the present and the past, out of which it creates a unity. Extratemporal being therefore, does not exhaust the entire meaning of *Time Regained*. It is, of course, *sub specie aeternitatis* that involuntary memory performs its miracle in time[91] and that the intelligence can encompass in the same look the distance of the heterogeneous and the simultaneity of the analogous. And it is indeed extratemporal being, when it makes use of the analogies offered by chance and by involuntary memory, as well as the work of the apprenticeship to signs, that brings the perishable course of things back to their essence "outside time" (III, p. 904). Nevertheless, this extratemporal being still lacks the power "to make me rediscover days that were long past" (ibid.). At this turning point the meaning of the narrative process constituting the tale about time is revealed. What remains to be done is to join together the two valences assigned side-by-side to "time regained."[92] Sometimes this expression designates the extratemporal, sometimes it designates the act of rediscovering lost time. Only the decision to write will put an end to the duality of meaning of time regained. Before this decision is made, this duality seems insurmountable. The extratemporal is, in fact, related to a meditation on the very origin of aesthetic creation, in a contemplative moment unconnected to its inscription in an actual work, and without any consideration of the labor of writing. In the extratemporal order, the work of art, considered with respect to its origin, is not the product of the artisan of words—its existence precedes us; it has only to be discovered. At this level, creating is translating.

Time regained, in the second sense of the term, in the sense of lost time revived, comes out of the fixing of this fugitive, contemplative moment in a lasting work. The question is then, as Plato said of Daedalus's statues that were always on the point of fleeing, to tie down this contemplation by inscribing it within duration. "To this contemplation of the essence of things I had decided therefore that in the future I must attach myself, so as somehow to immobilise it. But how, by what means, was I to do this?" (III, p. 909). It is here that artistic creation, taking over from aesthetic meditation, offers its mediation. "And this method, which seems to me the sole method, what was it but the creation of a work of art?" (III, p. 912). Swann's mistake, in this respect, was to have assimilated the happiness afforded by the phrase of the sonata to the pleasures of love: "he was unable to find it in artistic creation" (III, p. 911). It is here, too, that the deciphering of signs comes to the assistance of fugitive contemplation, not to substitute itself for the latter, and even less to precede it, but, under its guidance to clarify it.

So the decision to write has the capacity to transpose the extratemporal character of the original vision into the temporality of the resurrection of time lost. In this sense we may say, in all truth, that Proust's work *narrates the transition from one meaning of time regained to the other*; and it is for this reason that it is a tale about time.

It remains to say in what way the narrative character of the birth of a vocation is assured by the act of testing that follows the revelation of the truth of art as well as by the hero's involvement in the work to be accomplished. This testing takes through the challenge of death. It is not an overstatement to say that it is the relation to death that makes the difference between the two meanings of time regained: the extratemporal, which transcends "my anxiety on the subject of my death" and makes me "unalarmed by the vicissitudes of the future" (III, p. 904), and the resurrection in the work of lost time. If the fate of the latter is finally handed over to the labor of writing, the threat of death is no less in time regained than in time lost.[93]

This is what the narrator meant to indicate by having the narrative of the conversion to writing followed by the astonishing spectacle offered by the guests at the Prince de Guermantes's dinner party. This dinner, where all the guests appeared to have "put on a disguise [s'être 'fait une tête']" (III, p. 920)—actually, a death's head—is expressly interpreted by the narrator as a "spectacular and dramatic effect" (III, p. 959), which he says, "threatened to raise against my enterprise the gravest of all objections" (III, p. 959–60). What is this, if not the reminder of death, which, without any hold on the extratemporal, threatens its temporal expression, the work of art itself.

Who are the characters in this dance of death? "A puppet-show, yes, but one in which, in order to identify the puppets with the people whom one had known in the past, it was necessary to read what was written on several planes at once, planes that lay behind the visible aspect of the puppets and gave them depth and forced one, as one looked at these aged marionettes, to make a strenuous intellectual effort; one was obliged to study them at the same time with one's eyes and with one's memory. These were puppets bathed in the immaterial colours of the years, puppets which exteriorized Time, Time which by Habit is made invisible and to become visible seeks bodies, which wherever it finds it seizes, to display its magic lantern upon them" (III, p. 964).[94] And what do all these moribund figures announce, if not the hero's own approaching death? (III, p. 967). Here lies the danger. "I had made the discovery of this destructive action of Time at the very moment when I had conceived the ambition to make visible, to intellectualize in a work of art, realities that were outside Time" (III, p. 971). This admission is of considerable importance. Might not the old myth of destructive time be stronger than the vision of time regained through the work of art? Yes, if the second meaning of time regained is separated from the first one. And this is indeed the temptation that haunts the hero up to the end of the narrative. It is a powerful temptation, inasmuch as the labor of writing takes place in the same time as lost time. Worse, the narrative that has preceded has, in a certain way, precisely as a narrative, stressed the fugitive nature of the event, related to the discovery of its abolition in the supratemporal. But this is not the final word. For the artist who is capable of preserving the relation between revived time and the extratemporal, time reveals its other mythical side: the profound identity that beings preserve despite their altered appearance attests to "the power to renew in fresh forms that is possessed by Time, which can thus, while respecting the unity of the individual and the laws of life, effect a change of scene and introduce bold contrasts into two successive aspects of a single person" (III, pp. 977–78). When we shall later discuss recognition, as the key concept of the unity between the two foci of the ellipse of *Remembrance*, we should recall that what makes beings recognizable is still "Time, the artist" (III, p. 978). "He was an artist, moreover, who works very slowly" (ibid.).

A sign that this pact between the two figures of *Time Regained* can be made and preserved is seen by the narrator in the unexpected encounter, totally unforeseen in all that has gone before: the appearance of the daughter of Gilberte Swann and Robert de Saint-Loup, who symbolizes the reconciliation of the two "ways"—Swann's way through her mother, the Guermantes way through her father. "I thought her very beautiful: still rich in hopes, full of laughter, formed from those very years which I myself had lost, she was like my own youth" (III, p. 1088). Is this appearance, which concretizes a reconciliation, one announced or anticipated several times in the work, intended to suggest that artistic creation has a pact with youth—with "natality" as Hannah Arendt would say—which makes art, unlike love, stronger than death?[95]

Unlike the preceding ones, this sign is neither an announcement of something to come nor a premonition. Rather, it is a "spur." "The idea of Time was of value to me for yet another reason: it was a spur, it told me that it was time to begin if I wished to attain to what I had sometimes perceived in the course of my life, in brief lightening-flashes, on the Guermantes way and in my drives in the carriage of Mme de Villeparisis, at those moments of perception which had me think that life was worth living. How much more worth living did it appear to me now, now that I seemed to see that this life that we live in half-darkness can be illumined, this life that at every moment we distort can be restored to its true pristine shape, that a life, in short, can be realised within the confines of a book!" (III, p. 1088).

From Time Regained to Time Lost

At the end of this inquiry into *Remembrance of Things Past*, considered as a tale about time, we have still to describe the relation that the narrative establishes between the two foci of the ellipse: the apprenticeship to signs, with its lost time, and the revelation of art, with its exaltation of the extratemporal. It is this relation that characterizes time as time regained, more precisely as time *lost-regained*. In order to understand this adjective, we must interpret the verb—what is it, then to regain lost time?

To answer this question, we are interested, once again, only in the thoughts of the narrator, meditating on a work not yet written (in the fiction, this work is not the one we have just read). The result is that the meaning to be given to the act of regaining time is best designated by the difficulties expected of a work yet to be realized.

We find these difficulties condensed in the declaration by which the narrator attempts to characterize the meaning of his past life in relation to the work to be realized. "And thus my whole life up to the present day might and yet might not have been summed up under the title: A Vocation" (III, p. 936).

The ambiguity, carefully nourished, between the yes and the no deserves our attention. No, "literature had played no part in my life" (ibid.); yes, this whole life "formed a reserve," an almost vegetative domain in which the germinating organism was to be nourished. "In the same way my life *was linked to* [*en rapport avec*] what, eventually, would bring about its maturation" (ibid., my emphasis).

What difficulties, then, must the act of regaining lost time overcome? And why does their resolution bear the mark of an ambiguity?

An initial hypothesis presents itself. Could the relation upon which the act of regaining time on the scale of *Remembrance* as a whole is built be extrapolated from that discovered by reflection on the canonical examples of reminiscence that are elucidated and clarified? In turn, might not these infinitesimal experiences constitute the laboratory in miniature where the relation is forged that will confer unity upon the whole of *Remembrance*?

An extrapolation such as this may be read in the following statement: "what we call reality is a certain connexion between these immediate sensations and the memories which envelop us simultaneously with them—a connexion that is suppressed in a simple cinematographic vision, which just because it professes to confine itself to the truth in fact departs widely from it— a unique connexion which the writer has to rediscover in order to link for ever in his phrase the two sets of phenomena which reality joins together" (III, p. 924). Every element carries weight here: "unique connexion," as in the happy moments and in all the similar expressions of reminiscence, once these are clarified—a connection (or relation) to be "rediscovered"—a connection in which two different terms are "linked forever in his phrase."

The first trail is now open, and it leads us to look for others, those of the stylistic figures whose function is precisely to posit the relation between two different objects. This figure is *metaphor*. The narrator confirms this in one statement in which, along with Roger Shattuck, I am prepared to see one of the hermeneutical keys to *Remembrance*.[96] This metaphorical relation, brought to light by the elucidation of happy moments, becomes the matrix for all the relations in which two distinct objects are, despite their differences, raised to their essence and liberated from the contingencies of time. The entire apprenticeship to signs, which contributes to the considerable length of *Remembrance*, thus falls under the law that is apprehended in the privileged examples of a few premonitory signs, already bearing the twofold sense that the intelligence has only to clarify. Metaphor reigns where cinematographic vision, which is purely serial, fails to relate sensations and memories. The narrator has perceived the general application that can be made of this metaphorical relation when he holds it to be "analogous in the world of art to the unique connexion which in the world of science is provided by the law of causality" (III, p. 924). It is thus not an overstatement to say that sensations and memories, on the scale of *Remembrance* in its entirety, are enclosed within "the necessary links of a well-wrought style" (III, p. 925). Style, here, does not designate anything ornamental but the singular entity resulting from the union, in a unique work of art, of the questions from which it proceeds and the solutions it gives. Time regained, in this first sense, is time lost eternalized by metaphor.

This first trail is not the only one. The stylistic solution, placed under the aegeis of metaphor, calls for, as its complement, a solution that could be termed "optical."[97] The narrator himself invites us to follow this second trail, without pausing to identify the point where they cross, by declaring that "style for the writer, no less than colour for the painter, is a question not of technique but of vision" (III, 931).

By vision we are to understand something other than a revivification of what is immediate: a reading of signs, which, as we know, calls for an apprenticeship. If the narrator calls the experience of regained time "vision," it is insofar as this vision is crowned with a "recognition" that is the very mark of the extratemporal on lost time.[98] Once again, happy moments illustrate in miniature this stereoscopic vision set up as a form of recognition. But the idea of an "optical view" applies to the entire apprenticeship to signs. This apprenticeship, in fact, is shot through with optical errors, which retrospectively take on the sense of a misunderstanding. In this respect, the sort of dance of death—the death's heads at the Guermantes dinner party—which follows the great meditation, is not marked simply by the sign of death but also by that of non-recognition (III, pp. 971, 990, etc.). The hero even fails to recognize Gilberte. This is a crucial scene, for it places the entire foregoing quest retrospectively at once under the sign of a comedy of errors (optical errors) and on the path of a project of integral recognition. This overall interpretation of *Remembrance* in terms of recognition authorizes us to consider the meeting between the hero and Gilberte's daughter as an ultimate recognition scene, to the extent that, as I said above, the young girl incarnates the reconciliation between the two ways, that of Swann and that of the Guermantes.

The two trails we have just followed intersect at some point. Metaphor and recognition share the common role of elevating two impressions to the level of essence, without abolishing their difference. "For to 'recognize' someone, and, *a fortiori*, to learn someone's identity after having failed to recognize him, is to predicate two contradictory things of a single subject" (III, p. 982). This crucial text establishes the equivalence between metaphor and recognition, making the first the logical equivalent of the second ("to predicate two contradictory things of a single subject"), and the second the temporal equivalent of the first ("it is to admit that what was here, the person whom one remembers, no longer exists, and also that what is now here is a person whom one did not know to exist" [ibid]). Thus metaphor we may say is in the order of style what resemblance is in the order of stereoscopic vision.

The difficulty, however, reappears at this very point. Just what is the relation between style and vision? By this question we touch on the problem that predominates throughout *Remembrance*, that of the relation between writing and impressions, that is to say, in an ultimate sense, between literature and life.

A third sense of the notion of time regained will be discovered along this new trail. Time regained, I will now say, is *the impression regained*. But what is the impression regained? Once again, we must start from the exegesis of happy moments, and extend this to the entire apprenticeship to signs pursued throughout *Remembrance*. In order to be regained, the impression must first have been lost as an immediate pleasure, prisoner to its external object. The initial stage of the rediscovery is that of the complete internalization of the impression.[99] A second stage is the transposition of the impression into a law, into an idea.[100] A third stage is the inscription of this spiritual equivalent in a work of art. There is supposed to be a fourth stage, which is alluded to only once in *Remembrance*, when the narrator mentions his future readers. "For it seemed to me that they would not be 'my' readers but the readers of their own selves, my book being merely a sort of magnifying glass like those which the optician at Combray used to offer his customers—it would be my book, but with its help I would furnish them with the means of reading what lay inside themselves" (III, p. 1089).[101]

This alchemy of the impression regained perfectly presents the difficulty that the narrator perceives as he crosses the threshold of the work: How to prevent substituting literature for life, or again, under the patronage of laws and ideas, how to keep from dissolving the impression in a psychology or an abstract sociology, divested of all narrative character? The narrator replies to this danger by his concern for preserving an unsteady balance between impressions, of which he says, "their essential character was that I was not free to choose them, that such as they were they were given to me" (III, p. 913), and, on the other side, the deciphering of signs, guided by the conversion of the impression into a work of art. Literary creation therefore seems to go in two opposite directions at once.

On the one hand, the impression must act as "the very proof of the trueness of the whole picture" (ibid.).[102] Along this same line, the narrator comes to speak of life as an "inner book of unknown symbols" (ibid.). This book, we have not written, and yet "the book whose hieroglyphs are patterns not traced by us is the only book that really belongs to us" (III, p. 914).[103] Better, it is "our true life, . . . reality as we have felt it to be, which differs so greatly from what we think it is that when a chance happening brings us an authentic memory of it we are filled with an immense happiness" (III, p. 915). Writing the work to be realized is thus based on "the faculty of submitting to the reality within" (III, p. 917).[104]

On the other hand, reading the book of life is "an act of creation in which no one can do our work for us or even collaborate with us" (III, p. 913). Everything now seems to swing to the side of literature. The following text is well known. "Real life, life at last laid bare and illuminated—the only life in consequence which can be said to be really lived—is literature, and life thus defined is in a sense all the time immanent in ordinary man no less than in the artist. But most men do not see it because they do not seek to shed light upon it" (III, p. 931). This statement should not mislead us. It in no way leads to an apology for "The Book" as Mallarmé conceived it. Rather it posits an equation which, at the end of the work, should be completely reversible between life and literature, which is to say, finally, between the impression preserved in its trace and the work of art that states the meaning of the impression. This reversibility, however, is nowhere simply given. It must be the fruit of the labor of writing. In this sense *Remembrance* could be entitled the search for the lost impression, literature being nothing other than the impression regained— "the joy of rediscovering what is real" (III, p. 913).

A third version of time regained thus offers itself to our meditation. It is not so much added to the two preceding versions as it includes them both. In the impression regained, the two paths we have followed cross and reconcile what might be called the two "ways" of *Remembrance*: on the level of style, the way of metaphor; on the level of vision, the way of recognition.[105] In return, metaphor and recognition make explicit the *relation* upon which the impression regained is itself constructed, the relation between life and literature. And in every instance this relation includes forgetfulness and death.

Such is the wealth of meaning of time regained, or rather of the operation of rediscovering lost time. This meaning embraces the three versions that we have just explored. Time regained, we might say, is the metaphor that encloses differences "in the necessary links of a well-wrought style." It is also the recognition, which crowns stereoscopic vision. Finally, it is the impression regained, which reconciles life and literature. Indeed, inasmuch as life is the figure of the way of time lost, and literature the way of the extratemporal, we have the right to say that time regained expresses the recovery of lost time in the extratemporal, just as the impression regained expresses the recovery of life in the work of art.

The two foci of the ellipse formed by *Remembrance of Things Past* do not merge into one another—a distance remains between the lost time of the apprenticeship to signs and the contemplation of the extratemporal. But this will be a distance that is traversed.

And it is with this final expression, "traversal," that I shall conclude, for it marks the transition from the extratemporal, glimpsed in contemplation, to what the narrator calls "Time embodied" (III, p. 1105).[106] The extratemporal is only a point of passage; its virtue is to transform into a continuous duration the "retorts of discontinuous periods." *Remembrance*, then, is far from a Bergsonian vision of a duration free of all extension; instead, it confirms the *dimensional* character of time. The itinerary of *Remembrance* moves from the idea of a distance that separates to that of a distance that joins together. This is confirmed by the final figure of time proposed in *Remembrance*, that of an accumulated duration that is, in a sense, beneath us. Thus the narrator-hero sees people "perched upon living stilts which never cease to grow until sometimes they become taller than church steeples, making it in the end both difficult and perilous for them to walk and raising them to an eminence from which suddenly they fall" (III, p. 1107). As for himself, having incorporated into his present "all this length of Time," he sees himself "perched on its giddy summit" (III, p. 1106). This final figure of time regained says two things: that time lost is contained in time regained but also that it is finally Time that carries us within it. *Remembrance*, in fact, closes not with a cry of triumph but with "a sensation of weariness and almost of terror" (ibid.). For time regained is also death regained. *Remembrance* has generated, in the phrase of Hans Robert Jauss, only an interim time, that of a work yet to be accomplished, one that may be destroyed by death.

The fact, in the final analysis, that time envelops us, as we are told in the old myths, we have known from the start—the beginning of the narrative possessed the strange feature of referring us back to an indefinite earlier period. The narrative closure is not different. The narrative stops when the writer sets to work. All the tenses then pass from the future to the conditional. "But my task was longer . . . , my words had to reach more than a single person. My task was long. By day, the most I could hope for was to try to sleep. If I worked, it would only be at night. But I should need many nights, a hundred perhaps, or even a thousand. And I should live in the anxiety of not knowing whether the master of my destiny might not prove less indulgent than the Sultan Shahriyar, whether in the morning, when I broke off my story, he would consent to a further reprieve and permit me to resume my narrative the following evening" (III, p. 1101).[107]

Is it for this reason that the final words place the self and all other people back *in* Time? This is certainly "a very considerable place compared with the restricted one which is allotted to them in space" (ibid.) but nonetheless a place "in the dimension of Time" (III, p. 1107).

Conclusion

At the end of this second volume of my study of time and narrative, I should like to make an overall assessment as I did at the end of volume 1 (pp. 226–30).

The first conclusion to be drawn concerns the narrative model worked out in Part I of *Time and Narrative* under the title of "threefold mimesis." The study you have just read has claimed to remain strictly within the limits of mimesis₂, that is, within the confines of the mimetic relation that Aristotle identified with the rule-governed composition of a tale. Have I truly remained faithful to this important equation between mimesis and muthos?

I should like openly to express certain scruples that have been continually present throughout the writing of this volume.

The one that is easiest to formulate finds its answer in Aristotle's *Poetics*. Does not my use of the substantive "narrative," the adjective form "narrative," and the verb "to narrate" (or sometimes in English, "to recount," "to tell"), which I hold to be rigorously interchangeable, suffer from a serious equivocation, to the extent that these terms seem to cover at times the entire field of the mimesis of action, and at times just the diegetic mode, to the exclusion of the dramatic one? What is more, due to this equivocation, do we not find that I have surreptitiously transferred to the diegetic mode categories specific to the dramatic one?

The right to use the term "narrative" in a generic sense, while respecting in appropriate contexts the specific difference between the diegetic and the dramatic modes, appears to me to be founded in the very choice of the notion of a mimesis of *action* as my dominant category. Actually, muthos, from which my notion of emplotment is derived, is a category possessing the same scope as the mimesis of action. The result of this choice is that the distinction between the diegetic mode and the dramatic mode moves to the background. It answers the question of the "how" of mimesis and not the question of its "what." It is for this reason that examples of well-constructed plots may be drawn indifferently from Homer or from Sophocles.

153

The same scruple reappears, however, in another form when one looks at the order of my four chapters in this volume. One may no doubt grant that by broadening and deepening the notion of plot, as I announced in introducing the first two chapters of this volume, I confirmed and strengthened the priority of the generic sense of fictional narrative in relation to the specific sense of the diegetic mode. On the other hand, I might be reproached with having gradually confined my analyses to the diegetic mode by dealing in games with time. The distinction between utterance and statement, then the stress placed on the dialectic between the narrator's discourse and that of the character, and finally the fact that I concentrate at the end on point of view and narrative voice—do not all these aspects indicate a preference for the diegetic mode? Foreseeing this objection, I have taken great pains to consider in these games with time only their contribution to the composition of the literary work, following the lesson learned from Bakhtin, Genette, Lotman, and Uspensky. In this way, I believe that I have "enriched" the notion of plot, conforming to the promise made in my introduction, and have also kept it at the same level of generality as the mimesis of action, which thus remains my guiding concept. I am prepared to admit that my reply would be more convincing if analyses like those Henri Gouhier has devoted to dramatic art were able to show that the same categories—point of view and voice among others—are also at work in the dramatic order.[1] We would then have proof that concentrating on the novel represents simply a de facto restriction, the obverse of that practiced by Aristotle to the benefit of the tragic muthos. It is a fact that this proof is missing in the present work.

Unfortunately, this reference to the novel gives new life to my initial scruple, for a reason that has to do with the very nature of the genre. Does the novel constitute merely one example of fictional narrative among others? This is indeed what seems to be assumed in the choice of the three tales about time that are examined in the final chapter. Yet there are reasons to doubt that the novel allows itself to be neatly classified in a homogeneous taxonomy of narrative genres. Is not the novel an antigenre genre, which by this very fact makes it impossible to fit back together the diegetic mode and dramatic mode under the inclusive term of "fictional narrative"? This type of argument receives impressive reinforcement in the essays that Bakhtin devotes to the "dialogic imagination."[2] According to Bakhtin, the novel escapes all homogeneous classification because we cannot place in the same set those genres, of which the epic is the perfect example, that have run dry and the sole genre that has been born after the institution of writing and books, the only one that continues to develop but never ceases to rethink its own identity. Before the novel, genres with fixed forms tended to act to reinforce one another and in this way to form a harmonious whole, a coherent literary ensemble, and consequently were accessible to a general theory of literary composition. By upsetting the other genres, the novel dislocates this overall cohesiveness.

According to Bakhtin, three major factors prevent us from placing the epic and the novel under a common category. First, the epic places the history of its hero in a "perfect past," to employ Hegel's expression, a past that has no ties to the time of the narrator (or the storyteller) and his public. Next, this absolute past is connected to the time of recitation only through national traditions that command respect exclusive of any criticism and hence of any upheaval. Finally, and above all, tradition isolates the epic world and its heroic characters from the sphere of the collective and the personal experience of people today. The novel is born out of the destruction of this "epic distance." And it is principally under the pressure of laughter, of ridicule, of the "carnivalesque," and more generally out of the expressions of serious comedy—culminating in the work of Rabelais, so brilliantly celebrated by Bakhtin himself—that epic distance gave way to the contemporaneousness based on sharing the same ideological and linguistic universe that characterizes the relation between the writer, the characters, and the public in the age of the novel. In short, it is the end of epic distance that provides the definitive basis for opposing "low" literature to all the rest of "high" literature.

Does this global opposition between epic and novel render useless an analysis like my own that claims to assemble under the general title of fictional narrative all the works that, in one way or another, aim at creating a mimesis of action? I do not think so. However far we extend the opposition between "high" and "low" literature, however deeply we hollow the abyss that separates epic distance and contemporaneousness between the writer and the public, the general features of fiction are not abolished. Ancient epic was, no less than the modern novel, a critique of the limits of contemporary culture, as James Redfield has shown with regard to the *Iliad*. Conversely, the modern novel belongs to its time only at the price of another sort of distance, the distance of fiction itself. This is why contemporary critics, without denying the originality of the novel, can continue, as did Goethe and Schiller in their famous common work, along with Hegel in his *Phenomenology of Mind* and his *Aesthetics*, to characterize the novel as a form—a "low" form, if one likes—of the epic and to divide up literature—*Dichtung*—into epic, drama, and lyric. The end of epic distance certainly marks a break between "high" mimetic and "low" mimetic. But we have learned, from Northrop Frye, to maintain this distinction within the universe of fiction. Whether the characters are "superior," "inferior," or "equal" to us, Aristotle noted, they nonetheless all remain the agents of an imitated history. This is why the novel has only made infinitely more complex the problems of emplotment. We may even say, unparadoxically, and moreover with the support of Bakhtin, that the representation of a reality in full transformation, the painting of incomplete personalities, and the reference to a present held to be in suspense, "without any conclusion"—all this requires a more rigorous formal discipline on the part of the creator of tales than on the part of the storyteller of a heroic world that carries with it its own internal completion. But I shall not limit myself to just this defensive argument. I claim that the modern novel demands of literary criticism much more than a more subtle reformulation of the principle of the synthesis of the heterogeneous, by which I formally defined emplotment. It produces in addition an enrichment of the very notion of action, proportional to that of the notion of emplotment. If my final two chapters in this volume seemed to move away from a mimesis of action in the narrow sense of the term, to the benefit of a mimesis of the character, in order to end, in Dorrit Cohn's words, at a mimesis of consciousness, this drift of my analysis is more apparent than real. For the novel contributes to a genuine enrichment of the notion of action. At the limit, the "narrated monologue" to which the "Penelope" episode at the end of Joyce's *Ulysses* can be reduced, is the supreme illustration of the fact that saying is still doing, even when the saying takes refuge in the voiceless discourse of a silent thought, which the novelist does not hesitate to narrate.

This initial assessment has next to be completed by a confrontation of the conclusions of this study devoted to the configuration of time in fictional narrative with those I have drawn, at the end of volume 1, concerning the configuration of time by historical narrative.

Allow me to say first that these two analyses, dealing respectively with configuration in the historical narrative and with configuration in the fictional narrative, strictly parallel each other and constitute the two sides of one and the same investigation into the art of composition, which I placed in Part I under the title of mimesis$_2$. One of the restrictions on my analyses of historical narrative has thus been removed—the narrative field in its entirety is now open to reflection. With the same stroke, a serious lacuna in the studies currently dealing with narrativity is also filled. Historiography and literary criticism are both called upon and are invited together to form a grand narratology, where an equal right would be given to historical narrative and to fictional narrative.

There are several reasons why we should not be surprised by this congruence between historical and fictional narrative on the level of configuration. I shall not linger over the first of these reasons, namely, the fact that both narrative modes are preceded by the use of narrative in daily life. The largest part of our information about events in the world is, in fact, owing to knowledge through hearsay. In this way the act—if not the art—of narrating or recounting is part of the symbolic mediations of action that I have related to the preunderstanding of the narrative field, which I placed under the title of mimesis$_1$. In this sense we may say that all the arts of narration, and foremost among them those belonging to writing, are imitations of narrative as it is already practiced in the transactions of ordinary discourse.

However, this common source of historical and fictional narratives could not of itself preserve the kinship of the two narrative modes in their most elaborated forms, historiography and literature. A second reason for this persistent congruence has to be advanced. The reconstitution of the narrative field is possible only insofar as the configurating operations in both domains can be measured by the same standard. For me, this standard has been emplotment. In this respect, it is not surprising that we have rediscovered in fictional narrative the same configurating operation that historical explanation was confronted with, since the narrativist theories presented in Part II authorized the transference of literary categories of emplotment into the field of historical narrative. In this sense, we have simply returned to literature what history had borrowed from it.

This second reason, in turn, only holds if the transformations of the simple model of emplotment received from Aristotle conserve a discernible kinship even in their most divergent expressions. The reader will have observed in this regard a large resemblance between my attempts undertaken separately in the two narrative fields to give the notion of emplotment a broader extension and a more fundamental understanding than that conveyed by Aristotle's muthos, dependent as it is on his interpretation of Greek tragedy. I adopted as my guideline in these two efforts the same notions of "the temporal synthesis of the heterogeneous" and "discordant concordance" that carry the formal principle of Aristotelian muthos beyond its particular instantiation in overly determined genres and literary types, allowing it to be transposed without precautions from literature to history.

The deepest reason for the unity of the concept of "narrative configuration" depends finally on the kinship between the methods of derivation I called upon in both cases to account for the specificity of the new narrative practices that have appeared as much in the field of historiography as in that of narrative fiction. As regards historiography, we ought not to forget the reservations with which I received the narrativist theses that would make history a simple species of the genre "story," nor my preference for the long way of "questioning back," borrowed from Husserl's *Krisis*. In this way, I could do justice to the birth of a new form of rationality within the field of historical explanation, while at the same time preserving, through this genesis of meaning, the subordination of historical rationality to narrative understanding. Recall the notions of quasi-plot, quasi-character, and quasi-event, by means of which I tried to fit these new modes of historical configuration to the formal concept of emplotment, taken in the broad sense of a synthesis of the heterogeneous.

The first and second chapters of this volume lead to the same generalization of the concept of plot under the control of the idea of a temporal synthesis of the heterogeneous. By first interrogating the realm of traditionality that characterizes the development of literary genres as related to narrativity, we were able to explore the resources for deviance that the formal principle of narrative configuration can tolerate, and we ended with the wager that despite the warning signs of a schism threatening the very principle of narrative emplotment, this principle always succeeds in incarnating itself in new literary genres capable of assuming the perenniality of the age-old act of narrating. But it was in my examination of the attempts made by narrative semiotics to reformulate the surface structures of narratives as a function of their deep structures that we could observe the closest parallel between the epistemology of historical explanation and that of narrative grammar. My thesis was the same in both cases. It was a plea for the precedence of narrative understanding over narratological rationality. The universal character of the formal principle of narrative configuration was thereby confirmed, to the extent that what this understanding confronts is the emplotment, taken in its most extreme formality, namely, the temporal synthesis of the heterogeneous.

I have just emphasized the homology, from an epistemological point of view, between my analyses of the configurative operations on the planes of historical and fictional narrative. We may now place the accent on the dissymmetries that will only attain a complete elucidation in my next volume, when I remove the parentheses I have imposed on the question of truth. If it is indeed this question, ultimately, that distinguishes history, as a true narrative, from fiction, the dissymmetry that affects a narrative's power to refigure time—that is, following my convention regarding vocabulary, the third mimetic relation of narrative to action—announces itself already at the level where, as we have just been discussing, fictional narrative and historical narrative offer the greatest symmetry: the plane of configuration.

We could ignore this dissymmetry by recalling the most striking results of my parallel studies of historical and fictional narrative, insofar as, in speaking of the configuration of time by narrative, the principal accent was on the mode of intelligibility the configurating power of narrative could claim rather than on the time that was at stake in it.

For reasons that will appear only in the next volume, fictional narrative is richer in information about time, on this very plane of composition, than is historical narrative. It is not that historical narrative is completely impoverished in this regard. My discussion about the event and more precisely my observations regarding the return of the event by the detour of the long time-span made the time of history appear as a sufficiently wide field of variations to constrain us to formulate the notion of a quasi-event. Nevertheless other constraints, which I shall be able to account for only in volume 3, result in the fact that the various time-spans considered by historians obey laws relating to their placement within ever vaster currents, which despite undeniable qualitative differences relating to the rhythm, the tempo of events, make these time-spans and their corresponding speeds extremely homogeneous. This is why the order of chapters in Part II did not correspond to any notable progression in the apprehension of time. The same thing is not true with regard to the configuration of time by fictional narratives. The four chapters presented in this volume could be organized on the basis of an increasingly more detailed apprehension of narrative temporality.

In the first chapter, it was still simply a question of temporal aspects connected to the style of traditionality in the history of literary genres related to the narrative. I was thus able to define a sort of transhistorical, but not atemporal, identity of the operation of configuration, by linking together the three notions of innovation, perenniality, and decline, whose temporal implications are obvious. The second chapter went further into the problematic of time, during the debate between narrative understanding and narratological rationality, inasmuch as the latter requires for its models of the deep grammar of narrative an achronological status as a matter of principle, in relation to which the diachrony of transformations, displayed on the surface of a narrative, appears derived and inessential. To this I opposed the originary character of the temporal process inherent in emplotment as related to narrative understanding, which we see simulated by narratological rationality. But it was with the study of "games with time," in Chapter 3, that the fictional narrative appeared for the first time to develop the resources that the historical narrative seemed prevented from exploiting, for reasons which, once again, could not be clarified at this stage of my investigation. It is only with the fictional narrative that the maker of plots multiplies the distortions authorizing the division between the time taken to narrate and the time of the things narrated, a division that itself is initiated by the interplay between utterance and statement in the course of the narration. Everything occurs as though fiction, by creating imaginary worlds, opened up an unlimited career to the manifestation of time.

We took the last step in the direction of the specificity of fictive time in the final chapter, devoted to the notion of the fictive experience of time. By fictive experience, I mean a virtual manner of living in the world projected by the literary work as a result of its capacity for self-transcendence. This chapter is the exact counterpoint of that devoted to historical intentionality in Part II. The dissymmetry I am speaking about now, therefore, parallels very precisely the symmetry between historical narrative and fictional narrative on the level of narrative structure.

Is this to say that we have crossed, on the side of fiction as well as on that of history, the boundary that I marked out at the beginning between the question of sense and that of reference, or better as I prefer to say, between the question of configuration and that of refiguration? I do not think so. Even if I have to admit that at this stage the problematic of configuration is open to a very strong attraction exerted by the problematic of refiguration—and this is so by reason of the general law of language that *what* we say is governed by *that about which* we are speaking—I still affirm with equal force that the boundary between configuration and refiguration has not yet been crossed, as long as the world of the work remains a transcendence immanent in the text.

This asceticism in my analysis has its counterpart in a comparable asceticism practiced in Part II, where I dissociated the epistemological characteristics of the historical event from its ontological characteristics, which will be examined only in volume 3, with respect to the "reality" of the historical past. So, just as I abstained from deciding the question of the reference of the historical event to the actual past, I am also suspending any decision concerning the capacity of a fictional narrative to *disclose* and to *transform* the actual world of action. In this sense, the studies I devoted to the three tales about time prepare the way for—without actually realizing—the transition from the problems of narrative configuration to the problems of the refiguration of time by narrative, which will be the subject of Part IV. The threshold separating these problematics is, in fact, crossed only when the world of the text is confronted with the world of the reader. Only then does the literary work acquire a meaning in the full sense of the term, at the intersection of the world projected by the text and the life-world of the reader. This confrontation requires, in turn, that we pass by way of a theory of reading, inasmuch as the latter constitutes the privileged place for the intersection of an imaginary world and an actual one. Only after a theory of reading has been proposed in one of the concluding chapters of volume 3 will fictional narrative be able to assert its claims to truth, at the cost of a radical reformulation of the problem of truth. This will involve the capacity of the work of art to indicate and to transform human action. In the same way, only once the theory of reading has been presented will the contribution of the fictional narrative to the refiguration of time enter into opposition to and into composition with the capacity of historical narrative to speak of the actual past. If my thesis about the highly controversial problem of reference in the order of fiction possesses any originality, it is to the extent that it does not separate the claim to truth asserted by fictional narrative from that made by historical narrative but attempts to understand each in relation to the other.

The problem of the refiguration of time by narrative will, therefore, be brought to its conclusion only when we shall be in a position to make the respective referential intentions of the historical narrative and the fictional narrative *interweave*. Our analysis of the fictive experience of time will at least have marked a decisive turning point in the direction of the solution to this problem that forms the horizon of my investigation, by providing something like a *world of the text* for us to think about, while awaiting its complement, the *life-world of the reader*, without which the signification of the literary work is incomplete.

Notes

INTRODUCTION

1. Cf. Paul Ricoeur, *Time and Narrative*, vol. 1, trans. Kathleen McLaughlin and David Pellauer (Chicago: University of Chicago Press, 1984), chapter 3, especially pp. 64–70.

2. Tzvetan Todorov defines the three notions of literature, discourse, and genre in terms of one another. Cf. "La Notion de littérature" in *Les Genres du discours* (Paris: Seuil, 1978), pp. 13–26. If it is objected that individual works transgress all categorization, it nonetheless remains true that "transgression, to exist as such, requires a law that would be, precisely, transgressed" (ibid., p. 45). This law depends upon a certain codification of preexisting discursive properties, that is, in the institutionalizing of certain "transformations that certain speech acts undergo in order to produce a certain literary genre" (ibid., p. 54). The filiation between literary genres and ordinary discourse, as well as the autonomy of literature, are thus preserved. Todorov's initial analyses of the notion of literary genres can be found in his *The Fantastic: A Structural Approach to a Literary Genre*, trans. Richard Howard (Ithaca: Cornell University Press, 1973).

3. Cf. *Time and Narrative*, vol. 1, p. 64.

4. Strictly speaking, narratology should be termed the science of narrative structures, without considering the distinction between historical narrative and fictional narrative. However, according to the contemporary use of the term, "narratology" is centered on the fictional narrative, without excluding a few incursions into the domain of historiography. It is in view of this de facto division of roles that I am contrasting narratology and historiography.

5. I have chosen to devote studies of three literary texts to this question: Virginia Woolf's *Mrs. Dalloway*, Thomas Mann's *Der Zauberberg*, and Marcel Proust's *A la recherche du temps perdu*. See below, chapter 4.

6. My interpretation of the role of reading in literary experience in close to that proposed by Mario Valdés in *Shadows in the Cave: A Phenomenological Approach to Literary Criticism Based on Hispanic Texts* (Toronto: University of Toronto Press, 1982). "In this theory, structure is completely subordinated to the function and . . . the discussion of function shall lead us back ultimately into the reintegration of expression and experience in the intersubjective participation of readers across time and space" (ibid., p. 15). I also concur with the central thesis of Jacques Garelli, *Le Recel et la Dispersion: Essai sur le champ de lecture poétique* (Paris: Gallimard, 1978).

161

CHAPTER ONE

1. The term "paradigm" refers to the narrative understanding of a competent reader. It is fairly synonymous with a rule for composition. I have chosen to use "paradigm" as a general term covering three levels, that of the most formal principles of composition, that of the generic principles (tragedy, comedy, and so on), and finally that of the specific types (Greek tragedy, Celtic epic, and so on). Its contrary is the individual work considered in terms of its capacity for innovation and deviation. Taken in this sense, the term "paradigm" must not be confused with the two terms "paradigmatic" and "syntagmatic" which have to do with semiotic rationality in its simulation of narrative understanding.

2. See *Time and Narrative*, vol. 1, pp. 64–70.

3. An acknowledgement is due to Robert Scholes and Robert Kellogg, for their *The Nature of Narrative* (New York: Oxford University Press, 1966), where they precede their study of narrative categories, including that of plot, with a review of our narrative traditions, archaic, ancient, medieval, and modern.

4. The case of the English novel is especially noteworthy. Cf. Ian Watt, *The Rise of the Novel: Studies in Defoe, Richardson, and Fielding* (Berkeley: University of California Press, 1957). Watt describes the relationship between the rise of the novel and the growth of a new reading public, and with it the birth of a new need for expression of private experience. These are problems I shall return to in Part IV in volume 3 when I consider the place of reading in the range of meaning of the narrative work.

5. See also A. A. Mendilow, *Time and the Novel* (London: Peter Nevill, 1952, 2nd ed., New York: Humanities Press, 1972).

6. Cf. Hegel on *Le Neveu de Rameau* in G. W. F. Hegel, *Phenomenology of Spirit*, trans. A. V. Miller, (Oxford: Clarendon Press, 1977), pp. 317–18, 332.

7. Robinson Crusoe, although not a person on the same level as Don Quixote or Faust or Don Juan—our modern mythical heroes—may be taken as a hero before the fact of the *Bildungsroman*: placed in conditions of solitude unparalleled in real life, moved only by concern for profit and the single criterion of utility, he becomes the hero of a quest in which his perpetual isolation works like the secret nemesis of his apparent triumph over his adversities. He thus raises solitude, taken as the universal state of human existence, to the rank of a paradigm. Hence, far from the character breaking free of the plot, we should say that he engenders it. The theme of this novel, what I have called the hero's quest, reintroduces a principle of order more subtle than that in the conventional plots from the past. In this respect, everything that distinguishes Defoe's masterpiece from a simple narrative about a voyage and its adventures, and places it within the new space of the novel, can be attributed to the emergence of a configuration where the "fable" is tacitly governed by the theme—to allude here to Northrop Frye's translation of Aristotle's muthos as "fable and theme."

8. The mutual unfolding of the two spirals of character and action is not an absolutely new procedure. In his *The Genesis of Secrecy: On the Interpretation of Narrative* (Cambridge: Harvard University Press, 1979), Frank Kermode shows how it works in the simultaneous enriching, from one gospel to another, of the character of Judas and the events narrated involving him. Cf. ibid., pp. 84–95. And Auerbach had earlier shown, in his *Mimesis: The Representation of Reality in Western Literature* (trans. Willard R. Trask [Princeton: Princeton University Press, 1953]), how the biblical characters Abraham and Peter differed from Homeric ones. Whereas the latter are flat and lacking depth, the former have a rich background capable of narrative development.

9. Proust's *A la recherche du temps perdu*, which I shall also consider below, might be considered as both a *Bildungsroman* and a stream of consciousness novel. See below, pp. 130–52.

10. From *Pamela* to *Clarissa* we can see this procedure becoming more refined. Instead of a simple correspondence between the heroine and her father, as in the first novel, *Clarissa* knits together two exchanges of letters between the heroine and her confidant and between the hero and his confidant. In fact, the parallel unfolding of two series of correspondences allows Richardson to attenuate the disadvantages of the genre while maximizing its advantages by varying the points of view. We can, I think, call by the name "plot" this subtle epistolary combination, which makes the feminine and masculine visions alternate, along with the discretion and the volubility, the slowness of developments and the suddenness of the violent episodes. Richardson, well aware of what he was doing and a master of his art, could boast that there was no digression in his work that did not stem from its subject and also contribute to it, which is the formal definition of plot.

11. It was not by accident that the English work in this genre was called "novel." Mendilow and Watt cite a number of striking declarations from Defoe, Richardson, and Fielding that attest of their conviction that they are inventing a new literary genre, in the proper sense of this term. Similarly, the word "original," which during the Middle Ages denoted what had existed from the beginning, came to signify something underived, independent, first-hand, in short, something "novel or fresh in character or style" (*The Rise of the Novel*, p. 14). The story told therefore had to be "novel" and its characters had to be particular beings in particular circumstances. It would not be an exaggeration to tie this confidence in simple and direct language to the choice referred to above of characters from a low social background, concerning whom Aristotle would have said that they are neither worse nor better than us, but like us, as in real life. One corollary of this will to be faithful to experience is the abandonment of traditional plots, drawn from the storehouse of mythology, history, or earlier literature, along with the invention of characters without a legendary past and stories without a previous tradition.

12. Regarding this short-circuit between intimacy and printing, and the incredible illusion of the reader's identification with the hero that results, cf. *The Rise of the Novel*, pp. 196–97.

13. In the history of the English novel, Fielding's *Tom Jones* occupies a special place. If for a long time Richardson's *Pamela* or *Clarissa* was preferred to it, it was because critics found in these novels a more elaborated picture of the characters, at the expense of the plot in the narrow sense of this term. Modern criticism has restored *Tom Jones* to a certain preeminence due to its very elaborate treatment of narrative structure from the point of view of the interplay between narrated time and the time of the things narrated. Its central action is relatively simple, but subdivided into a series of narrative units, relatively independent of one another and of different lengths, devoted to episodes separated by shorter or longer intervals of time and themselves covering quite different lengths of time—in fact, there are three groups with six subgroups making up 18 books of 7 to 20 chapters each. Such vast problems of composition required a great variety of procedures, incessant changes, and surprising counterpoints. It is no accident that Fielding was more sensitive to the continuity between the novel and the older forms of the narrative tradition than either Defoe or Richardson, who disdained the epic stemming from Homer, or that he should have assimilated the novel to "an epic in prose." Ian Watt, who cites this formula, relates it to Hegel's comment in the *Aesthetics* that the novel is a manifestation of the spirit of epic influenced by a modern and prosaic concept of reality (*The Rise of the Novel*, p. 239).

14. In this sense, neither T. S. Kuhn's notion of a paradigm shift, nor Michel Foucault's idea of an epistemic break contradict in radical fashion an analysis of tradition based on Gadamer's work. Epistemic breaks would become insignificant—in the strict sense of this term—if they did not characterize the very style of our traditionality, the

unique way in which it has structured itself. It is in terms of such breaks that we are submitted to the efficacy of history, which Gadamer calls *Wirkungsgeschichte*, a notion that I will consider on its own terms in Part IV in volume 3.

15. Northrop Frye, *Anatomy of Criticism: Four Essays* (Princeton: Princeton University Press, 1957).

16. Paul Ricoeur, "*Anatomy of Criticism* or the Order of Paradigms," in Eleanor Cook, Chaviva Hošek, Jay Macpherson, Patricia Parker, and Julian Patrick, eds., *Centre and Labyrinth: Essays in Honour of Northrop Frye* (Toronto: University of Toronto Press, 1983), pp. 1–13.

17. The parallel between fictional modes is assured by the link between muthos and dianoia in Aristotle's *Poetics* along with Longinus's treatise on the sublime. "Fable and theme" together constitute the story, the dianoia designating "the point of the story."

18. In this respect, the realistic novel might be accused of confusing symbol and sign. The novelistic illusion, at least in its beginnings, is born from the fusion of two heterogeneous enterprises in one principle: compose an autonomous verbal structure and represent real life.

19. Henri De Lubac, *Exégèse Médiévale: Les Quatre Sens de l'Ecriture* (Paris: Aubier, 1959–64), 4 vols.

20. My own attempt to separate configuration and refiguration only as an abstraction rests on a conception close to Frye's stages of the symbol. Refiguration, in effect, is in many ways a reprise at the level of mimesis$_3$ of features of the world of action already understood at the level of mimesis$_1$, across their narrative configuration (mimesis$_2$)—or, in other words, across the "fictional" and "thematic modes" of Northrop Frye.

21. "Poetry can be made out of other poems, novels out of other novels. Literature shapes itself" (*Anatomy of Criticism*, p. 97).

22. Archetypal criticism, in this sense, does not differ fundamentally from the criticism practiced by Gaston Bachelard in his theory of a "material" imagination, governed by the "elements" of nature: water, sir, earth, and fire—whose metamorphosis Frye takes up within the setting of language. It is also akin to the way in which Mircea Eliade sets out hierophanies in terms of the cosmic dimensions of sky, water, life, etc., which are always accompanied by spoken or written rituals. For Northrop Frye, too, the poem, in its archetypal phase, imitates nature as a cyclical process expressed in rites (cf. *Anatomy of Criticism*, p. 145). But it is civilization that thinks of itself in this attempt to extract a "total human form" from nature.

23. When put in terms of the major symbol of the Apocalypse, the myth of the four seasons, in which this symbol readily takes up residence, loses once and for all its naturalistic character. In the archetypal phase of the symbol, nature still contains humanity. In its anagogical phase, humanity is what contains nature, under the sign of the infinitely desirable.

24. In my essay referred to above, I discuss Frye's attempt to make the narrative modes correspond to the myths of Spring, Summer, Fall, and Winter.

25. "In the great moments of Dante and Shakespeare, in, say *The Tempest* or the climax of the *Purgatorio*, we have a feeling of converging significance, the feeling that we are close to seeing what our whole literary experience has been about, the feeling that we have moved into the still center of the order of words" (*Anatomy of Criticism*, p. 117).

26. Cited by Frye, p. 122. Frye writes, "The conception of a total Word is the postulate that there is such a thing as an order of words" (ibid., p. 126). However it would be a serious error to find a theological resonance in this statement. Religion for Northrop Frye is too devoted to what *is* and literature is too devoted to what *may be* for them to be identified with each other. Culture and the literature that expresses it find their

autonomy precisely through the mode of the imaginary. This tension between the possible and the actual prevents Frye from giving the concept of fiction the scope and englobing power Frank Kermode confers upon it in the work I shall consider next, where the Apocalypse occupies a place comparable to the one Frye grants it in his criticism.

27. *Aristotle's Poetics*, trans. James Hulton (New York: W. W. Norton, 1982), p. 52.

28. Cf. John Kucich, "Action in the Dickens Ending; *Bleak House* and *Great Expectations*," *Nineteenth Century Fiction* 33 (1978): 88–109. (The whole of this special issue is devoted to narrative endings.) Kucich calls "crucial" endings those endings that bring about a break that gives rise to the sort of activity Georges Bataille characterizes as "wasteful." He also expresses his debt to the work of Kenneth Burke, especially *A Grammar of Motives* (New York: Prentice-Hall, 1945) and *Language as Symbolic Action* (Berkeley: University of California Press, 1966). His final remark is worth citing: "In all crucial endings, the means of causing that gap to appear *is* the end" (p. 109, his emphasis).

29. J. Hillis Miller, "The Problematic of Ending in Narrative," *Nineteenth Century Fiction* 33 (1978): 3–7. He declares, "no narrative shows either its beginning or its ending" (ibid., p. 4). And he also states that the "aporia of ending arises from the fact that it is impossible ever to tell whether a given narrative is complete" (ibid., p. 5). It is true that he takes as his reference the relationship between knotting (*desis*) and unknotting (*lusis*) in Aristotle's *Poetics* and that he develops the aporias of this metaphor of the knot with gusto. But the place of this text in the *Poetics* is much debated insofar as the operation of knotting and unknotting escapes the criterion of a beginning and an end so clearly stated in the canonical chapter Aristotle devotes to plot. The incidents recounted may be interminable and are in fact so in real life, but the narrative as a muthos is terminable. What happens after this ending is not pertinent to the configuration of the poem. This is why there is a problem about good endings and, as we shall see below, of "anticlosure."

30. One of the many merits of Barbara Herrnstein Smith's work, *Poetic Closure: A Study of How Poems End* (Chicago: University of Chicago Press, 1968), is that it provides the theory of narrative with not only a noteworthy model of analysis but also precise suggestions about how to extend to "poetic closure" in general its specific comments about "lyric closure." The transposition is easily justified. On both sides, we have to do with poetic works, that is, with works that are built upon the foundation of transactions in ordinary language and that therefore interrupt these transactions. Furthermore, it is a matter, in both cases, of mimetic works in the particular sense of this term that they imitate an ordinary "utterance"—an argument, a declaration, a lamentation. Hence literary narrative imitates not just an action but also ordinary narrative taken from the transactions of everyday life.

31. Barbara Herrnstein Smith speaks in this regard of "self-closural reference" (ibid., p. 172), where the work refers to itself as such by its way of ending or not ending.

32. Smith distinguishes between "anticlosure" which still preserves some tie with the need for an ending through its application of the reflexive resources of language to the thematic incompleteness of the work and its recourse to ever more subtle forms of ending, and what is "beyond closure." As regards anticlosure and its techniques of "sabotaging" language, she says, "If the traitor, language, is not to be exiled, one may disarm him and make him a prisoner of war" (ibid., p. 254). As for what is beyond closure, "the traitor, language, has here been brought to his knees and not only disarmed but beheaded" (ibid., p. 266). She does not take this step because of her conviction that, as the imitation of an utterance, poetic language cannot escape the tension between literary and nonliterary language. When the aleatory, for example, is sub-

stituted for the deliberate surprise, as in concrete poetry, there is no longer something to read, only something to look at. Then criticism finds itself confronted with an intimidating message that tells it, "All linguistic baggage must be deposited at this point" (p. 267). But art cannot break with the powerful institution of language. This is why her closing words recall Frank Kermode's "yet . . . however" concerning the resistance of paradigms to erosion: "Poetry ends in many ways, but poetry, I think, has not yet ended" (ibid., p. 271).

33. Frank Kermode, *The Sense of an Ending: Studies in the Theory of Fiction* (New York: Oxford University Press, 1966).

34. I shall return to Kermode's illuminating comments about the *aevum*, the perpetual or sempiternal. He sees in such tragic time a "third order of duration, distinct from time and eternity" (ibid., p. 70), which medieval theory attributed to angels. For myself, in Part IV, I will connect these temporal qualities to other features of narrative time that indicate its liberation from simple rectilinear succession.

35. Kermode rightly links this horrible rending of time in *Macbeth* to the Augustinian *distentio*, as it was experienced by the author of the *Confessions* in the torments of a continually deferred conversion: "I kept crying 'How long shall I go on saying "tomorrow, tomorrow"' [Quamdiu, Quamdiu, 'cras et cras']?" (VIII, 12:28). However, in *Macbeth* this quasi-eternity of the put-off decision is the opposite of Christ's patience in the garden on the Mount of Olives as he awaits his *kairos*, "the season . . . filled with significance" (Kermode, p. 46). This opposition between *chronos* or rectilinear time and *kairos* or sempiternal time points us toward the theme of my Part IV.

36. Kermode's emphasis on this point is significant: cf. ibid., pp. 25, 27, 28, 30, 38, 42, 49, 55, 61, and, above all, 82 and 89.

37. See here especially Kermode's fourth essay, "The Modern Apocalypse." There he describes and discusses our age's claim to uniqueness, its sense of being caught up in a perpetual crisis. He also considers what Harold Rosenberg calls the tradition of the new. As regards the contemporary novel in particular, I note that the problem of the end of paradigms is posed in terms opposite to those used in the early days of the novel. In the beginning, the security of realistic representation concealed the insecurity of novelistic composition. Today, at the other end of the development of the novel, the insecurity, revealed by the conviction that reality is chaotic, turns against the very idea of an orderly composition. Writing becomes a problem for itself and its own impossibility.

38. "Crisis, however facile the conception, is unescapably a central element in our endeavours towards making sense of our world" (ibid., p. 94).

39. Cf. Kermode's discussion of Robbe-Grillet and his "*écriture labyrinthine*" (pp. 19–24). He correctly emphasizes the intermediary role played by the narrative technique developed by Sartre and Camus, in *Nausea* and *The Stranger*, as contributing to the dissidence proclaimed by Robbe-Grillet.

40. Quoted by Kermode, p. 102.

41. The expression "the consoling plot" becomes almost a pleonasm. No less important than the influence of Nietzsche is that of the poet Wallace Stevens, especially in the last section of his "Notes Toward a Supreme Fiction."

42. Whence also the overdetermination of the very term "ending." The end is the end of the world, or Apocalypse; the end of the book, or the book of the Apocalypse; the end without an end of crisis, or the myth of the *fin de siècle*; the end of the tradition of paradigms, or schism; the impossibility of giving a poem an ending, or the incomplete work; and finally death, the end of desire. This overdetermination explains the irony of the indefinite pronoun in the title: *The Sense of an Ending*. We are never done with the end. Or as Wallace Stevens says, "The imagination is always at the end of an era" (cited by Kermode, p. 31).

43. Another exploration of the relationship between fiction and broken myth is possible, one that would focus upon the substitutionary function of literary fiction with regard to those narratives that have functioned authoritatively in our culture in the past. A suspicion of another form of order then comes to light, the suspicion that fiction has usurped the authority of these foundational narratives, that this shift in power calls for, in return, in an expression of Edward Said's, an effect of "molestation," if we understand by this the wound the writer inflicts on himself when he becomes aware of the illusory and usurped character of the authority he exercises as an author (*auctor*), capable not only of influencing but also of making the reader submit to his power. Cf. Edward Said, *Beginnings: Intention and Method* (New York: Basic Books, 1975), pp. 83–85 and passim. For a more detailed analysis of the pair authority/molestation, cf. idem, "Molestation and Authority in Narrative Fiction," in J. Hillis Miller, ed., *Aspects of Narrative* (New York: Columbia University Press, 1971), pp. 47–68.

44. We ought to emphasize, in this respect, the failure of a simply biological or psychological justification of the desire for concordance, even if it turns out that it is founded on some basis in the *Gestalt* of perception, as in the work of Barbara Herrnstein Smith, or as Kermode suggests using the example of the ticking of a clock. "We ask what it *says*: and we agree that it says *tick-tock*. By this fiction we humanize it, make it talk our language. . . . *Tick* is a humble genesis, *tock* a feeble apocalypse; and tick tock is in any case not much of a plot" (ibid., pp. 44–45, his emphases). These biological and perceptive rhythms invariably send us back to language: a "supplement" of plot and fiction insinuates itself as soon as we *talk* about a clock, and with this supplement comes "the time of the novelist" (ibid., p. 46).

45. Jurij Lotman, *The Structure of the Artistic*, trans. Ronald Vronn (Ann Arbor: University of Michigan Press, 1977), gives a properly structural solution to the problem of the perenniality of the forms of concordance. He outlines a series of concentric circles that progressively enclose a central circle, that of the plot, whose own center in turn is the notion of an event. He begins from a general definition of language as a system of communication using signs that are ordered in some way. From this, we obtain the notion of a text conceived of as a sequence of signs transformed by special rules into one unique sign. Next we pass to the notion of art as a secondary modeling system, and then to verbal art or literature as one of the secondary systems built from our natural languages. Along this chain of included elements we see a principle of "demarcation" unfolding, hence of inclusions and exclusions, which appear as inherent to the notion of a text. Marked by some frontier, a text is transformed into an integral unit of signals. The notion of closure is not far off. It is introduced by the notion of a "frame," which is related to this same concept in painting, the theater (the footlights, the curtain), architecture, and sculpture. In one sense, the beginning and the end of a plot only specify this notion of the frame, which is directly related to that of the text. There is no plot without a frame, that is, "the boundary separating the artistic text from the non-text" (ibid., p. 209). This is why, as I shall indicate in Part IV, the work of art, "being limited spatially, can be the finite model of the infinite universe—a world external to the work" (ibid., p. 217). Open-ended or even nonending stories are only interesting because of the deviations and violations they impose on the rule of closure. The notion of an event thus figures for Lotman as the center of this ring game (cf. ibid., pp. 233ff.). The decisive determination that makes the event a more precise concept, and thereby specifies the plot as one of the possible temporal frames, is quite unexpected and, to my knowledge, is without parallel in the literature on this subject. Lotman begins by imagining what a text without any plot or events would be. It would be a purely classificatory system, a simple inventory—for example, a list of places, as on a map. As regards culture, it would be a fixed system of semantic fields (strikingly arranged in binary fashion: rich vs. poor, noble vs. base, etc.). When does

an event occur then? "When a character crosses the frontiers of some semantic field" (ibid., p. 233). A fixed image of the world is required, therefore, so that someone can transgress its internal barriers and prohibitions. The event is this crossing, this transgression. In this sense, "a text possessing a plot is built upon the base of the plotless text of which it is the negation" (ibid.). Is this not an admirable commentary on Aristotle's peripeteia and Kermode's discordance? Can we conceive of a culture that would contain neither a determined semantic field nor a crossing of some frontier?

46. Eric Weil, *Logique de la philosophie* (Paris: Vrin, 1967).

47. In Walter Benjamin, *Illuminations*, ed. Hannah Arendt, trans. Harry Zohn (New York: Schocken Books, 1969), pp. 83–109.

48. Barbara Herrnstein Smith and Frank Kermode, as I have indicated, come together here: "Poetry ends in many ways but poetry, I think, has not yet ended," says Smith (p. 271). "The paradigms survive, somehow. . . . The survival of paradigms is as much our business as their erosion," says Kermode (p. 43).

CHAPTER TWO

1. Cf. Roland Barthes, "Introduction to the Structural Analysis of Narratives," in *A Barthes Reader*, ed. Susan Sontag (New York: Hill and Wang, 1982), pp. 251–95.

2. Roland Barthes, *Poétique du récit* (Paris: Seuil, 1977), p. 14. Regarding this presumed homology between language and literature, Tzvetan Todorov cites Valéry's remark that literature is only an "extension and application of certain properties of language" (*Poetics of Prose*, trans. Richard Howard [Ithaca: Cornell University Press, 1977], p. 28). In this respect, the procedures of style (including the rhetorical figures) and the procedures for organizing a narrative, along with the cardinal notions of meaning and interpretation, all constitute so many manifestations of linguistic categories in the literary narrative (cf. ibid., pp. 29–41). This homology becomes even more precise once we try to apply to narrative the grammatical categories of the proper noun, the verb, and the adjective to describe the agent-subject and the action-predicate, hence the state of equilibrium or disequilibrium. A "grammar" of narrative is therefore possible. Yet we should not forget that these grammatical categories are better understood if we are acquainted with their manifestation in narratives (cf. ibid., pp. 108–19, 218–33). I would like to emphasize that the grammar of narrative finds its originality in relation to the grammar of *langue* when we pass from the phrase to sentences to a higher syntactic unit or to *sequence* (cf. ibid., p. 116). It is at this level that the grammar of narrative is supposed to become equal to the operation of emplotment.

3. *Poétique du récit*, pp. 131–57. I have thought it better to pursue this distinction in the next chapter.

4. See below, pp. 38–44.

5. Barthes sees here Benveniste's distinction between the form that produces the units through segmentation and the meaning that gathers these units into units of a higher order.

6. Cf. "Introduction to the Structural Analysis of Narrative," p. 270.

7. This demand is satisfied to its most extreme consequences by Claude Lévi-Strauss in his *Mythologiques*. However readers of his *Structural Anthropology* will also recall his essay on "The Structural Study of Myth" and its structural analysis of the myth of Oedipus. (Claude Lévi-Strauss, "The Structural Study of Myth," in idem, *Structural Anthropology*, trans. Claire Jacobson and Brooke Grundfest Schoepf [New York: Basic Books, 1963], pp. 206–31. See also his "The Story of Asdiwal" in *Structural Anthropology*, vol. II, trans. Monique Layton [New York: Basic Books, 1976], pp. 146–97.) As is well known, there the anecdotal unfolding of the myth is abolished

in favor of a combinatory law that does not bind together temporal sentences but what Lévi-Strauss calls bundles of relations, such as the overrating of blood relations as opposed to their underrating, and the relation of dependence on the earth (autochthony) opposed to emancipation from it. The structural law of this myth will be the logical matrix of the solution brought to these contradictions. I shall forego here any incursion into the realm of mythology, having fictional narrative begin with epic by abstracting from its filiation and dependence upon myth. I shall observe this same reservation in Part IV, particularly in discussing the calendar, by not taking up the problem of the relations between historical time and mythic time.

8. Monique Schneider, from whom I am borrowing this decisive insight (Monique Schneider, "Le Temps du Conte," in Dorian Tiffeneau, ed., *La Narrativité* [Paris: Editions du Centre National de la Recherche Scientifique, 1980], pp. 85–123, cf. pp. 85–87) has, for example, emphasized the transformation of the "marvelous" character of the folktale, which it owes to its prior insertion in an initiatory practice, into a thoroughly intelligible object, proposing to "reawaken those powers that allow the folktale to resist this logical seizure" (ibid., p. 87). It is not these powers linked to the "marvelous" character of the folktale that interest me, but rather those resources of intelligibility it already possesses as first being a cultural creation.

9. In his "Introduction to the Structural Analysis of Narrative," Roland Barthes declared that "analysis today tends to 'dechronologize' the narrative continuum and to 'relogicize' it, to make it dependent on what Mallarmé called with regard to the French language, 'the primitive thunderbolts of logic'" (Barthes, p. 270). And he added, regarding time, that "the task is to succeed in giving a structural description of the chronological illusion—it is for narrative logic to account for narrative time" (ibid.). For Barthes, at this time, it was to the extent analytic rationality is substituted for narrative intelligibility that time is transformed into a "chronological illusion." In fact, his discussion of this assertion takes us beyond the framework of mimesis$_2$: "Time belongs not to discourse strictly speaking but to the referent; both narrative and language know only a semiotic time, 'true' time being a 'realist,' referential illusion, as Propp's commentary shows. It is as such that structural description must deal with it" (ibid., pp. 270–71). I shall discuss this alleged referential illusion in Part IV. What we are considering in this chapter concerns what Barthes himself calls semiotic time.

10. Recall Le Goff's similar comment concerning the historian's reluctance to adopt the vocabulary of synchrony and diachrony, mentioned in volume 1, p. 218.

11. Vladimir Propp, *Morphology of the Folktale*, 1st edition, trans. Laurence Scott, 2nd edition rev. and ed. Louis A. Wagner (Austin: University of Texas Press, 1968). This work constitutes one of the culminating points in the form of literary study known as "Russian formalism" developed during the years 1915–30. For a summary of the principal methodological achievements of this movement and a comparison with subsequent developments based on linguistics during the 1960s, cf. Tvzetan Todorov, "The Methodological Heritage of Formalism," in *The Poetics of Prose*, pp. 247–67. See also his discussion in the volume he edited, *Théorie de la littérature: Textes des formalistes russe* (Paris: Seuil, 1965). Particularly important for our discussion are the notions of "literariness" (*littérarité*), immanent system, level of organization, distinctive feature (or sign), motif and function, and typological classification. Most important is the notion of "transformation," which I shall take up below.

12. Propp's ambition to become the Linnaeus of the fairy tale is clearly stated (cf. ibid., p. xii). Indeed they both share the same goal: to discover the amazing unity hidden beneath the labyrinth of appearances. Their means are also the same: to subordinate the historical approach to the structural one (ibid., p. 15), motifs (that is, thematic contents) to "formal structural features" (ibid., p. 6). As for Goethe, he provides no less than five exergues for the preface and the chapters of this work, which for

some reason are left out of the English translation as "nonessential" (see the translator's note on p. x).

13. This number is almost the same as that of the phonemes in a phonological system.

14. This limitation in his field of investigation explains Propp's extreme prudence regarding an extrapolation beyond this domain. Within this domain, freedom in creation is strictly limited by the constraint of the sequence of the functions in the unilinear series. The teller of the tale is only free to omit some of the functions, to choose the species within the genus of actions defined by a function, to give this or that attribute to the characters, and to choose from the storehouse of language his means of expression.

15. If the scheme can serve as a measuring unit for individual tales, it is no doubt because there is no problem of deviation for the fairy tale as there is for the modern novel. To use the vocabulary of the preceding chapter concerning traditionality, in the folktale the paradigm and the particular work tend to overlap. Undoubtedly it is due to this almost complete overlapping that the fairy tale provides so fertile a field for the study of narrative constraints, the problem of "rule-governed deformations" reducing to the omission of certain functions or the specifying of generic features which define a function.

16. In fact, Propp precedes the definition of each function with a narrative proposition that mentions at least one character. This comment, as we shall see, will lead Claude Bremond to his definition of a "role" as the conjunction of an actant and an actor. Yet Propp had already written at the beginning of his work: "Function is understood as an act of a character, defined from the point of view of its significance for the course of the action" (*Morphology of the Folktale*, p. 21).

17. Once again it is appropriate to recall Frank Kermode's discussion of this point in *The Genesis of Secrecy*, pp. 75–99, where he demonstrates how in the gospels the characters Peter and Judas become more specific as the sequences involving them become larger and more complex in the Passion narratives.

18. The French translation of Propp says "sequence" instead of "move." In the English translation, "sequence" is used for what the French calls *l'ordre*, that is, the uniform succession of the functions. Cf. *Morphology of the Folktale*, pp. 21–22.

19. The remainder of this chapter in Propp is devoted to the different ways the tale may combine "moves": addition, interruption, parallelism, intersection, etc.

20. I have excluded from my analysis everything concerning the contribution of *Morphology of the Folktale* to the history of the genre "fairy tale." I said earlier how Propp carefully subordinates questions of history to description, in agreement on this point with Saussurian linguistics. He does not abandon his initial reserve on this point in his concluding chapter. Yet he does risk suggesting a link between religion and fairy tales: "A way of life and religion die out, while their contents turn into tales" (ibid., p. 106). For example, the quest, so characteristic of the tale, might stem from the wandering of souls in the otherworld. Perhaps this comment is not out of bounds if we recall that the fairy tale itself is on the way to extinction. "There are no new formations at present" (ibid., p. 114). If such is the case, is the propitious moment for structural analysis one where a certain creative process has been exhausted?

21. Claude Bremond, *La Logique du récit* (Paris: Seuil, 1973). For a brief version in English, cf. "The Logic of Narrative Possibilities," *New Literary History* 11 (1980): 387–411. My references are to the French volume.

22. For example, their interconnection may occur by simply setting things "end to end" (malevolence, a misdeed, etc.), or by enclosing one sequence within another (the test as part of the quest), or by parallels between independent series. As for the syntactic connections that hold these complex sequences together, they too come in many

forms: pure succession, causal connection, influence, a relation of means to an end, and so on.

23. Let us also note that this first dichotomy seems to be analytically contained within the concept of a role inasmuch as the role joins together a subject noun and a predicate verb. This point does not apply to the following cases.

24. See Arthur C. Danto, *Analytical Philosophy of Action* (New York: Cambridge University Press, 1973); A. I. Goldman, *A Theory of Human Action* (Englewood Cliffs, N.J.: Prentice-Hall, 1970).

25. Bremond applies this idea of a "good form" to Propp's sequence type (*Logique*, p. 38).

26. Cf. Todorov, "The Grammar of Narrative," in *Poetics of Prose*, pp. 108–19. A narrative statement proceeds from the conjoining of a proper noun (a grammatical subject devoid of internal properties) and two types of predicates, one describing a state of equilibrium or disequilibrium (adjectival), the other the passage from one state to another (verbal). The formal units of narrative are thus parallel to the parts of discourse: nouns, adjectives, verbs. However, it is true that beyond the proposition the syntax corresponding to a sequence attests that "there is hardly any linguistic theory of discourse" (ibid., p. 116). And this is to admit that the minimal complete plot consists of the statement of an equilibrium, then of a transforming action, and finally of a new equilibrium stemming from a specific grammar applied to the rules for narrative transformations (cf. also "Narrative Transformations," ibid., pp. 218–33).

27. "Our analysis having decomposed the plot into its constitutive elements, the roles, it remains to consider the inverse and complementary process that brings about their synthesis in the plot" (ibid., p. 136).

28. To the question of whether "another system of roles, just as satisfactory, or even better, is conceivable" (ibid., p. 327), Bremond replies, "We need to prove that the logic of roles that we have made use of imposes itself, always and everywhere, as the only principle for a coherent organization of the events in a plot" (ibid). And speaking of the metaphysics of the faculties of human existence upon which this system is constructed, he adds, "It is the narrative activity itself that imposes these categories upon us as the conditions for shaping the narrated experience" (ibid.).

29. Bremond prefers another way of putting it. "A basis in a metaphysics of the faculties of human existence for organizing the universe of roles is essential therefore to our undertaking" (ibid., p. 314). In fact, this assumption already governed the constitution of the elementary sequence as contingency, passage to an action, completion. It is what teaches us that we can be either the sufferer or the agent of any modification. It is not surprising, therefore, that it also governs the concepts of evaluation, influence, initiative, and retribution. It also presides over the subsequent constitution of the syntactic connection briefly referred to above: a relationship of simple coordination between successive developments, of cause to effect, of means to end, of implication (degradation implies the possibility of protection, disesteem implies the possibility of punishment). Bremond also claims the right of making recourse to natural language "to communicate to the reader an intuitive feeling for the logical organization of the roles in narrative" (ibid., p. 309).

30. A.-J. Greimas, *Structural Semantics: An Attempt at a Method*, trans. Daniele McDowell, Ronald Schleifer, Alan Velie (Lincoln: University of Nebraska Press, 1983); *Du Sens: Essais sémiotiques* (Paris: Seuil, 1970); *Maupassant. La sémiotique du texte: Exercises pratiques* (Paris: Seuil, 1976). The theoretical core of *Du Sens* lies in the two studies (pp. 135–86) entitled "The Interaction of Semiotic Constraints," written in collaboration with François Rastier and first published in *Yale French Studies* 41 (1968): 86–105, and "Eléments d'une Grammaire Narative," first published in *L'Homme* 9:3 (1969): 71–92. See also A.-J. Greimas and J. Courtes, *Semiotics and*

Language: An Analytical Dictionary, trans. Larry Christ, Daniel Patte, et al. (Bloomington: Indiana University Press, 1982). A new volume by Greimas appeared just as the French edition of this volume was going to press: A.-J. Greimas, *Du Sens*, vol. 2 (Paris: Seuil, 1983).

31. Etienne Souriau, *Les Deux Cent Mille Situations Dramatiques* (Paris: Flammarion, 1950).

32. "The test, because of this, could be considered as the irreducible nucleus accounting for the definition of the story diachronically" (ibid., p. 237).

33. Greimas himself turns this consideration against Propp's treatment of the whole sequence of functions as one fixed sequence, for the test constitutes in contradiction to this a certain manifestation of freedom. But may not the same argument be turned against Greimas's own attempt to construct a paradigmatic model lacking any originary diachronic dimension. In fact, he openly concedes this: "If a diachronic residue no longer existed, the whole narrative could then be reduced to this simple structure in the form of the functional pair 'confrontation vs. success' . . . which does not let itself be transformed into an elementary semic category" (ibid., p. 236).

34. In a similar vein, he adds, "the alternative which the narrative presents is the choice between the individual's freedom (that is to say, the absence of the contract) and the accepted social contract" (ibid.).

35. "Consequently, it is the contest (F)—the only functional pair not analyzable in achronic structure . . . which must account for the transformation itself" (ibid., pp. 244–45).

36. This thesis finds support in Todorov's use of the concept of "transformation" in his "Narrative Transformations," referred to above. The advantage of this concept is that it combines the paradigmatic point of view of Lévi-Strauss and Greimas with the syntagmatic view of Propp. Among other things, it splits the predicates of action, of doing something, running from modalities (ought, could, does) to attitudes (likes to do). Furthermore, it makes narrative possible by bringing about the transition from the action predicate to the sequence as a synthesis of difference and resemblance. In short, "it links two facts without their being able to be identified" (ibid., p. 233). This synthesis is nothing other than what has already occurred and been understood, in my opinion, as the synthesis of the heterogeneous on the level of our narrative understanding. I also agree with Todorov when he opposes transformation to succession in his *Les Genres du discours*. The notion of transformation does seem to be assigned to narratological rationality, in opposition to my notion of configuration, which I see as arising from narrative understanding. And, strictly speaking, we cannot speak of "transformation" unless we give it a logical formulation. But, to the extent that narrative gives rise to other transformations than negation, dependent upon disjunctions and conjunctions—for example, the passage from ignorance to recognition, the reinterpreting of already occurred events, or submission to ideological imperatives (cf. ibid., pp. 67f.)—it seems difficult to give a logical equivalent of all the narrative forms of organization for which we have acquired a competence, thanks to our familiarity with the plot-types inherited from our culture.

37. "The Interaction of Semiotic Constraints," p. 87.

38. I discuss the question of the logical structure of the semiotic square in two long notes (numbers 4 and 11) to my essay, "La grammaire narrative de Greimas," *Documents de recherches sémio-linguistiques de l'Institut de la langue française* no. 15 (1980): 5–35. The notes are on pp. 29–30 and 32–33.

39. At this stage, narrative sentences and action sentences are indiscernible. Danto's criterion for a narrative sentence is not yet applicable. This is why we can only speak of a program statement at this point.

40. The final statement of the performance—called the attribution—is "the equiva-

lent on the superficial plane of the logical assertion in the basic grammar" (ibid., p. 175). In my essay mentioned above (pp. 8–9), I also discuss the logical pertinence of this equivalence.

41. "A syntax of operators has to be constructed independently of the syntax of operations. A metasemiotic level has to be laid out to justify the transference of values" (ibid).

42. In an interview with Frédéric Nef published in Frédéric Nef et al., *Structures élémentaires de la signification* (Brussels: Complexe, 1976), Greimas asserts, "If we now consider narration in terms of the syntagmatic perspective where each narrative program appears as a process made up of acquisitions and losses of values, of enrichings and impoverishings of a subject, we see that each step taken along the syntagmatic axis corresponds to 'and is defined by' a topological deplacement along the paradigmatic axis" (ibid., p. 25).

43. "Two Friends," in Guy de Maupassant, *Selected Short Stories*, trans. Roger Colet (New York: Penguin Books, 1971), pp. 147–56.

44. The pair sender/receiver extends Propp's concept of a mandate or the concept of an inaugural contract in Greimas's own first actantial model, the contract thanks to which the hero receives the ability to do something. However this pair sender/receiver is now situated on a more radical formal plane. There are, in fact, social and even cosmic senders as well as individual ones.

45. Cf. Jacques Escande, *Le Récepteur face à l'Acte persuasif. Contribution à la théorie de l'interprétation (à partir de l'analyse de textes évangéliques)*, thèse de 3ᵉ cycle en sémantique générale dirigée par A.-J. Greimas (Paris: EPHESS, 1979).

46. *Maupassant* suggests other even more refined distinctions having to do with doing something. The index entry for *faire* at the end of the book gives some idea of the ramifications that theory is called upon to produce by works that are considerably more subtle than are popular tales. It is the distinction between "doing something" and "being" that seems to be to be the one most difficult to maintain within the framework of narrativity inasmuch as it is no longer inscribed within "doing something" alone. What is more, the being which is in question is connected to doing something through the intermediary of the idea of a state or an enduring disposition—for example, joy, which indicates entry into a euphoric state, or the freedom the "two friends," who have been deprived of all ability to do something following their capture by the Prussians, exercise when they choose to be able not to do something, that is, their refusal to obey the Prussian officer, and hence their entering a "state of being free," which is expressed at the end of the story by their ability to die standing upright.

47. See above, note 38.

48. Someone may object that I am confusing anthropomorphic categories from the surface level with human categories from the figurative level (characterized by the existence of goals, motives, and choices), or, in short, with the practical categories I described in volume 1 under the heading mimesis₁. But I doubt that we can define "doing something" without any reference to human action, even if it is only through such categories as the quasi-character, the quasi-plot, and the quasi-event, which I introduced in chapter 6 of that volume.

49. Paul Ricoeur, "Le Discours de l'action," in Paul Ricoeur and Le Centre de Phénoménologie, *La Sémantique de l'action* (Paris: Editions du Centre National de la Recherche Scientifique, 1977), pp. 3–137. Cf. especially Anthony Kenny, *Action, Emotion and Will* (London: Routledge and Kegan Paul, 1963).

50. The situation here is no different from the one described in our examination of Bremond's *Logique du récit*. There, too, the logic of narrative rested upon a phenomenology and a semantics of action, which Bremond called a "metaphysics."

51. Cf. Max Weber, *Economy and Society: An Outline of Interpretive Sociology*,

trans. Ephraim Fischoff et al., (New York: Bedminster Press, 1968; reprinted, Berkeley: University of California Press, 1978), chapter 1, section 8. The preceding categories are those of social action, social relationship, the orientation of action (customs and manners), of legitimate order (convention, law), and the basis of legitimacy (tradition, faith, law).

52. In his interview with Frédéric Nef ("Entretien," p. 25), Greimas says that it is the polemical structure of narration that allows extending the initial paradigmatic articulation of the taxonomic model to the whole syntagmatic unfolding of the narration. By opposing an antisubject to a subject, and an antiprogram to a program, and even by multiplying the actantial squares by splitting every actant into an actant, a not-actant, an antiactant, and a not-antiactant, the polemical structure assures the infiltration of the paradigmatic order into the whole syntagmatic order. There is "nothing surprising therefore about the fact that the analysis of even the least complex texts requires a multiplying of the actantial positions which reveal in this way, on the side of the syntagmatic unfolding, the paradigmatic articulation of narrativity" (ibid., p. 24). But we might also put it the opposite way. Because something happens as a conflict between two subjects, we can project this on the square. And this projection is possible in turn because this square itself has been treated "as the place where the logical operations occur" (ibid., p. 26); in short, because it has already been narrativized. All progress in applying the square of opposition—*la carréfication*—from one level to another, may then appear as the step-by-step advance of the paradigmatic into the heart of the syntagmatic, or as the addition of new syntagmatic dimensions (quest, struggle, etc.), secretly directed by the double paradigmatic and syntagmatic structure of the completed narrative.

53. As regards the coherence of the topological syntax as such, and the role attributed to the relationship of presupposition that brings the traversal of the corners of the semiotic square back to its beginning, cf. my "La grammaire narrative de Greimas," pp. 22–24.

54. Greimas comes close to acknowledging this later in his interview with Nef. "However it is only a question here of a syntax manipulating, with the help of disjunctions and conjunctions, statements about *states of affairs*, which only give the narrative a static representation of a series of narrative states of affairs. Since the taxonomic square ought only to be considered as the place where the logical operations take place, the series of statements about the states of affairs are organized and manipulated by the statements about doing something and by the transformative subjects inscribed in them" ("Entretien," p. 26).

CHAPTER THREE

1. As early as the medieval philosophers we find the wholehearted assertion of the reflective nature of judgment. It is Kant, however, who introduces the fruitful distinction between a determining judgment and a reflective one. A determining judgment is wholly caught up in the objectivity it produces. A reflective judgment turns back upon the operations through which it constructs aesthetic and organic forms on the basis of the causal chain of events in the world. In this sense, narrative forms constitute a third class of reflective judgment, that is, a judgment capable of taking as its object the very sort of teleological operations by which aesthetic and organic entities take shape.

2. Emile Benveniste, "The Correlations of Tense in the French Verb," in his *Problems in General Linguistics*, trans. Mary Elizabeth Meek (Coral Gables, Florida: University of Miami Press, 1977), pp. 205–15; Käte Hamburger, *The Logic of Literature*, 2nd., rev. ed., trans. Marilynn J. Rose (Bloomington: Indiana University Press, 1973); Harald Weinrich, *Tempus: Besprochene und erzählte Welt* (Stuttgart: Kohlhammer,

1964). I shall cite the French translation by Michèle Lacoste, *Le Temps: le récit et le commentaire* (Paris: Seuil, 1973), which is, in fact, an original work by the author for the divisions and analyses often differ from the German text.

3. Benveniste's hesitation in this regard is instructive. Having repeated that "In order for them to be recorded as having occurred, these events must belong to the past," (ibid., p. 206), he adds, "No doubt it would be better to say that they are characterized as past from the time they have been recorded and uttered in a historical temporal expression" (ibid.). The criterion of the speaker's nonintervention in the narrative allows him to pass over the question whether it is the time of the narrative that produces the effect of being past, or whether the quasi-past of the fictional narrative has some connection with the real past in the sense the historian gives this term.

4. As a matter of fact, the separation between verb tenses and lived time is presented by Benveniste with a certain amount of prudence: "In the idea of time alone, we do not find the criterion that will decide the position or even the possibility of a given form with the verbal system" (ibid., p. 205). The analysis of compound forms, to which a large part of his essay is devoted, poses similar problems concerning the notion of action that is completed or not completed and that of the anteriority of an event in relation to another reported event. The question remains whether these grammatical forms can be entirely disconnected from relations connected to time.

5. Benveniste is joined on this point by Roland Barthes in his *Le Degré zéro de l'écriture*. (Roland Barthes, *Writing Degree Zero and Elements of Semiology*, trans. Annette Lavers and Colin Smith [Boston: Beacon Press, 1976].) For Barthes, the use of the preterite connotes the literary character of the narrative more than it denotes the pastness of the action. Cf. also Gérard Genette, *Nouveau Discours du récit*, p. 53. A study should be done of the implications for narrative theory of the linguistics of Gustave Guillaume presented in his *Temps et Verbe* (Paris: Champion, 1929, 1965). He opens the door to such study by distinguishing operations of thinking behind every architonic of time. He distinguishes, for example, on the level of modes, the passage of time *in posse* (the infinitive and participle modes), then time *in fieri* (the subjunctive mode), and finally time *in esse* (the indicative mode). The distinction, on the level of time *in esse*, of two species of the present—of two "chronotypes" (ibid., p. 52)—the one real, and decadent, the other virtual and incidental, is at the heart of this chronogenesis. André Jacob, *Temps et Langage: Essai sur les structures du sujet parlant* (Paris: Armand Colin, 1967), has gone another step in the direction of the inquiry I am suggesting with his operative conception of language, directed toward a general anthropology wherein the constitution of human time and of the speaking subject intersect.

6. Hamburger uses the general term *Dichtung* to designate the three great genres: epic, drama, and lyric. Epic covers the entire narrative domain, drama covers that of action brought on stage by characters who dialogue in front of the spectators, and lyric is the expression, using poetic techniques, of the thoughts and feelings experienced by the writer. Only the epic and dramatic genres, then, belong to fiction, epic still being called mimetic, with Plato in mind. Employed in this sense, the term "epic" recalls how it was used in the discussion between Goethe and Schiller on the comparable merits of the two genres: "Uber epische und dramatische Dichtung" (1797) in W. Goethe, *Sämtliche Werke* (Stuttgart and Berlin: Jubliläums-Ausgabe, 1902–07), vol. 36, pp. 149–52. It should be noted that in this comparison the "perfect past" (*vollkommen vergangen*) of the epic is opposed to the "perfect present" (*vollkommen gegenwärtig*) of drama. The novel is not at issue, unless it be as a modern variety of the epic, which explains Hamburger's terminology.

7. The "absence of the Real I-Origo and the functional character of fictional narration are one and the same phenomenon" (*The Logic of Fiction*, p. 137). The introduc-

tion of a personified fictive narrator would, in Hamburger's eyes, weaken the break between narrating and asserting. Thus she is obliged to maintain that the field of fiction "is not the range of experience of a narrator but the product of the narrative function" (ibid., p. 230). Between the author and his or her fictive characters there is no place for another I-Origo.

8. I cannot give here the reasons why the narrator is held to be a fictive subject of discourse irreducible to a mere neutral function (*das Erzählen*). I shall take up this problem again below in my discussion of the concepts of "point of view" and "voice."

9. Another problem dealt with by Hamburger, that of the tenses in free indirect discourse or narrated monologue (*erlebte Rede*), calls for the same kind of supplementary explication. In *erlebte Rede* the words of a character are reported in the third person and in the past tense, unlike in the reported monologue where the character expresses himself or herself in the first person and in the present tense. For example, in *Mrs. Dalloway*, we read, "He dropped her hand. Their marriage was over, he thought, with agony, with relief. The rope was cut; he mounted; he was free, as it was decreed that he, Septimus, the lord of men, should be free; alone . . . he, Septimus was alone. . . ." Hamburger sees in this the confirmation that the grammatical past does not signify the past, since the words belong to the fictive present—a timeless present too, by the way—of the character. She is not mistaken in this, if by past we can only mean the "real" past, relating to memory or to history. The *erlebte Rede* is more thoroughly explained, however, if it is interpreted as the translation of the discourse of a character into the discourse of the narrator, where the latter imposes her/his tense and narration in the third-person. The narrator must then be held to be a subject of discourse in fiction. I shall return to this problem below in terms of a dialectic of the narrator and the character in first- as well as in third-person fiction.

10. My argument cannot be complete until we have introduced the ideas of "point of view" and of "voice." The epic preterite will then be able to be interpreted as the fictive past of the narrative voice.

11. By "text" Weinrich means "a meaningful succession of linguistic signs between two obvious breaks in communication" (*Le Temps*, p. 13), such as the pauses in spoken communication, or the two covers of a book in written communication, or, finally, "cuts that are introduced deliberately and which, in a metalinguistic sense, smooth over obvious breaks in communication" (ibid.). The types of opening and closing characteristic of narrative are, in this respect, "cuts that are introduced deliberately."

12. I found it difficult to follow the French translator of *Tempus*, who translates *Besprechung* by *commentaire* (commentary), but finally decided to do so. This term does not take into account the "attitude of tension" characteristic of this type of communication. To a French ear, there is more detachment in the reception of a commentary than in that of a narrative. On the other hand, translating *Besprechung* by *débat* (debate, discussion) which seems preferable to me, introduces a polemical note which itself is unnecessary. Nevertheless we can "debate" or discuss something without an adversary.

13. Another enumeration is also offered. On the side of commentary are listed "poetry, drama, dialogue in general, a journal, literary criticism, scientific description" (ibid., p. 39). On the side of narrative are "the short story, the novel, and narratives of all kinds (except for dialogues)" (ibid.). What is important is that this division has nothing in common with a classification of forms of discourse in terms of "genres."

14. Weinrich notes that "the idea of tension . . . has only very recently penetrated poetics under the influence of an informational aesthetics, through notions such as 'suspense'" (ibid., p. 35). He is referring here to Todorov's *The Poetics of Prose*.

15. "The boundary between poetry and truth does not correspond to that between narrated world and commented world. The commented world has its truth (the con-

traries here are error and lies) and the narrated world has its truth as well (the contrary here is fiction). In the same way, both have their poetry. For the former it is lyric poetry and drama, for the latter the epic" (ibid., p. 104). Drama and epic poetry are once again separated, as they were in Aristotle's *Poetics*.

16. I suggest in this connection that the notion of a long time-span in Braudel be compared with Weinrich's notion of a background. The distribution of temporality in terms of three levels is wholly a work of putting-into-relief.

17. I have said nothing here about the complementary role played by other syntactic signals that have a temporal value, such as pronouns, adverbs, etc. According to Weinrich, establishing whether distributional regularities are displayed in the form of privileged combinations is a task belonging to a general survey of combinations. The affinity of the preterite with the third-person is well-known, following Benveniste's celebrated article. The affinity of certain adverbs of time such as "yesterday," "at this moment," "tomorrow," and so on, with tenses of commentary and others such as "the day before," "at that moment," "the following day," and so on, with tenses of narrative is just as noteworthy. Even more so, in my opinion, is the affinity of many adverbial phrases with tenses that put-into-relief. Their abundance is particularly striking. Weinrich enumerates more than forty of them in a single chapter of Flaubert's *Madame Bovary* (ibid., p. 268) and almost as many in a chapter from Malraux's *la Voie royal*. So many adverbs for just two tenses! To which must be added the adverbs that mark narrative tempo: "sometimes," "at times," "from time to time," "always," etc., in combination, generally, with the imperfect. Finally, "all at once," "suddenly," "abruptly," etc. are most often found in combination with the preterite. Added to this are all the adverbs replying to the question "When?" or "to an analogous question connected to Time" (ibid., p. 270): "sometimes," "often," "finally," "next," "then," "always," "once more," "already," "now," "this time," "one more time," "little by little," "all of a sudden," "one after the other," "unceasingly," and so on. This abundance suggests that adverbs and adverbial phrases weave a considerably finer network for the schematiziation of the narrated world than do the verbs with which they are combined.

18. Temporal transitions also draw assistance from the combination of tenses and adverbs. What is true of the paradigmatic aspect of the problem applies even more to the syntagmatic one. The adverbs mentioned above are more aptly described as accompanying temporal transitions, reinforcing them, and making them more precise. In this way, the adverbs—"now," "then," "once," "one morning," "one evening"—stress the heterogeneous transition from background (imperfect) to foreground (preterite), while "and then," as an adverb of narrative sequence, is better suited to homogeneous transitions within the narrated world. I shall discuss below the resources this syntax of narrative transitions offers for the utterance of narrative configurations.

19. What Weinrich says of the notions of opening, closing, and simulated end (so subtly marked by Maupassant, for example, using what has been termed the imperfect tense of rupture) should be noted once again in this regard. Here, the narrative's relief is indistinguishable from the narrative structure itself.

20. Cf., for example, Edmund Husserl, *Ideas Pertaining to a Pure Phenomenology and to a Phenomenological Philosophy. First Book: General Introduction to a Pure Phenomenology*, trans. F. Kersten (The Hague: Martinus Nijhoff, 1982) §109, "The Neutrality Modification," pp. 257–59.

21. Eugen Fink, *De la Phénoménologie*, trans. Didier Franck (Paris: Minuit, 1974), pp. 15–93. The German original, "Vergegenwärtigen und Bild: Beitrage zur Phänomenologie der Unwirklichkeit," is available in Eugene Fink, *Studien zur Phänomenologie, 1930–1939* (The Hague: Martinus Nijhoff, 1966), pp. 1–78.

22. This problem will be discussed further in the concluding chapter of this volume.

23. The notion of narrative voice will below (cf. p. 98) provide a more complete response to what is at issue here.

24. This can be connected to Greimas's semiotics, with regard to what he calls the "aspectuality" of transformations, which he places (it will be recalled) half-way between the logical-semantic plane and the properly discursive plane. To express this aspectuality, language has available to it expressions about duration (and about frequency) and expressions about events. In addition, it marks the transitions from permanence to incidental occurrences by means of the features of inchoativity and terminativity.

25. Other syntactic signs, such as adverbs and adverbial phrases, the abundance and variety of which we referred to above, reinforce the expressive power of the tenses.

26. The remarks that follow are in close harmony with my interpretation of metaphorical discourse as the "redescription" of reality in the seventh and eighth studies of my *Rule of Metaphor*.

27. I shall attempt below, at my own risk, to interpret *Der Zauberberg* from the point of view of the experience of time, which this *Zeitroman* projects beyond itself, without ceasing to be a fiction.

28. *Morphologische Poetik*, ed. Elena Müller (Tubingen: M. Niemeyer, 1968) is the title that was adopted by Müller for a collection of his essays dating from 1964–68.

29. It is worth recalling that Propp was also inspired by Goethe, as we saw in chapter 2.

30. Goethe himself is at the origin of this ambiguous relation between art and nature. On the one hand, he writes, "Kunst ist eine andere Natur." But he also says that "Kunst . . . is eine eigene Weltgegend [an original region of the world]" (cited by Müller, p. 289). The second conception opens the way for Goethe's formal investigations into narrative, to which we owe his well-known "schema" of the *Iliad*. Müller refers to this as a model for his own investigations (cf. ibid., pp. 270, 280, 409). Cf. also "Goethes Morphologie in ihrer Bedeutung für die Dichtungskunde" (ibid., pp. 287–98).

31. The term *Aussparung* emphasizes both what is omitted (life itself, as we shall see) and what is retained, chosen, or picked out. The French word *épargne* sometimes has these two meanings: what is spared is what is available to someone and it is also what is not touched, as when we say that a village was spared by (*épargné par*) the bombing. The word "savings" (*l'épargne*), precisely, includes what is put aside for one to make use of and what is left aside and sheltered.

32. Müller is somewhat ill at ease in speaking of this time of the narrative in itself, which is neither narrated nor read, a sort of disembodied time, measured by the number of pages, in order to distinguish it from the time of reading, to which each reader contributes his own *Lesetempo* (ibid., p. 275).

33. For example, the study of Goethe's *Lehrejahre* begins with a comparison between the 650 pages taken as "the measure of the physical time required by the narrator to tell his story" (ibid., p. 270) and the eight years covered by the narrated events. It is, however, the incessant variations in relative lengths that create the work's tempo. I shall say nothing here of his study of *Mrs. Dalloway*, as I give an interpretation of it in the next chapter that takes account of Müller's careful analysis of the insertions and the internal digressions, so to speak, that allow the depth of remembered time to rise to the surface of the narrated time. Müller also begins his study of the *Forsyte Saga*, a typical example of the "family history novel," with careful quantitative analysis. In 1100 pages the novel covers a span of forty years. In this vast interval of time the author has isolated five periods ranging from a few days, to a few months, to two years. Returning to the grand scheme of the *Iliad* proposed by Goethe, Müller reconstructs the temporal schema of Volume II of the *Forsyte Saga*, with its specific dates and its reference to days of the week.

34. A detailed analysis of the highly technical nature of these varied processes of narrative composition may be found in the studies dealing with the "Zeitgerüst des Erzählens" in Jürg Jenatsch (ibid., pp. 388–418) and with "Zeitgerüst des Fortunatus-Volksbuch" (ibid., pp. 570–89).

35. This intending of the time of life through narrated time is finally what is at stake in each of the brief monographs referred to above. It is said that the relation between the two temporal orders in the *Lehrejahr* "suits" (*fügt sich*) or is adapted to the particular object of the narrative, human metamorphosis and *Ubergänglichkeit* (ibid., p. 271). As a result, the *Gestaltsinn* of this poetic work is not arbitrary and makes the apprenticeship—*Bildung*—analogous to the biological process that generates living forms. The same thing can be said about the "family history novel." But, whereas in the *Bildungsroman* of Lessing and Goethe, the upsurge of vital forces governs the metamorphosis of a living being, Galsworthy's family history novel strives to show the aging, the necessary return to darkness, and, beyond the fate of the individual, the ascension of new life through which time reveals itself to be both salvific and destructive. In the three examples referred to, "the putting into form of narrated time has to do with the domain of reality that is manifested in the *Gestalt* of a narrative poetry [*einer erzählenden Dichtung*]" (ibid., p. 285). The relation and the tension existing between the time taken to narrate and narrated time are thus referred back to something that, over and beyond the narrative, is not narrative but life. Narrated time is itself defined as *Raffung* with respect to the ground against which it stands out, namely, nature as unmeaningful, or rather as indifferent to meaning.

36. In another essay in the same collection, "Zeiterlebnis und Zeitgerüst," Müller introduces another pair of terms indicated by the title (ibid., pp. 229–311). The "armature of time" is the interplay between the time taken to narrate and narrated time. As for the lived experience of time, it is, in Husserlian terminology, the ground of life indifferent to meaning. No intuition gives the meaning of this time, which is never more than interpreted, intended indirectly by the analysis of the *Zeitgerüst*. New examples taken from authors who are concerned with the stakes as well as with the game show this even more clearly. For one, Andreas Gruphius, time is only a chain of disconnected instants, which the reference to eternity alone saves from nothingness. For others, such as Schiller and Goethe, it is the very course of world time that constitutes eternity. For another, Hofmannsthal, time is strangeness itself, the immensity that swallows everything up. For another, Thomas Mann, time is the numinous par excellence. With each of these authors we touch upon the "*poietische Dimension*" of "lived" time (ibid., p. 303).

37. In the essay "Uber die Zeitgerüst des Erzählens", we read, "Since Joseph Conrad, Joyce, Virginia Woolf, Proust, Faulkner, the way in which the evolution of time is handled has become a central problem in epic representation, a terrain for narrative experimentation, in which it is first of all a matter not of speculation on time but of the 'art of narrating'" (ibid., p. 392). This avowal does not imply that temporal "experience" ceases to be what is at stake, but that the game takes precedence over the stakes. Genette will draw a more radical consequence from this reversal. Müller does not seem inclined to reduce the stakes to the game. The focus put on the art of narrating results from the fact that the narrator does not have to speculate about time in order to intend this poetic time; this is done by giving a configuration to narrated time.

38. Gérard Genette, "Frontiers of Narrative," in *Figures of Literary Discourse*, trans. Alan Sheridan (New York: Columbia University Press, 1982), pp. 127–44; *Narrative Discourse: An Essay in Method*, trans. Jane E. Lewin (Ithaca: Cornell University Press, 1980); *Nouveau Discours du récit* (Paris: Seuil, 1983).

39. The term "diegesis" (*diégèse*) is borrowed from Etienne Souriau, who first proposed it in 1948, in order to oppose the place of the signified in film to the screen-universe as the place of the signifier. Genette specifies, in *Nouveau Discours du récit*,

that the adjective "diegetic" is constructed on the model of the substantive "diégèse," without reference to Plato's *diegesis* which Genette assures us in his 1983 work, "has nothing to do with diegesis" (*diégèse*) (ibid., p. 113). In fact Genette had himself referred to Plato's famous text in his "Frontiers of Narrative" (p. 128). His intention then, however, was polemical. For it was a question of getting rid of the Aristotelian problem of mimesis, identified with the illusion of reality created by the representation of action. "Literary representation, the mimesis of the ancients . . . is narrative, and only narrative. . . . *Mimesis is diegesis*" (ibid., pp. 132–33, his emphasis). The question is taken up more briefly in *Narrative Discourse* (pp. 162–66). "Language signifies without imitating" (ibid., p. 164). To avoid any equivocation, however, it should be recalled that in the *Republic*, III, 392c, Plato does not oppose diegesis to mimesis. Diegesis is the only generic term discussed. It is divided into "plain" diegesis when the poet narrates events or discourse with his own voice and diegesis "by imitation" (*dia mimēseōs*) when the poet speaks as if he were someone else, simulating as much as possible the voice of this other person, which is equivalent to imitating it. The relationship between diegesis and mimesis is just the opposite in Aristotle, for whom *mimēsis praxeōs* is the generic term and diegesis the subordinate "mode." We have constantly to be on guard, therefore, against letting these two kinds of terminology become superimposed, since they have to do with two different kinds of usage. Cf. *Time and Narrative*, vol. 1, pp. 33–34 and 238, n. 14.

40. Narrative theory has never, in fact, stopped oscillating between bipartition and tripartition. The Russian formalists recognize the distinction between *sjužet* and *fabula*, the subject and the tale. For Schklovsky, the tale designates the material used in forming the subject; the subject of *Eugene Onegin*, for example, is the elaboration of the tale, and hence a construction. Cf. *Théorie de la littérature. Textes des formalistes russes*, collected, presented, and translated by Tzvetan Todorov, Preface by Roman Jakobson (Paris: Seuil, 1965), pp. 54–55. Tomaschevski adds that the development of the tale may be characterized as "the passage from one situation to another" (ibid., p. 273). The subject is what the reader perceives as resulting from the techniques of composition (ibid., p. 208). In a similar sense, Todorov himself makes a distinction between discourse and story ("Les catégories du récit littéraire"). Bremond uses the terms "narrating narrative" and "narrated narrative" (*Logique de récit*, p. 321, n. 1). Cesare Segre, however, proposes the triad: discourse (signifier), plot (the signified in the order of literary composition), and fabula (the signified in the logical and chronological order of events) (*Structures and Time: Narration, Poetry, Models*, trans. John Meddemmen [Chicago: University of Chicago Press, 1979]). It is thus time, considered as the irreversible order of succession, that serves as the discriminating factor. The time of discourse is that of reading, the time of plot that of the literary composition, and the time of the fabula that of the events recounted. On the whole, the pairs subject/tale (Schklovsky, Tomashevski), discourse/story (Todorov), and narrative/story (Genette) correspond rather well. Their reinterpretation in Saussurean terms constitutes the difference between the Russian and the French formalists. Ought we to say then that the reappearance of a tripartition (in Cesare Segre and Genette himself) marks the return to a Stoic triad: what signifies, what is signified, what occurs?

41. "One of the objects of this study would be to list and classify the means by which narrative literature (and in particular the novel) has tried to organize in an acceptable way, within its own *lexis*, the delicate relations maintained within it between the requirements of narrative and the necessities of discourse" ("Frontiers," p. 142). *Nouveau Discours du récit* is clear and unequivocal in this regard: a narrative without a narrator is simply impossible. This would be a statement without utterance, hence without any act of communication (ibid., p. 68). Whence the very title "Discours du récit."

42. On these complex relations, cf. the various attempts at ordering proposed by Seymour Chatman, *Story and Discourse: Narrative Structure in Fiction* (Ithaca: Cornell University Press, 1978); Gerald Prince, *Narratology: The Form and Function of Narrative* (The Hague: Mouton, 1982); Shlomith Rimmon-Kenan, *Narrative Fiction: Contemporary Poetics* (New York: Methuen, 1983).

43. We might wonder in this regard if the time of reading, from which the time of the narrative is borrowed, does not belong for this reason to the plane of utterance, and if the transposition brought about through the metonymy does not conceal this filiation by projecting onto the plane of the statement what rightfully belongs to the plane of utterance. In addition, I would not call this a pseudo-time, but precisely a fictive time, so closely is it tied, for narrative understanding, to the temporal configurations of fiction. I would say that the fictional is transposed into the pseudo when narrative understanding is replaced by the rationalizing simulation that characterizes the epistemological level of narratology, an operation that I reemphasize once again is both legitimate and of a derivative nature. *Nouveau Discours du récit* makes this more precise: "the time of the (written) narrative is a 'pseudo-time' in the sense that it exists empirically for the reader of a text-space that only reading can (re)convert into duration" (ibid., p. 15).

44. The study of anachronies (prolepsis, analepsis, and their combinations) may be superimposed rather easily on Harald Weinrich's study of "perspective" (anticipation, retrospection, zero degree).

45. I refer the reader here to the lovely page in *Narrative Discourse* where Genette evokes Marcel's general "play" with the principal episodes of his existence, "which until then were lost to significance because of their dispersion and are now suddenly reassembled, now made significant by being bound all together. . . . chance, contingency, arbitrariness now suddenly wiped out, his life's portrait is now suddenly 'captured' in the web of a structure and the cohesiveness of a meaning" (ibid., pp. 56–67).

46. The reader cannot help comparing this remark by Genette to Müller's use of the notion of *Sinngehalt*, discussed above, as well as the opposition between meaningful and unmeaningful (or indifferent) inherited from Goethe. This opposition, in my opinion, is entirely different from the opposition between signifier and signified coming from Saussure.

47. Cf. Auerbach, *Mimesis*, p. 544, cited by Genette, *Narrative Discourse*, p. 70.

48. Genette readily admits that to "the extent that they bring the narrating instance itself directly into play, these anticipations in the present constitute not only data of narrative temporality but also data of *voice*: we will meet them later under that heading" (ibid., p. 70).

49. The notion of *Raffung* in Müller, therefore, finds an equivalent here in that of acceleration.

50. "The duration of these contemplative halts is generally such that it is in no danger of being exceeded by the duration of the reading (even a very slow reading) of the text that 'tells of' them" (ibid., p. 102).

51. In his *Maupassant*, Greimas introduces the same categories of the iterative and the singulative, and, in order to account for them, adopts the grammatical category of "aspect." The alternation of iterative and singulative also forms a parallel with Weinrich's category of "putting into relief."

52. Genette quotes the beautiful page from *The Captive* where we read, "This ideal morning filled my mind full of a permanent reality, identical with all similar mornings, and infected me with . . . cheerfulness" (cited by Genette, ibid., p. 124).

53. Genette is, moreover, the first to "deplore this quartering of the problems of narrative temporality" (ibid., p. 157, n. 88). But are there grounds for saying that "any other distribution would have the effect of underestimating the importance and

the specificity of the narrating instance"? (ibid.).

54. However, if the temporality of the narration governs that of the narrative, we cannot speak of the "game with time" in the work of Proust, as Genette does in his decisive pages (pp. 155–60), which I shall discuss below, until we have considered utterance and the time that goes along with it, thereby preventing the analyses of temporality from being pulled in so many directions at once.

55. E. Vendryes, for example, defined "voice" as: "a mode of action of the verb in its relation with the subject" (quoted by Genette, ibid., p. 31). *Nouveau Discours du récit* adds no new element concerning the time of utterance and the relation between voice and utterance. On the other hand, this text contains a wealth of observations concerning the distinction between the question of voice—Who is speaking?—and the question of perspective—Who is looking?—the latter being reformulated in terms of "focalization"—Where is the focus of perception? Cf. ibid., pp. 43–52.

56. As I stated above, the principal weight of the analysis of the time of the narrative in *Remembrance* bears on the relation between narrative and diegesis, a relation that is examined in the first three chapters under the headings of "order," "duration," and "frequency" (*Narrative Discourse*, pp. 33–161), while only a few of the pages dealing with "voice" (ibid., pp. 215–27) are, as an afterthought, reserved for the time of narration. This disproportion is partly explained by the addition of the triad time, mood, voice, borrowed from the grammar of verbs, to the threefold division into utterance, statement, and object. It is finally these three new classes that determine the order of the chapters on narrative discourse. "The first three (Order, Duration, Frequency) deal with time; the fourth, with mood; the fifth and last, with voice" (ibid., p. 32, n. 13). A certain amount of competition can be observed between the two schemata, such that "*tense* and *mood* both operate on the level of connections between *story* and *narrative*, while *voice* designates the connections between *narrating* and *narrative* and between *narrating* and *story*" (ibid., p. 32, his emphases). This competition explains why the main emphasis is placed on the relation between the time of the narrative and the time of the story, and why the time of the utterance is treated in less detail, in the discussion of voice in the last chapter.

57. "There is simply the narrative's halt at the point when the hero has discovered the truth and the meaning of his life: at the point, therefore when this 'story of a vocation'—which, let us remember, is the avowed subject of Proustian narrative—comes to an end. . . . So it is necessary that the narrative be interrupted before the hero overtakes the narrator; it is inconceivable for them both to write together: The End" (ibid., pp. 226–27).

58. We ought to be able to say of the metaphysical experience of time in *Remembrance of Things Past* exactly what Genette says of the "I" of the book's hero, namely, that he is neither entirely Proust nor entirely another. This is by no means a "return to the self," a "presence to the self" that would be postulated by an experience expressed in the fictional mode, but instead a "semi-homonymy" between real experience and fictive experience, similar to that which the narratologist discerns between the hero-narrator and the work's signatory (cf. ibid., pp. 251–52).

59. We saw above the grammatial means through which Genette introduces these notions in *Narrative Discourse*. Below, we shall examine what he adds to this in his *Nouveau Discours du récit*.

60. If I do not engage in a detailed discussion here of the concept of "implied author" introduced by Wayne Booth in his *Rhetoric of Fiction* (Chicago: University of Chicago Press, 1961), this is due to the distinction I am making between the contribution of voice and point of view to the (internal) composition of the work and their role in (external) communication. It is not without reason that Booth places his analysis of the implied author under the auspices of a rhetoric and a poetics of fiction. This is why

I am reserving my discussion of the implied narrator for a later analysis of the relation of the work to the reader. It goes without saying, nonetheless, that all my analyses concerning the narrator's discourse are incomplete until they have been connected with a rhetoric of fiction that I shall incorporate into the theory of reading to be present in Part IV in volume 3.

61. On the triad plot, character, thought in Aristotle's *Poetics*, cf. *Time and Narrative*, vol. 1, pp. 36–42.

62. We have examined above Käte Hamburger's contribution to the theory of verb tenses. However, if the epic preterite (that is, the diegetic preterite) loses, in her opinion, its power to signify real time, this is because this preterite is linked to mental verbs designating the action of *Ich-Origos* that are themselves fictive.

63. It is "epic persons," (*epische Personen*) she says, that "render a piece of narrative literature just that" (ibid., p. 63). Also, "epic fiction is the sole epistemological instance where the I-originarity (or subjectivity) of a third person *qua* third person can be portrayed [*dargestellt*]" (ibid., p. 83).

64. Dorrit Cohn, *Transparent Minds: Narrative Modes for Presenting Consciousness in Fiction* (Princeton: Princeton University Press, 1978).

65. In first-person narrative fiction, the narrator and the main character are one and the same; but only in autobiography are the author, the narrator, and the main character the same. Cf. Philippe Lejeune, *Le Pacte autobiographique* (Paris: Seuil, 1975). I shall, therefore, not consider autobiography here. However, I ought not to avoid referring to it in the context of the refiguration of time performed jointly by history and fiction. It is actually the only place that can be assigned to autobiography by the strategy operating in *Time and Narrative*.

66. Two of the texts I will study in the next chapter—*Mrs. Dalloway* and *The Magic Mountain*—are third-person fictional narratives. The third is a first-person fictional narrative, *Remembrance of Things Past*, which includes a narrative in the third-person, *Swann in Love*. The equally fictive character of the "I" and the "he" is a powerful factor in integrating one narrative within the other. As concerns the permutation between the "I" and the "he," *Jean Santeuil* (trans. Gerard Hopkins [London: Weidenfeld & Nicolson, 1955]) stands as unimpeachable evidence. This exchange of personal pronouns does not signify that the choice of one technique or the other is not based on concrete reasons or that it is without particular narrative effects. It is not my purpose to weigh the advantages and drawbacks of these two narrative strategies.

67. "All comprehension is imagination" (Jean Pouillon, *Temps et Roman* [Paris: Gallimard, 1945], p. 45).

68. Cf. Robert Alter, *Partial Magic: The Novel as a Self-Conscious Genre* (Berkeley: University of California Press, 1975).

69. Quotation marks generally serve as a guide here. But this sort of mark may be missing in the contemporary novel. Nevertheless the quoted or self-quoted monologue respects the grammatical tense (usually the present) and the person (the first person) and consists in an interruption of the narrative by the character, who then speaks. The text tends toward unreadability when these two marks are avoided, as in Joyce's successors.

70. Pouillon's *Temps et Roman* anticipates the typology of narrative situations with its distinction between seeing "with," seeing "from behind," and seeing "from outside." However, unlike more recent analyses, it takes as its basis not the dissimilarity but the deep kinship between narrative fiction and "real psychological understanding" (ibid., p. 69). In both cases, understanding is the work of the imagination. It is therefore essential to move, in turn, from psychology to the novel and from the novel to psychology (ibid., p. 71). Nonetheless, a certain privilege is given to self-understanding, to the extent that "the author of a novel tries to give the reader the same

understanding of the characters as the reader has of himself or of herself" (ibid., p. 69). This privilege runs through the proposed categorization. For example, since all understanding consists in grasping an inside through an outside, seeing "from outside" suffers from the same drawbacks as behaviorist psychology, which thinks it can infer the inside on the basis of the outside, and even contests the relevance of the notion of "inside." As for seeing "with" and seeing "from behind," they correspond to two other uses of the imagination in understanding. In one case, it shares "with" the character the same unreflective self-consciousness (ibid., p. 80); in the other, the seeing is "disconnected," not in the same way as in seeing "from outside," but in the way that reflection objectifies unreflective consciousness (ibid., p. 85). Thus, for Pouillon, the distinction between the narrator's point of view and that of the character, which is taken directly from novelistic technique, remains closely related to the distinction, coming from Sartre, between prereflective and reflective consciousness. On the other hand, the most lasting contribution made by Pouillon seems to me to be that of the second part of his work, "The Expression of Time." The distinction he makes there between "novels of duration" and "novels of eternity" is directly related to what I am calling here the fictive experience of time (cf. below, chapter 4).

71. Franz Stanzel, *Narrative Situations in the Novel: Tom Jones, Moby-Dick, The Ambassadors, Ulysses*, trans. James P. Pusack (Bloomington: Indiana University Press, 1971). A more dynamic, less taxonomical, reformulation can be found in idem, *Theorie des Erzählens* (Gottigen: Van den Hoeck & Rubrecht, 1979). The first monograph devoted to this problem was Käte Friedmann, *Die Rolle des Erzählers in der Epik* (Leipzig, 1910).

72. The term *Mittelbarkeit* preserves a dual meaning. By offering a "medium" for presenting the character, literature "transmits" the content of the fiction to the reader.

73. "Author" is always taken here in the sense of narrator, that is, the internal locutor responsible for the composition of the work.

74. Cf. Jonathan Culler, "Defining Narrative Units," in Roger Fowler, ed., *Style and Structure in Literature: Essays in The New Stylistics* (Ithaca: Cornell University Press, 1975), pp. 123–42.

75. Seymour Chatman, in "The Structure of Narrative Transmission" (in *Style and Literature*, pp. 213–57), attempts to account for the reader's competence on the basis of an open-ended list of "discursive features" that are isolated in the same way as are the inventories of illocutionary force in speech acts by John Austin and John Searle. This is a plausible alternative to the search for taxonomies that would be both systematic and dynamic.

76. One attempt that is particularly careful to combine the systematic emphasis of typology with the power to produce ever more varied "narrative modes" is sketched out by Ludomir Doležel in "The Typology of the Narrator: Point of View in Fiction," in *To Honor Roman Jakobson*, vol. 1 (The Hague: Mouton, 1967), pp. 541–52. Unlike Stanzel's typology, Doležel's rests on a series of dichotomies, beginning with the most general one, that of texts with or without a locutor. This first kind can be distinguished through a certain number of "marks"—the use of personal pronouns, verb tenses and appropriate diegetic levels, the relation of allocution, subjective implication, personal style. The second kind are "unmarked" in various ways. Narrations that are said to be "objective" belong to this category. Texts with locutors are divided according to whether the above-mentioned marks characterize the locutor as narrator or as character (narrator's speech vs. characters' speech). After this follows the distinction between areas of activity (or passivity) as regards the narrator. Finally, all these dichotomies include as well that between *Er-* and *Ich-Erzählung*. Doležel's typology is further developed in his *Narrative Modes in Czech Literature* (Toronto: University of Toronto Press, 1973). It adds to the preceding study a structural analysis of the narrative modes that can be assigned either to the narrator's speech or to that of the charac-

ters. These modes are distinguished on a textual basis that is as independent as possible of anthropological terminology ("omniscient" narrator and so forth). In this way, the narrator exercizes the functions of "representing" events, "mastering" the textual structure, "interpretation," and "action," in correlation with the character who exercizes the same functions in inverse proportion. By combining these features with the major division between *Er-* and *Ich-Erzählung*, and by completing the functional model with a verbal one, a model is obtained in which the binary divisions extend the initial dichotomy between the narrator's speech and the character's speech. The detailed study of prose narrative in modern Czech literature (in particular, Kundera) permits the dynamism in the model to unfold by adapting it to the variety of styles encountered in the works considered. The notion of point of view is thus identified with the schematism resulting from this series of dichotomies. What I said earlier with respect to the structural analyses studied in Chapter 2 may also be applied to this analysis, heir to Russian and Prague Structuralism, namely, that it results from a second-order rationality that makes explicit the deep logic of first-order narrative understanding. The dependence of the former with respect to the latter, and the acquired competence of the reader that expresses it, seems to me to be more obvious in a typology of the narrator than in a typology in the manner of Propp, based on the actions imitated by fiction, due to the irreducibly anthropomorphic character of the roles of narrator and character. The first is someone who recounts something, the second someone who acts, thinks, feels, and speaks.

77. Cf. Boris Uspensky, *A Poetics of Composition: The Structure of the Artistic Text and a Typology of Compositional Form*, trans. Valentina Zavanin and Susan Wittig (Berkeley: University of California Press, 1973). Uspensky defines his undertaking as a "typology of compositional options in literature as they pertain to point of view" (ibid., p. 5). This is a typology but not a taxonomy, inasmuch as it does not claim to be exhaustive or closed. Point of view is only one of the ways to reach the articulation of the structure of a work of art. This concept is common to all art concerned with representing some part of reality (film, theater, painting, etc.), that is, all the art forms presenting the duality of content and form. Uspensky's concept of the work of art is similar to that of Lotman referred to above. He, too, calls the text "any semantically organized sequence of signs" (ibid.). Lotman and Uspensky both refer to the pioneering work of Mikhail Bakhtin, *Problem of Dostoevski's Poetics*, trans. R. W. Rotsel (Ann Arbor: Ardis Publications, 1973), to which I shall return below.

78. Lotman particularly emphasizes the stratified structure of the artistic text (*Structure of the Artistic Text*, pp. 59–69). This multilayered structure brings together the modeling activity of the work of art as regards reality and also its playful activity, which itself engages in forms of behavior that take place on at least two planes at once—that of everyday practice and that of the conventions of playing. By so conjoining regular and aleatory processes, the work of art proposes a variety of more or less rich, but also true, pictures of life (ibid., p. 65). In Part IV, I shall return to this "game effect" [*effet de jeu*] (ibid., p. 67), which in French wipes out the difference between "game" [*jeu*] and "play" [*jeu*].

79. Once again, the most noteworthy narrative technique from the point of view of the games with verb tenses, known as *erlebte Rede*—the *style indirect libre* of French critics, or the "narrated monologue" of English-speaking critics—results from the contamination of the narrator's discourse by that of the character, who superimposes his or her grammatical person and verb tense. Uspensky notes all the nuances resulting from the variety of roles played by the narrator, depending on whether he/she records, edits, or rewrites the discourse of the character.

80. This may be compared with the study of anisochronies in Proust carried out by Genette and also with Cohn's analysis of the two opposing models that predominate in the first-person narrative: the clearly retrospective and dissonant narrative of Proust,

where there is a vast distance between the narrator and the hero, and Henry James's synchronic and consonant narrative, where the narrator is contemporary with the hero.

81. The Russian language also offers the grammatical resources of "aspect" to express the iterative and durative features of behavior or of a situation.

82. For an excellent summary of the problem to 1970, cf. Françoise van Rossum-Guyon, "Point de vue ou perspective narrative," *Poétique* 4(1940): 476–97.

83. In *Nouveau Discours du récit*, Genette proposes to substitute the term "focalization" for that of point of view. The personalization inevitably required by the category of narrator is then associated with the notion of voice.

84. This is why in so many German and English-language critics we find the adjective "*auktorial*" (Stanzel) or "authorial" (Cohn). These adjectives offer the advantage of establishing another sort of relation—between author and authority, the adjective "authoritative" linking together both constellations of meaning. On the relation between author and authority, cf. Said, *Beginnings*, pp. 16, 23, 83–84. This theme is linked to his idea of "molestation," referred to above, chap. 1, n. 43.

85. Cf. also Tzvetan Todorov, *Mikhail Bakhtine: Le principe dialogique*, followed by *Ecrits du Cercle du Bakhtine* (Paris: Seuil, 1981).

86. The pages devoted to dialogue, as the general "metalinguistic" principle of language in all its speech acts, deserve attention just as much as the study of the particular forms of the polyphonic novel (cf. *Dostoevsky's Poetics*, pp. 150–227).

87. Cf. ibid., p. 23. Stressing the rapidity with which changes occur in the course of the narrative, Bakhtin notes that "dynamics and speed . . . signify not the triumph of time, but the triumph over time, for speed is the only means of overcoming time in time" (ibid., p. 24).

88. Here we find the fourteen distinctive features that Bakhtin recognizes in carnivalistic literature (ibid., pp. 93–97). In this regard he does not hesitate to speak of "an internal logic determining the inseparable coupling of all its elements" (ibid., p. 98). In addition, the secret spot linking the concealed discourse and the depths of a character with the discourse shown upon the surface of another character forms a powerful factor of composition.

89. On the notion of "subsequent" narration, cf. Genette's *Narrative Discourse*, pp. 35, 223. *Nouveau Discours du récit* adds the following: a narrator who announces ahead of time a subsequent development of the action that is being narrated "thereby posits without any possible ambiguity that this narrative act is posterior to the story told, or at least with respect to the part of the story that he anticipates in this way" (ibid., p. 54). We shall see in the final chapter of volume 3 in what way this posterior position of the narrative voice in the fictional narrative favors the historization of fiction, which compensates for the fictionalization of history.

90. I shall return at the end of volume 3 to the role of this quasi-intuition in the fictionalization of history.

91. On reading as the response to the narrative voice of the text, cf. Valdés, *Shadows in the Cave*, p. 23. The text is trustworthy to the extent that the fictional voice itself is (ibid., p. 25). This question is particularly urgent in the case of parody. The characteristic parody found in *Don Quixote*, for example, must finally be able to be identified by unmistakable signs. This "address" of the text, uttered by the narrative voice, constitutes the intentionality of the text as such (cf. ibid., pp. 26–32; see also Valdés's interpretation of *Don Quixote*, pp. 141–62).

CHAPTER FOUR

1. Cf. above, p. 5.

2. Cf. the work by Fink referred to above, Chap. 3, n. 21. In a similar sense, Lotman places inside the "frame" that marks out every work of art, the compositional

process that makes it "a finite model of an infinite universe" (*The Structure of the Artistic Text*, p. 210).

3. This notion of immanent transcendence exactly overlaps that of intentionality as it is applied by Mario Valdés to the text as a whole. It is in the act of reading that the intentionality of the text is actualized (*Shadows in the Cave*, pp. 45–76). This analysis should be combined with that of narrative voice considered as that which presents the text. The narrative voice is the bearer of the intentionality belonging to the text, which is actualized only in the intersubjective relationship that unfolds between the solicitation coming from the narrative voice and the response of reading. This analysis will be taken up again in a systematic way in volume 3.

4. A. A. Mendilow, *Time and the Novel*, p. 16.

5. The expression "imaginative variations" will take on its full meaning only when we are in a position to confront the range of solutions it offers to the aporias of time with the resolution provided by the constitution of historical time, in the next volume of *Time and Narrative*.

6. Virginia Woolf, *Mrs. Dalloway* (London: Hogarth Press, 1924; reprinted, New York: Harcourt Brace Jovanovitch, 1953).

7. James Hafley, contrasting *Mrs. Dalloway* with Joyce's *Ulysses*, writes, "[Virginia Woolf] used the single day as a unity . . . to show that there is no such thing as a single day" (*The Glass Roof*, p. 73, quoted by Jean Guiguet, *Virginia Woolf and Her Works*, trans. Jean Stewart [London: The Hogarth Press, 1965], p. 389).

8. Virginia Woolf was quite proud of discovering this narrative technique and of putting it to use. In her diary she called it "the tunnelling process." "It took me a year's groping to discover what I call my tunnelling process, by which I tell the past by installments, as I have need of it" (*A Writer's Diary*, ed. Leonard Woolf [London: The Hogarth Press, 1959], p. 60, quoted by Guiguet, p. 229). During the period when the first draft of *Mrs. Dalloway* was still called *The Hours*, she wrote in her diary: "I should say a good deal about *The Hours* and my discovery: How I dig out beautiful caves behind my characters: I think that gives exactly what I want; humanity, humour, depth. The idea is that the caves shall connect and each comes to daylight at the present moment" (*A Writer's Diary*, p. 60, quoted by Guiguet, pp. 233–34). The alternations between action and remembering thus become an alternation between the superficial and the profound. The two fates of Septimus and Clarissa essentially communicate through the closeness of the subterranean "caves" visited by the narrator. On the surface, they are brought together through the character of Dr. Bradshaw, who belongs to two subplots. The news of Septimus's death, brought by the doctor, thus assumes, on the surface, the unity of the plot.

9. Exploring the character of each protagonist is the main interest of the third chapter ("*Mrs. Dalloway* and *To the Lighthouse*") of Jean Alexander's *The Venture of Form in the Novels of Virginia Woolf* (Port Washington, New York: Kennikat Press, 1974), pp. 85–104. *Mrs. Dalloway* is judged to be the only one of Virginia Woolf's novels that "evolves from a character" (ibid., p. 85). By isolating the character of Clarissa in this way, Jean Alexander can point out the tinsel that is mixed with the brilliance, the compromises with a social world that, for Clarissa, never loses its solidity and its glory. Clarissa thus becomes a "class symbol," which Peter Walsh has perceived as being hard as wood and yet hollow. But the hidden relation with Septimus Warren Smith shifts the perspective by bringing to light the dangers that Clarissa's life is thought to disarm, namely, the possible destruction of the personality through the interplay of human relationships. This psychological approach gives rise to an apt analysis of the range of sentiments of fear and terror that the novel explores. Alexander's comparison with Sartre's *Nausea* (ibid., p. 97) seems completely justified to me in this regard.

10. David Daiches, *The Novel and the Modern World* (Chicago: University of Chi-

cago Press, 1939, rev. ed. 1960), considers this process to be the most advanced element in the art of fiction in Virginia Woolf. It allows the interweaving of the modes of action and introspection. This conjunction induces a "twilight mood of receptive reverie" (ibid., p. 189), which the reader is invited to share. Virginia Woolf herself also referred to this "mood" so characteristic of her entire work in her essay "On Modern Fiction": "life is a luminous halo, a semi-transparent envelope surrounding us from the beginning of consciousness to the end" (*The Common Reader* [London: The Hogarth Press, 1925–32, 2 vols.], quoted by Daiches, p. 192). Daiches proposes a simple schematism that accounts for this subtle, yet easy-to-analyze technique. Either we keep ourselves immobile and take in with our gaze the various events occurring simultaneously in space, or we fix ourselves in space, or better in a character, considered a fixed "place," and let ourselves follow back or move along with the time-consciousness of this same character. The narrative technique thus consists in alternating the dispersion of characters in a single point in time with the dispersion of memories within one character. Cf. the diagram given by Daiches, ibid., pp. 204–5. In this regard, Virginia Woolf is much more careful than Joyce is to set out unequivocal guideposts to direct the course of this alternation. For a comparison with *Ulysses*, which also keeps the infinitely complex skein of its excursions and incursions within the span of a single day, cf. ibid., pp. 190, 193, 198–99. Daiches relates the difference in technique of these two authors to the difference in their intentions. "Joyce's aim was to isolate reality from all human attitudes—an attempt to remove the normative element from fiction completely, to create a self-contained world independent of all values in the observer, independent even (as though it is possible) of all values in the creator. But Virginia Woolf refines on values rather than eliminates them. Her reaction to crumbling norms is not agnosticism but sophistication" (ibid., p. 199). Daiches has returned to and furthered his interpretation of *Mrs. Dalloway* in *Virginia Woolf* (Norfolk, Conn.: New Directions, 1942; London: Nicholson and Watson, 1945, pp. 61–78; revised edition, New Directions, 1963, pp. 187–217), to which I shall refer. Jean Guiguet in the work already referred to, based principally on Virginia Woolf's diary published only in 1953, returns to the question of the relationship between Joyce's *Ulysses* and *Mrs. Dalloway*, pp. 241–45.

11. Clarissa reads this refrain while stopping at the window of a bookshop. It constitutes at the same time one of the bridges built by the narrative technique between Clarissa's fate and that of Septimus, so taken, as we shall see, with Shakespeare.

12. Furtive figure of authority: the glimpse of the Prince of Wale's car (and is not the Queen, if it is she, "the enduring symbol of the State"? [*Mrs. Dalloway*, p. 23]). Even the shop windows of the antique dealers recall their role: "sifting the ruins of time" (ibid.). Also there is the airplane and its trail of advertising in the form of imposing capital letters. Figures of authority: the lords and ladies of the sempiternal parties and even honest Richard Dalloway, faithful servant of the state.

13. "Here is my Elizabeth," says Clarissa, with all that the possessive form implies. This will receive a reply in Elizabeth's final appearance, rejoining her father, just when the curtain is about to fall on Mrs. Dalloway's party. "And suddenly he realised that it was his Elizabeth" (ibid., p. 295).

14. Could Virginia Woolf here not help but be thinking of Shakespeare's words in *As You Like It*: Rosalind: "I pray you, what is't o'clock?" Orlando: "You should ask me, what time o'day. There's no clock in the forest." Rosalind: "Then there is no true lover in the forest; else sighing every minute and groaning every hour would detect the lazy foot of Time as well as a clock." Orlando: "And why not the swift foot of Time? Had not that been as proper?" Rosalind: "By no means, sir. Time travels in divers paces with divers persons. I'll tell you who Time ambles withal, who Time trots withal, who Time gallops withal, and who he stands still withal" (act 3, scene 2, 11. 301ff.)

15. Cf. John Graham, "Time in the Novels of Virginia Woolf," *University of Toronto Quarterly* 18 (1949): 186–201; reprinted in *Critics on Virginia Woolf*, ed. Jacqueline E. M. Latham (Coral Gables, Florida: University of Miami Press, 1970), pp. 28–35. This critic pushes the interpretation of Septimus's suicide quite far indeed. It is the "complete vision" of Septimus (ibid., p. 32) that gives Clarissa "the power to conquer time" (ibid.). Clarissa's reflections on the young man, which I shall refer to below, support this. Clarissa intuitively understands, John Graham says, the meaning of Septimus's vision, which he can communicate only through death. Consequently, returning to her party symbolizes for Clarissa "the transfiguration of time" (ibid., p. 33). I hesitate to follow this interpretation of Septimus's death all the way: "In order to penetrate to the center like Septimus, one must either die, or go mad, or in some other way lose one's humanity in order to exist independently of time" (ibid., p. 31). On the other hand, this critic well notes that "the true terror of his vision is that it destroys him as a creature of the time-world" (ibid., p. 30). It is then no longer time that is mortal, it is eternity that is the bringer of death. But how can one separate this "complete vision"—this gnosis—from Septimus's madness that has all the aspects of paranoia? Let me add that John Graham's interpretation of Septimus's revelations does give us an opportunity to build a bridge between the interpretation of *Mrs. Dalloway* and that of *Der Zauberberg* that I shall attempt below, when the theme of eternity and its relation to time comes to the forefront.

16. A note by Virginia Woolf in her diary warns against a clearly defined separation between madness and health: "I adumbrate here a study of insanity and suicide; the world seen by the sane and the insane stay side by side—something like that" (*A Writer's Diary*, p. 52). The madman's vision is not disqualified because of his "insanity." It is its reverberation in Clarissa's soul that finally is important.

17. *Time and Narrative*, vol. 1, pp. 22–30.

18. A. D. Moody sees in Mrs. Dalloway the living image of the superficial life led by the "British ruling class," as London society is called in the book itself (*"Mrs. Dalloway* as Comedy," in *Critics on Virginia Woolf*, pp. 48–58). It is true that she incarnates at the same time criticism of her society but without possessing the power to dissociate herself from it. This is why the "comic" aspect, nourished by the narrator's ferocious irony, predominates up to the final scene at the party, marked by the presence of the Prime Minister. This interpretation seems to me to suffer from an oversimplification that is the inverse of that which, above, saw in Septimus's death, transposed by Clarissa, the power to transfigure time. The tale about time in *Mrs. Dalloway* is situated halfway between comedy and gnosis. As Jean Guiguet justly notes, "the social criticism intended by the author is grafted onto the psycho-metaphysical theme of the novel" (p. 235). Guiguet is alluding here to an observation made by Virginia Woolf in her diary: "I want to give life and death, sanity and insanity; I want to criticize the social system, and show it at work at its most intense" (*A Writer's Diary*, p. 57, quoted by Guiguet, p. 228). This priority of the psychological investigation over the social criticism is demonstrated by Jean O. Love in her *Worlds in Consciousness: Mythopoetic Thought in the Novels of Virginia Woolf* (Berkeley: University of California Press, 1970).

19. This expression comes from Virginia Woolf herself in her Preface to the American edition of *Mrs. Dalloway*. Septimus "is intended to be her double" (cf. Isabel Gamble, "Clarissa Dalloway's Double," in *Critics on Virginia Woolf*, pp. 52–55). Clarissa becomes Septimus's "double" when she realizes "that there is a core of integrity in the ego that must be kept intact at all costs" (ibid., p. 55).

20. We know, from her Preface, that in an initial version Clarissa was to commit suicide. By adding the character of Septimus and by having him commit suicide, the author allowed the narrator—the narrative voice that tells the story to the reader—to

draw Mrs. Dalloway's line of destiny as close to suicide as possible but to extend it beyond the temptation of death.

21. Graham, "Time in the Novels of Virginia Woolf," pp. 32–33.

22. We must, no doubt, refrain from giving this gift of presence the dimension of a message of redemption. Clarissa will continue to be a woman of the world, for whom monumental time is a magnitude with which one must have the courage to deal. In this sense, Clarissa remains a figure of compromise. The concluding sentence "For there she was," notes Jean Guiguet, "contains everything and states nothing precisely" (*Virginia Woolf and Her Works*, p. 240). This somewhat harsh judgment is justified if we leave Clarissa alone confronting the prestige of the social order. It is the kinship between the destinies of Septimus and Clarissa, at another depth—that of the "caves" that the narrator "connects"—that governs not only the plot but the psycho-metaphysical theme of the novel. The self-assured tone of this claim resonates louder than the striking of Big Ben and all the clocks, stronger than the terror and the ecstacy that from the beginning of the story struggle to capture Clarissa's soul. If Septimus's refusal of monumental time was able to direct Mrs. Dalloway back toward transitory life and its precarious joys, this is because it set her on the path to a mortal time that is fully assumed.

23. It would be a serious mistake to consider this experience, however puzzling it may be, as the illustration of a philosophy constituted outside the novel, even if it be that of Bergson. The monumental time that both Septimus and Clarissa confront has nothing to do with Bergson's spatialized time. It exists, so to speak, in its own right and is not the result of a confusion between space and duration. This is why I compared it instead to Nietzsche's monumental history. As for the internal time, brought to light by the narrator's excursions into underground caves, it has more in common with the upsurge of the moment than with the melodic continuity of duration in Bergson. The very resonance of the hour is one of those moments that is defined differently every time depending on the present mood (cf. Guiguet, pp. 388–92). Regardless of the similarities and differences between time in Virginia Woolf and time in Bergson, the major shortcoming here is not giving fiction per se the power to explore the modes of temporal experience that escape philosophical conceptualization, due to its aporetic character. This will be the central theme in my concluding volume.

24. Thomas Mann, *The Magic Mountain*, trans. H. T. Lowe-Porter (New York: Alfred A. Knopf, 1927; Vintage Books, 1969).

25. Concerning this relation, cf. Hermann Weigand, *The Magic Mountain* (New York: D. Appleton-Century, 1933; reprinted, Chapel Hill: The University of North Carolina Press, 1964).

26. Cf. above, pp. 77–81.

27. The narrator returns to this theme of the reading time at several points. He does so in the decisive episode, "Soup-Everlasting" (*Ewigkeitssuppe*) (*Magic Mountain*, pp. 183–203). At the beginning of Chapter 7, he wonders, more precisely, if one can tell, that is narrate, time itself (ibid., p. 541). If, the narrator says, one cannot narrate time, at least one can "von der Zeit erzählen zu wollen" (one can "desire to tell a tale *about* time," says the English translator [ibid., p. 542, her emphasis]). The expression *Zeitroman* then takes on its twofold sense of a novel that is spread out in time, and thereby requires time to be told, and of a novel *about* time. The narrator returns to this same ambiguity in one of the Mynheer Peeperkorn episodes, and at the beginning of "The Great God Dumps" (ibid., p. 624).

28. This calculated ambiguity serves as a warning. *The Magic Mountain* will not simply be the symbolic history that runs from the sickness unto death of European culture, before the thunderbolt of 1914; nor will it be simply the tale of a spiritual quest. Between the sociological symbolism and the hermetic symbolism, we do not have to choose.

29. A positive evaluation of the hero's apprenticeship was proposed in 1933 by Hermann J. Weigand in the work referred to above. Weigand was the first to characterize *The Magic Mountain* as a "pedagogical novel." But he sees in this "novel of self-development" (ibid., p. 4) "a quest for *Bildung* that transcends any specific practical aims" (ibid.), where the main emphasis is placed on the progressive integration of a total experience from which emerges an affirmative attitude regarding life as a whole. Even in the major crises reported in the first part (the temptation to run away, Dr. Behrens's summons making Hans a patient at the Berghof, Walpurgis-Night), the hero is found to be capable of choice and of "elevation" (*Steigerung*). Of course, Weigand freely admits that the end of the first part marks the culminating point of the sympathy with death. He calls *Der Zauberberg* "the epic of disease" (ibid., p. 39). But the second part will show the subordination of the fascination exerted by death to the fascination exerted by life (ibid., p. 49). The "Snow" episode bears witness to the "spiritual climax of clarity that marks the acme of his capacity to span the poles of cosmic experience . . . that he owes to the resource which enables him ultimately to sublimate even his passion for Clavdia into this interested friendship." In the spiritualism seance, Weigand sees the experience of the hero confined to mysticism (the final chapter of his book is devoted expressly to mysticism) but, according to the author, the occult seance never leads Hans Castorp to lose control of his will to live. Moreover, the exploration of the unknown, of the forbidden, extends to the revelation of "the essential ethos of sin for Thomas Mann" (ibid., p. 154); this is the "Russian" side of Castorp, the Clavdia side. From her he learns that there is no curiosity without a certain amount of perversity. The question is nevertheless to know whether the hero has integrated, as Weigand claims, this chaos of experiences ("synthesis is the principle that governs the pattern of the *Zauberberg* from first to last" [ibid., p. 157]). The reader will find in Hans Meyer's *Thomas Mann* (Frankfurt: Suhrkamp, 1980), a more negative estimate of Hans Castorp's apprenticeship at the Berghof. Meyer, passing over the *Zeitroman* in silence, clearly places the accent on "the epic of life and death" (ibid., p. 114). The outcome of the hero's education is, of course, the establishing of a new relationship with sickness, death, and decadence, as the *Faktum* of life, a relationship that contrasts with the nostalgia for death, coming from Novalis, and that predominates in *Death in Venice*, the work by Thomas Mann that preceded *The Magic Mountain*. Mann himself confirms this in his Lübeck lecture: "Was ich plante, war eine groteske Geschichte, worin die Faszination durch den Tod, die das venezianischen Novelle gewesen war, ins Komische gezogen werden sollte: etwas wie ein Satyrspeil alzo zum 'Tod in Venedig'" (cited by Meyer, ibid., p. 116). According to Meyer the ironic tone adopted in this pedagogical novel establishes a second contrast, not only with the romantic heritage but also with the Goethean *Bildungsroman*. Instead of a continuous development of the hero, *Der Zauberberg* is held to depict an essentially passive hero (ibid., p. 122), receptive to extremes, but always at an equal distance from things, in the middle like Germany itself, torn between humanism and antihumanism, between the ideology of progress and that of decadence. The only thing that the hero can have learned is to remove himself (*Abwendung*) (ibid., p. 127) from all the impressions, lectures, and conversations he has to undergo. As a result, the accent must be placed as much on the pedagogical influence exerted by the other protagonists—Settembrini, Naphta, Madame Chauchat, and Peeperkorn—if we want accurately to measure the rich social fresco that brings *The Magic Mountain* close to Balzac, as it moves away from Goethe and, with all the more reason, from Novalis. Hans Meyer is certainly not unaware of the opposition between the time up above and the time down below; he even expressly compares it to the opposition Bergson makes between the level of action and the level of dreams. But, as concerns Hans Castorp himself, Meyer holds that, among the bourgeois parasites of the Berghof, all condemned to die, Hans Castorp could learn nothing, for there was nothing to learn (ibid.,

p. 137). It is here that my interpretation differs from his, without concurring with that of Weigand. What there was to learn at the Berghof is a new way of relating to time and to its effacement, *the model of which is to be found in the ironic relation of the narrator to his own narrative*. In this respect, I find support in the remarkable study that Meyer devotes to the passage from irony to parody in Thomas Mann (cf. ibid., pp. 171–83).

30. Richard Thieberger in *Der Begriff der Zeit bei Thomas Mann von Zauberberg zum Joseph* (Baden-Baden: Verlag für Kunst und Wissenschaft, 1962), pp. 25–65 ("Die Zeitaspekte im *Zauberberg*"), has attempted to gather together all the considerations on time that occur either in conversations, in thoughts (in other words, in the internal discourse) attributed to the characters in the narrative, or in the narrator's commentary. I am indebted to him for the selection of the most typical remarks on this subject.

31. Chapter 2 plunges into the past. This flashback—moreover quite common in nineteenth- and early-twentieth-century novels—is not unrelated to the construction of the perspectival effect which I referred to above. The chapter does indeed set up the *Urerlebnisse*, as Weigand puts it (Weigand, pp. 25–39), that will act as underground guides for the spiritual growth that parallels the diminishing interest in measured time. The sense of the continuity of generations, symbolized by the transmission of the baptismal basin; the double sense of death, at once sacred and indecent, felt for the first time before the mortal remains of his grandfather; the irrepressible sense of freedom, depicted by the taste for experimentation, for adventure; the erotic penchant, subtly evoked by the episode of borrowing the pencil from Pribislav Hippe, the same pencil in the *Walpurgisnacht* scene Clavdia Chauchat will ask Hans to return to her. In addition to the fact that these *Urerlebnisse* contain tenacious energies that will make the negative experience of time an experience of internal *Steigerung*, the fact of evoking them *after* the "arrival" scene and *before* the agitated narrative of the first day serves the specific function of getting the major experience of the effacement of time underway. It was first necessary to have given time this antiquity, this thickness, and this density in order to give the full measure of the loss that is experienced when the measurements of time fade away.

32. "'But lately [*neulich*]—let me see, wait a minute, it might be possibly eight weeks ago—' 'Then you can hardly say lately,' Hans Castorp pounced on him crisply. 'What! Well, not lately, then, since you're so precise. I was just trying to reckon. Well, then, some time ago'" (*The Magic Mountain*, p. 53).

33. "'*O dio!* Three weeks! Do you hear, Lieutenant? Does it not sound to you impertinent to hear a person say: "I am stopping for three weeks and then I am going away again"? We up here are not acquainted with such a unit of time as the week—if I may be permitted to instruct you, my dear sir. Our smallest unit is the month. We reckon in the grand style [*im grossen Stil*]—that is a privilege we shadows have'" (ibid., p. 58).

34. Joachim himself, by the headstart he still has over Hans, helps to sharpen the perplexity of his cousin. "Yes, when you watch it, the time, it goes very slowly. I quite like measuring, four times a day; for then you know what a minute—or seven of them—actually amounts to, up here in this place, where the seven days of the week whisk by the way they do!" (ibid., pp. 65–66). The narrator adds, referring to Hans, "He was unaccustomed to philosophize, yet somehow felt an impulse to do so" (ibid., p. 66).

35. "'Keep quiet! I'm very clear-headed today. Well, then, what *is* time?' asked Hans Castorp" (ibid.). It is amusing to follow our hero's parody of Augustine, of whom he is supposed to be unaware. But this certainly does not apply to the narrator!

36. "I've still a great many ideas in my head about time—a whole complex, if I may say so" (ibid., p. 67). " 'Good Lord, is it still only the first day? It seems to me I've been up here a long time—ages.' 'Don't begin to philosophize again about time,' said Joachim. 'You had me perfectly bewildered this morning.' 'No, don't worry, I've forgotten all of it,' answered Hans Castorp, 'the whole "complex." I've lost all the clear-headedness I had—it's gone' " (ibid., p. 82). " 'And yet, in another way, it seems as though I had been here a long time, instead of just a single day—as if I had got older and wiser since I came—that is the way I feel.' 'Wiser, too?' Settembrini asked" (ibid., p. 85).

37. The narrator, intervening shamelessly, says, "We have introduced these remarks here only because our young Hans Castorp had something like them in mind" (ibid., p. 105).

38. "But even the phenomena of everyday life held much that Hans Castorp had still to learn: faces and facts already noted had to be conned, new ones to be observed with youth's receptivity" (ibid., p. 106). In the same sense the narrator speaks of Hans Castorp's enterprising spirit (*Unternehmungsgeist*). Thieberger compares this *Exkurs* to Joachim's apology for music, which, at least, preserves an order and precise divisions. Settembrini goes even further. "Music quickens time, she quickens us to the finest enjoyment of time; she quickens—and in so far she has moral value. Art has moral value, in so far as it quickens" (ibid., p. 114). But Hans Castorp receives this moralizing diatribe, which remains that of a schoolmaster, with disinterest.

39. Among the *Leitmotive*, let us recall the christening basin—"that symbol of the passing and the abiding, of continuity through change" (ibid., p. 154), and also the grandfather's trembling head (during Walpurgis-Night).

40. The two voices of the narrator and the hero join together to exclaim, "Ah, time is a riddling thing, and hard it is to expound its essence!" (ibid., p. 141). Lucidity hangs upon this question.

41. After two weeks, the daily routine of those up here "had begun to take on, in his eyes, a character of sanctity. When, from the point of view of 'those up here,' he considered life as lived down in the flat-land, it seemed somehow queer and unnatural" (ibid., p. 148).

42. It is noteworthy that, in his disdain for the Russians and their prodigious negligence with respect to time, the Italian tutor praises Time. "Time is a gift of God, given to man that he might use it—use it, Engineer, to serve the advancement of humanity" (p. 243). Weigand stresses here the subtle play between the German, the Italian, and the Slavic mind. This constitutes one of the numerous overdeterminations of this tale about time.

43. The author once again takes his reader by the hand. "We have as much right as the next person to our private thoughts about the story we are relating; and we would here hazard the surmise that young Hans Castorp would never have overstepped so far the limits originally fixed for his stay if to his simple soul there might have been vouchsafed, out of the depth of his time, any reasonably satisfying explanation of the meaning and purpose of man's life" (ibid., pp. 229–30).

44. Does this not irresistibly call to mind the dinner among the death's-heads in *Remembrance of Things Past*, after the crucial vision in the Duke of Guermantes' library?

45. The irony of the final words, "And went out" leaves the reader not knowing what Clavdia and Hans did the rest of this carnival night. Later, the confidence made to poor Wehsal will excite our curiosity without satisfying it. The ironic author then notes, "there seems every reason, on our part and on his, not to go into it very much" (ibid., p. 428). Later, upon her return, he will say to Clavdia, "I have told you I regard

it as a dream, what we had together" (ibid., pp. 597–97). Mynheer Peeperkorn's curiosity will not succeed in lifting the veil.

46. "Hans Castorp revolved these queries and their like in his brain. . . . For himself, it was precisely because he did not know the answers that he put the question" (ibid., pp. 244–45).

47. Thieberger is certainly correct in mentioning Mann's Joseph novels here, Joseph in whom the passion for observing the heavens was bound up with the archaism of myths as much as with ancient wisdom.

48. "The more I think of it, the surer I am that the bed of repose—by which I mean my deck-chair, of course—has given me more food for thought in these ten months than the mill down in the flat-land in all the years before. There's simply no denying it" (ibid., p. 376).

49. The long ski escapades are not unrelated to this conquest of freedom. They even provide him with an active use of time, which sets the stage for the critical "Snow" episode.

50. His ramblings sometimes do have time as a theme. Naptha decries "the exploitation of time," a "universal God-given dispensation" (ibid., p. 403). Cf. also his apology for communist time, "when no one would be allowed to receive interest" (ibid., p. 408).

51. "In a word, Hans Castorp was valorous up here—if by valour we mean not mere dull matter-of-factness in the face of nature, but conscious submission to her, the fear of death cast out by irresistible oneness" (ibid., p. 477).

52. Note the irony of the title *Als Soldat und brav* (ibid., p. 498). Joachim has been forced to leave the profession of soldier in order to return to die in a sanatorium. His interment, however, is that of a soldier; a premonition of all the interments marking the Great War, the same war that, at the end of Chapter 7, will roll over the Berghof like a thunderbolt.

53. Does the kiss on the mouth, in the Russian manner, which the narrator compares with Dr. Krokowski's manner of treating the subject of life "in that slightly fluctuating sense" (ibid., p. 599), mark a victory or a defeat? Or, more subtly, is it not the ironic reminder of the fluctuating sense of the word "love," oscillating between piety and voluptuousness?

54. "He saw on every side the uncanny and the malign, and he knew what it was he saw: life without time, life without care or hope, life as depravity, assiduous stagnation; life as dead" (ibid., p. 627).

55. "Augenblicke kamen, wo dir aus Tode und Körperunzucht ahnugsvoll und regierungsweise ein Traum von Liebe erwuchs."

56. Marcel Proust, *Remembrance of Things Past*, trans. C. K. Scott Moncrieff, Terence Kilmartin, and Andreas Mayor (New York: Random House, 1981), 3 vols. I shall refer to this work throughout this chapter by volume and page number.

57. Gilles Deleuze, *Proust and Signs*, trans. Richard Howard (New York: George Braziller, 1972).

58. The quasi-synchronic table of signs in Deleuze's work and the hierarchy of temporal configurations that correspond to this grand paradigm of signs must not make us forget either the historicity of this apprenticeship or, especially, the singular historicity that marks the event of the Visitation itself, which changes after-the-fact the meaning of the earlier apprenticeship, and first and foremost its temporal signification. It is the eccentric character of the signs of art in relation to all the others that engenders this singular historicity.

59. Anne Henry, *Proust romancier: le tombeau égyptien* (Paris: Flammarion, 1983).

60. Henry (ibid., pp. 33 and 40) gives two significant extracts from Part VI of *The System of Transcendental Idealism*. Cf. F. W. J. Schelling, *The System of Transcendental Idealism* (1800), trans. Peter Heath (Charlottesville: University of Virginia Press, 1978).

61. Schopenhauer, *The World as Will and Representation*, trans. E. F. J. Payne (New York: Dover Books, 1966), 2 vols.

62. "The realization of Identity did foresee its place of accomplishment as the artist's consciousness, but it was a metaphysical essence, not a psychological subject—a feature that the novel will inevitably end up concretizing" (Henry, p. 44). And further along: "Proust thought only about placing himself in the intermediary zone between the system and concrete reality which the genre, novel, permits" (ibid., p. 55).

63. Anne Henry is not unaware of the problem. "Nothing will have been accomplished so long as one has not yet shed light on this ever so peculiar presentation that Proust gives of Identity, its realization at the heart of reminiscence" (ibid., p. 43). But the answer she gives leaves the difficulty intact, when the key to the psychologizing process to which the aesthetics of genius is subjected is still sought outside the novel in a mutation of intellectual culture at the end of the nineteenth century. This reversal of the relationship between the theoretical foundation and the narrative process leads to the question what revolution *Remembrance* provoked in the tradition of the *Bildungsroman*, which Thomas Mann's *Der Zauberberg* reoriented in the way I have tried to indicate above. The decentering brought about by *Remembrance* of the redemptive event in relation to the long apprenticeship to signs leads us rather to understand that, by placing his work within the tradition of the *Bildungsroman*, Marcel Proust subverts the law of the novel of apprenticeship in a different way than Mann does. Proust breaks with the optimistic vision of a continuous, ascending development of the hero in quest of himself. Compared in this way to the tradition of the *Bildungsroman*, Proust's novelistic creation resides in the invention of a plot that joins together, by strictly narrative means, the apprenticeship to signs and the maturation of a vocation. Anne Henry herself mentions this kinship with the *Bildungsroman* but, for her, the choice of this novel formula participates in the overall degradation that affects the philosophy of lost identity when it becomes a psychology of lost time.

64. The problem posed is not without analogy to that posed by Genette's structural analysis. He also saw in the "art of Poetry" inserted into the hero's meditation on the eternity of the work of art, an intrusion of the author into the work. My retort was to introduce the notion of a world of the work and of an experience that the hero of the work has within the horizon of this world. This accorded the work the power to project itself beyond itself in an imaginary transcendence. The same reply holds with respect to Anne Henry's explanation. It is to the extent that the work projects a narrator-hero who *thinks* about his experience that it can include, within its transcendent immanence, the scattered debris of philosophical speculation.

65. Nevertheless, this voice can be easily recognized in the aphorisms and maxims that allow us to see the exemplary character of the experience recounted. It is also readily apparent in the latent irony that prevails throughout the narrative of the hero's discoveries in the world of society. Norpois, Brichot, Madame Verdurin, and, one after the other, bourgeois and aristocrats fall victim to the cruelty of a cutting remark, perceptible to an ear with a moderate amount of experience. On the other hand, it is only on the second reading that the reader who knows the outcome of the work perceives what, in deciphering the signs of love, would be the equivalent of irony in deciphering worldly signs: a tone of disillusionment, which forces the day of disappointment and thus ascribes meaning without expressly stating it—the meaning of time lost that comes out of every amorous experience. In other words, it is the narrative voice that is

responsible for the overall pejorative tone that predominates in deciphering the signs of love. The narrative voice is more restrained in deciphering sensory signs, and yet their voice insinuates a questioning tone, an interrogation, a request for meaning at the heart of impressions, to the point of breaking this charm and dissolving their spell. The narrator thus constantly makes the hero a consciousness who is awakening to underlying reality.

66. These moments between waking and sleeping serve as an initial pivot for the inset memories, one within the other: "my memory had been set in motion" (I, p. 9). A second pivot is provided by the association of one bedroom with another: Combray, Balbec, Paris, Doncières, Venice (ibid.). The narrator does not fail to recall, at the appropriate moment, this inset structure. "And so it was that, for a long time afterwards, when I lay awake at night and revived old memories of Combray, I saw no more of it than this sort of luminous panel, sharply defined against a vague and shadowy background" (I, p. 46). This will be the case until the conclusion of this sort of "prelude" (as Hans Robert Jauss calls it in his *Zeit und Erinnerung in Marcel Prousts "A la Recherche du Temps Perdu"* [Heidelberg: Carl Winter, 1955]) in which all the narratives of childhood, as well as the story of Swann's love, are included.

67. As we would expect, this ritual is recounted in the *imparfait*: "that frail and precious kiss which Mamma used normally to bestow on me when I was in bed and just going to sleep had to be transported from the dining-room to my bed-room where I must keep it inviolate all the time that it took me to undress" (I, p. 24).

68. "I ought to have been happy; I was not" (I, p. 41).

69. The trap lies in the transitional question, "Will it ultimately reach the clear surface of my consciousness, this memory, this old, dead moment, which the magnetism of an identical moment has travelled so far as to importune, to disturb, to raise up out of the very depths of my being? I cannot tell" (I, p. 50).

70. The entire section *Time Regained* is announced in this statement by the narrator, reflecting on the hero's effort to make the ecstacy return: "And then for the second time I clear an empty space in front of it; I place in position before my mind's eye the still recent taste of that first mouthful, and I feel something start within me, something that leaves its resting-place and attempts to rise, something that has been embedded like an anchor at great depth; I do not know yet what it is but I can feel it mounting slowly; I can measure the resistance, I can hear the echo of great spaces traversed" (I, p. 49). The expression "great spaces traversed" will be, as we shall see, our final word.

71. Hans Robert Jauss interprets the experience of the madeleine as the first coincidence between the narrating self and the narrated self. In addition, he sees in this the primary *nunc*, always already preceded by an abyssal before, yet still able to open the door to the hero's forward progress. A double paradox, therefore: from the start of the narrative the self that narrates is a self remembering what preceded it. By narrating backwards, however, the narrative offers the hero the possibility of beginning his journey forward. And by virtue of this, to the end of the novel, the style of "the future in the past" is preserved. The problem of the relations between the orientation toward the future and the nostalgic desire for the past is at the center of the chapters devoted to Proust in Georges Poulet's *Etudes sur le temps humain* (Paris: Plon, Ed. du Rocher, 1952–68), vol. 1, pp. 400–438; vol. 4, pp. 299–355.

72. "An edifice occupying, so to speak, a four-dimensional space—the name of the fourth being Time—extending through the centuries its ancient nave, which, bay after bay, chapel after chapel, seemed to stretch across and conquer not merely a few yards of soil, but each successive epoch from which it emerged triumphant" (I, p. 66). It is not by chance that, closing the circle, *Time Regained* ends with a final evocation of the Combray church. The steeple of Saint Hilaire is already one of the symbols of time; in Jauss's expression, one of its symbolical figures.

73. Georges Poulet, *Proustian Space*, trans. Elliot Coleman (Baltimore: Johns Hopkins University Press, 1977), pp. 57–69.

74. The different epochs are never dated: "That year" (I, p. 158); "that autumn" (I, pp. 167, 169); "at that moment, too" (I, p. 170).

75. "It is perhaps from another impression which I received at Montjouvain, some years later, an impression which at the time remained obscure to me, that there arose, long afterwards, the notion I was to form of sadism. We shall see, in due course, that for quite other reasons the memory of this impression was to play an important part in my life" (I, p. 173). This "we shall see, in due course" followed by "was to" helps to rebalance in a forward direction the overall backward orientation of the work. The scene is at once recollected and projected toward its own future, and so placed at a distance. On the relation between temporality and desire in Proust, cf. Ghislaine Florival, *Le Désir chez Proust* (Louvain/Paris: Nauwelaerts, 1971), pp. 107–73.

76. "And these dreams reminded me that, since I wished some day to become a writer, it was high time to decide what sort of books I was going to write. But as soon as I asked myself the question, and tried to discover some subject to which I could impart a philosophical significance of infinite value, my mind would stop like a clock, my consciousness would be faced with a blank, I would feel either that I was wholly devoid of talent or that perhaps some malady of the brain was hindering its development" (I, pp. 188–89). And a bit further on: "And so, utterly despondent, I renounced literature for ever, despite the encouragement Bloch had given me" (I, pp. 189–90).

77. "Without admitting to myself that what lay hidden behind the steeples of Martinville must be something analogous to a pretty phrase, since it was in the form of words which gave me pleasure, that it had appeared to me, I borrowed a pencil and some paper from the doctor, and in spite of the jolting of the carriage, to appease my conscience and to satisfy my enthusiasm, composed the following little fragment, which I have since discovered and now reproduce with only a slight revision here and there" (I, p. 197).

78. "But by the same token, and by their persistence in those of my present-day impressions to which they can still be linked, they give those impressions a foundation, a depth, a dimension lacking from the rest" (I, p. 197).

79. "Thus would I often lie until morning, dreaming of the old days at Combray . . . and, by an association of memories, of a story which, many years after I had left the little place, had been told me of a love affair in which Swann had been involved before I was born . . ." (I, p. 203).

80. For the reader, a passage such as the following speaks clearly and distinctly: "Swann found in himself, in the memory of the phrase that he had heard, in certain other sonatas which he had made people play to him to see whether he might not perhaps discover his phrase therein, the presence of one of those invisible realities in which he had ceased to believe and to which, as though the music had had upon the moral barrenness from which he was suffering a sort of recreative influence, he was conscious once again of the desire and almost the strength to consecrate his life" (I, p. 230). And again: "In its airy grace there was the sense of something over and done with, like the mood of philosophic detachment which follows an outburst of vain regret" (I, p. 238).

81. It is not without importance that Swann is a failure as a writer. He will never write his study on Vermeer. As is already suggested, in his relation to the phrase of the Vinteuil sonata, he will die without ever having known the revelation of art. *Time Regained* states this clearly (III, p. 902).

82. In order to anchor his narrative of "Swann in Love" in the main narrative, the narrator common to the third- and the first-person narratives is careful to have Odette appear for the last time (at least the first Odette, who the reader is unable to guess will

later be Gilberte's mother in the hero's fictive autobiography) "in the twilight of a dream" (I, p. 411), and then in his thoughts as he awakes. In this way, "Swann in Love" ends in the same semi-dreamlike region as the "Combray" narrative.

83. The author—and no longer the narrator—is in no way bothered by having the young Marcel and the Gilberte encountered on the little footpath in Combray meet on the Champs-Elysées (her indelicate gesture in those early days [I, p. 154] will remain an enigma until *Time Regained* [III, pp. 711–12]). Novelistic coincidences do not disturb Proust. For it is the narrator who, transforming them first into the peripeteia of his story, then ascribing an almost supernatural sense to chance encounters, succeeds in transforming all coincidences into destiny. *Remembrance* is full of these unlikely encounters that the narrative makes productive. The final, and most meaningful, will be, as we shall see below, the joining together of *Swann's Way* and *The Guermantes Way* in the appearance of the daughter of Gilberte and Saint-Loup in the final pages of the book.

84. "When I found how incurious I was about Combray" (III, p. 709). "But, separated as I was by a whole lifetime from places I now happened to be passing through again, there was lacking between them and me that contiguity from which is born, even before we have perceived it, the immediate, delicious and total deflagration of memory" (III, p. 710).

85. Even the famous pastiche of the Goncourts (III, pp. 728–36), which serves as a pretext for the narrator to thrash out at a memorialist type of literature, based on the immediate capacity for "looking and listening" (III, p. 737) helps to reinforce the general tone of the narrative in which it is interpolated, through the disgust that the reading of the pages, fictitiously attributed to the Goncourts, inspires in the hero with respect to literature and by the obstacles it sets up to the advancement of his vocation (III, pp. 728, 737–38).

86. It is true that the transfiguration of the Parisian sky by the light of the searchlights and the way the airmen are taken for Wagnerian Valkyries (III, p. 781, 785–86) adds to the spectacle of Paris at war a touch of aestheticism, with respect to which it is hard to say whether it contributes to the spectral character of all the surrounding scene, or whether it already partakes of the literary transposition consubstantial with time regained. In any case, frivolity continues alongside the danger of death. "Social amusements fill what may prove, if the Germans continue to advance, to be the last days of our Pompeii. And if the city is indeed doomed, that in itself will save it from frivolity" (III, p. 834).

87. "And then it had turned out that their two lives had each of them a parallel secret, which I had not suspected" (III, p. 879). The rapprochement between these two disappearances gives the narrator the opportunity to engage in a meditation on death, which will later be incorporated into the perspective of time regained. "Yet death appears to be obedient to certain laws" (III, p. 881); more precisely, accidental death, which, in its own way, combines chance and destiny, if not predestination (ibid.).

88. "But it is sometimes just at the moment when we think that everything is lost that the intimation arrives which may save us; one has knocked at all the doors which lead nowhere, and then one stumbles without knowing it on the only door through which one can enter—which one might have sought in vain for a hundred years—and it opens of its own accord" (III, p. 898).

89. Note that this narrativized speculation is related too in the *imparfait*, the background tense according to Harald Weinrich, in contrast to the preterite, the tense of occurrence, from the point of view of what in the narrative is put into relief (cf. above, p. 71). The meditation on time indeed constitutes the background against which the decision to write stands out. A new preterite of anecdotal occurrence is required in order to interrupt this meditation. "At this moment the butler came in to tell me that the

first piece of music was finished, so that I could leave the library and go into the rooms where the party was taking place. And thereupon I remembered where I was" (III, p. 957).

90. "A minute freed from the order of time has re-created in us, to feel it, the man freed from the order of time" (III, p. 906).

91. Speaking of this extratemporal being that the hero had been without knowing it in the episode of the madeleine, the narrator specifies, "And only this being had the power to perform that task which had always defeated the efforts of my memory and my intellect" (III, p. 904).

92. The narrator anticipates this role of mediator between the two valences of time regained, when he admits, "And I observed in passing that for the work of art which I now, though I had not yet reached a conscious resolution, felt myself ready to undertake, this distinctness of different events would entail very considerable difficulties" (III, p. 903). It should be noted, as Georges Poulet points out, that the fusion in time is also a fusion in space: "Always, when these resurrections took place, the distant scene engendered around the common sensation had for a moment grappled, like a wrestler, with the present scene" (III, p. 908).

93. The "universal language" (III, p. 941) into which impressions must be translated is also not unrelated to death. Like history for Thucydides, the work of art, for the narrator of *Remembrance*, may "make out of those who are no more, in their truest essence, a lasting acquisition for the minds of all mankind" (III, p. 941). Lasting? Under this ambition is hidden the relation to death: "Sorrows are servants, obscure and detested, against whom one struggles, beneath whose dominion one more and more completely falls, dire and dreadful servants whom it is impossible to replace and who by subterranean paths lead us towards truth and death. Happy are those who have first come face to face with truth, those for whom near though the one may be to the other, the hour of truth has struck before the hour of death!" (III, p. 948).

94. I shall return in my Conclusion to this visibility of "externalized" time, which illuminates mortals by the light of its magic lantern. Later on, in the same sense, we also read, "now it was not merely what had become of the young men of my own youth but would one day become of those of today that impressed upon me with such force the sensation of Time" (III, p. 987). It is still a question of "the sensation of time having slipped away" (III, p. 1000) and of the alteration of beings as "an effect operative not so much upon a whole social stratum as within individuals—of Time" (III, p. 1010). This figuration of time, in the dance of death, is to be included in the "gallery of symbolic figures" (Jauss, pp. 152–66) which, throughout *Remembrance*, constitute the many figurations of invisible time: Habit, Sorrow, Jealousy, Forgetfulness, and now Age. This system of emblems, I would say makes visible to "the artist, Time."

95. "Time, colourless and inapprehensible Time, so that I was almost able to see it and touch it, had materialised itself in this girl, moulding her into a masterpiece, while correspondingly, on me alas! it had merely done its work" (III, p. 1088).

96. This statement follows the one just cited and is worth quoting in its entirety. "He can describe a scene by describing one after another the innumerable objects which at a given moment were present at a particular place, but truth will be attained by him only when he takes two different objects, states the connexion [*rapport*] between them—a connexion analogous in the world of art to the unique connexion which in the world of science is provided by the law of causality—and encloses them in the necessary links of a well-wrought style; truth—and life too—can be attained by us only when, by comparing a quality common to two sensations, we succeed in extracting their common essence and in reuniting them to each other, liberated from the contingencies of time, within a metaphor" (III, pp. 924–25). Cf. Roger Shattuck, *Proust's*

Binoculars: A Study of Memory, Time, and Recognition in "A la Recherche du Temps Perdu" (New York: Random House, 1963). Shattuck begins his study, the merits of which I shall acknowledge below, with this famous passage.

97. For the remarks that follow I am endebted to Shattuck's book cited in the previous note. He does not just confine himself to noting the optical images scattered throughout *Remembrance* (magic lantern, kaleidoscope, telescope, microscope, magnifying glass, etc.) but also attempts to discover the rules governing a Proustian dioptics based on binocular contrast. Proustian optics is not a direct but a split optics which allows Shattuck to describe *Remembrance* as a whole as a "stereo-optics of Time." The canonical passage in this regard reads as follows. "For all these reasons a party like this at which I found myself . . . was like an old-fashioned peepshow, but a peepshow of the years, the vision not of a moment but of a person situated in the distorting perspective of time" (III, p. 965).

98. Shattuck points this out very nicely. The high point of Proust's work is not a happy moment but one of recognition (*Proust's Binoculars*, p. 37): "After the supreme rite of recognition at the end, the provisional nature of life disappears in the discovery of the straight path of art" (ibid., p. 38).

99. "Since every impression is double and the one half which is sheathed in the object is prolonged in ourselves by another half which we alone can know, we speedily find means to neglect this second half, which is the one on which we ought to concentrate" (III, p. 927).

100. "In fact, both in one case and in the other, whether I was concerned with impressions like the one which I had received from the sight of the steeples of Martinville or with reminiscences like that of the unevenness of the two steps or the taste of the madeleine, the task was to interpret the given sensations as signs of so many laws and ideas, by trying to think—that is to say, to draw forth from the shadow—what I had merely felt, by trying to convert it into its spiritual equivalent" (III, p. 912).

101. We shall return to this final phase of the alchemy of writing in the course of Part IV in my next volume, within the framework of my reflections on the way the work finds its completion in the act of reading.

102. "I had not gone in search of the two uneven paving-stones of the courtyard upon which I had stumbled. But it was precisely the fortuitous and inevitable fashion in which this and the other sensations had been encountered that proved the trueness of the past which they brought back to life, of the images which they released, since we feel, with these sensations, the effort that they make to climb back towards the light, feel in ourselves the joy of rediscovering what is real" (III, p. 913).

103. The entire problematic of the trace, to be taken up again in volume 3, is contained here. "This book, more laborious to decipher than any other, is also the only one which has been dictated to us by reality, the only one of which the 'impression' has been printed in us by reality itself. When an idea—an idea of any kind—is left in us by life, its material pattern, the outline of the impression that it made upon us, remains behind as the token of its necessary truth" (III, p. 914).

104. In this respect, artists no less than historians owe a debt to something that precedes them. This is another topic I shall take up in volume 3. But here is another passage indicative of it: "the essential, the only true book, though, in the ordinary sense of the word it does not have to be 'invented' by a great writer—for it exists already in each of us—has to be translated by him. The function and the task of a writer are those of a translator" (III, p. 926).

105. Meditating on the outcome in the person of Mademoiselle de Saint-Loup of the two "ways" along which the hero had taken so many walks and engaged in so many reveries, the narrator tells himself that his entire work will be made of all the "cross-

sections" reuniting impressions, epochs, and sites; as many ways as cross-sections, as distances traversed.

106. The figuration corresponding to this embodied time is the repetition, at the beginning and the end of *Remembrance*, of the same memory of the church in Combray, Saint Hilaire: "it occurred to me suddenly that, if I still had the strength to accomplish my work, this afternoon—like certain days long ago at Combray which had influenced me—which in its brief compass had given me both the idea of my work and the fear of being unable to bring it to fruition, would certainly impress upon it that form of which as a child I had had a presentiment in the church at Combray but which ordinarily, throughout our lives, is invisible to us: the form of Time" (III, p. 1103). (To relate this final illumination, the narrator uses the preterite joined to the adverb "suddenly.") One last time the church at Combray restores proximity in the distance that, from the beginning of *Remembrance*, has marked the evocation of Combray. *Time Regained* is, then, a repetition. "This notion of Time embodied, of years past but not separated from us, it was now my intention to emphasize as strongly as possible in my work. And at this very moment, in the house of the Prince de Guermantes, as though to strengthen me in my resolve, the noise of my parents' footsteps as they accompanied M. Swann to the door and the peal—resilient, ferruginous, interminable, fresh and shrill—of the bell on the garden gate which informed me that at last he had gone and that Mamma would presently come upstairs, these sounds rang again in my ears, yes, unmistakably I heard these very sounds, situated though they were in a remote past" (III, p. 1105).

107. On the question of writing, that is, of the impossibility of writing, cf. Gérard Genette, "La Question de l'écriture," and Léo Bersani, "Déguisement du moi et art fragmentaire," in Roland Barthes et al., *Recherches de Proust* (Paris: Seuil, 1980), pp. 7–12 and 13–33.

Conclusion

1. Cf. Henri Gouhier, *L'Théâtre et l'existence* (Paris: Aubier-Montaigne, 1952, 1973); *L'essence du théâtre* (Paris: Aubier-Montaigne, 1968); *Antonin Artaud et l'essence du théâtre* (Paris: Vrin, 1974).

2. *The Dialogic Imagination: Four Essays*, ed. Michael Holquist, trans. Caryl Emerson and Michael Holquist (Austin: University of Texas Press, 1981).

Index

Actants, 31, 44, 46, 51, 53, 170
Action, 3, 9, 10, 12, 20, 28, 31, 33, 36, 38, 39, 40, 41, 42, 43, 44, 45, 46, 51, 54, 58, 69, 71, 74, 82, 83, 88, 95, 97, 101, 103, 115, 129, 130, 153, 154, 155, 156, 158, 160, 162, 165, 169, 171, 172, 173, 174, 175, 180, 185, 186, 187, 191; analytic theory of, 42, 43; narrated, 65, 66; semantics of, 42, 44, 57, 58, 173; spheres of, 36. *See also* Praxis
Aeschylus, 109
Alexander, Jean, 187
Alter, Robert, 183
Analogy, 30, 114, 120, 128, 144, 148
Analytic philosophy, 57, 58
Apocalypse, 19, 23, 28, 164, 166, 167
Arendt, Hannah, 147
Aristophanes, 16
Aristotle, 4, 5, 7, 8, 9, 12, 14, 15, 20, 23, 24, 32, 35, 37, 48, 53, 54, 65, 68, 69, 73, 88, 99, 115, 133, 153, 154, 155, 157, 162, 163, 164, 165, 168, 177, 180, 183
Auerbach, Eric, 83, 162, 181
Augustine, 4, 5, 32, 47, 48, 99, 101, 110, 124, 130, 166, 192
Austen, Jane, 90
Austin, John, 184
Author, 25, 66, 92, 93, 94, 95, 96, 99, 102, 114, 131, 176, 183, 184, 186, 195, 198; implied, 182
Axiology, 47, 51, 53, 54, 56

Bachelard, Gaston, 112, 164
Bakhtin, Mikhail, 96–98, 99, 154, 155, 185, 201

Balzac, H. de, 9, 64, 191
Barthes, Roland, 30, 31, 168, 169, 175
Bataille, Georges, 165
Beckett, Samuel, 10, 26
Being and Time, 110
Benjamin, Walter, 28, 168
Benveniste, Emile, 63–65, 67, 68, 69, 72, 82, 168, 174, 175, 177
Bergson, Henri, 190, 191
Bersani, Léo, 201
Bible, 23
Bildungsroman, 9, 81, 116, 117, 120, 125, 127, 129, 143, 162, 179, 191, 195
Booth, Wayne, 96, 182
Braudel, Ferdinand, 79, 177
Bremond, Claude, 31, 38–44, 170, 171, 173, 180
Bultmann, Rudolf, 26
Burke, Kenneth, 165

Camus, Albert, 166
Catharsis, 16
Character(s), 9, 10, 21, 31, 33, 34, 36, 37, 38, 39, 40, 44, 46, 53, 65, 66, 69, 74, 88, 89, 90, 91, 93, 94, 97, 98, 99, 101, 102, 104, 108, 112, 139, 154, 155, 156, 162, 163, 168, 170, 175, 176, 183, 184, 185, 187, 188, 192; point of view, 184
Chatman, Seymour, 181, 184
Chronology, 25, 34, 43, 47, 78, 79, 80, 84, 85, 105, 106, 112, 113, 114, 115, 124, 139, 180; chronological illusion, 169
Cohn, Dorrit, 89–91, 94, 156, 183, 185, 186
Conrad, Joseph, 80, 179
Cook, Eleanor, 164

Index

Courtes, J., 171
Creativity, 56, 74, 81, 133, 144, 145, 150, 170
Culler, Jonathan, 184

Daiches, David, 187
Dante, A. 109, 164
Danto, Arthur, 43, 171, 172
Death, 26, 28, 101, 107, 108, 110, 111, 113, 115, 116, 119, 122, 123, 126, 127, 128, 129, 130, 139, 142, 143, 145, 146, 147, 151, 152, 189, 190, 191, 192, 194, 198, 199
Defoe, Daniel, 11, 163
Deleuze, Giles, 131–32, 138, 194
De Lubac, Henri, 17, 164
Descartes, René, 71
Diachrony, 5, 30, 32, 44, 46, 47, 159, 169, 172
Dialectic, 47, 66, 132, 134, 154, 176
Discourse, 12, 26, 28, 30, 31, 40, 45, 52, 62, 63, 64, 65, 66, 67, 69, 72, 82, 88, 89, 93, 94, 96, 97, 98, 103, 110, 154, 156, 161, 169, 171, 176, 180, 182, 183, 185, 192; free indirect, 72, 90, 92, 98, 176, 185
Distentio animi, 105, 166
Doležel, Ludomir, 184
Don Quixote, 7, 186

Eliade, Mircea, 108, 164
Eliot, T. S., 26
Emotion. *See* Feeling
Emplotment, 4, 5, 10, 19, 29, 31, 37, 38, 44, 51, 61, 73, 84, 96, 102, 153, 155, 156, 157, 158, 168
Epistemology, 4, 7, 20, 23, 29, 38, 132, 158, 160, 181
Escande, Jacques, 173
Eternity, 101, 109, 110, 121, 122, 123, 125, 126, 127, 141, 144, 184, 189, 195
Event, 56, 73, 81, 84, 103, 104, 119, 144, 146, 156, 158, 160, 162, 167, 168, 171, 175, 178, 180, 185
Experience, 5, 11, 13, 18, 28, 62, 64, 66, 68, 73, 74, 81, 84, 85, 87, 92, 100, 102, 103, 108, 116, 123, 128, 129, 131, 143, 148, 155, 171, 176, 182, 190, 191, 192, 195, 196; aesthetic, 74; of configuration, 21; fictive, 6, 74, 86, 87, 88, 100, 105, 133, 134, 159, 160, 182, 183; imaginative,

18; literary 19; of the particular, 12; of time, 6, 62, 62, 67, 74, 80, 81, 100, 105, 108, 110, 111, 112, 115, 117, 124, 130, 133, 134, 149, 159, 160, 178, 179, 184
Explanation, 4, 32, 70, 133, 157, 158

Faulkner, William, 179
Feeling, 10, 11, 16, 21, 41, 88, 89, 90, 91, 97, 98, 119, 125, 127, 141, 175, 185, 200
Fiction, vii, 3, 13, 14, 17, 23, 26, 27, 28, 32, 62, 65, 67, 71, 73, 74, 89, 91, 107, 116, 124, 155, 158, 165, 167, 175, 183, 186, 190; entry into, 25, 66, poetics of, 182, rhetoric of, 21, 182, 183
Fielding, Henry, 78, 163
Fink, Eugen, 177, 186
Flaubert, Gustave, 90, 177
Florival, Ghislaine, 197
Foucault, Michel, 163
Fowler, Roger, 184
Freedom, 123, 126, 170, 172, 173, 192
Friedmann, Käte, 184
Frye, Northrop, 15–19, 22, 26, 27, 41, 155, 162, 164, 165

Gadamer, H.-G., 163, 164
Galsworthy, John, 79, 179
Gamble, Isabel, 189
Garelli, Jacques, 161
Genette, Gérard, 61, 75, 80, 81–88, 154, 175, 179, 180, 182, 185, 186, 195, 201
Genres, 3, 7, 8, 9, 14, 20, 29, 97, 157, 158, 159, 161, 162, 175, 176, 195
Goethe, J. W. von, 9, 33, 35, 37, 38, 73, 74, 75, 79, 80, 87, 116, 155, 175, 178, 179, 181, 191
Goldman, A. I., 171
Gombrich, E. H., 26
Gouhier, Henri, 154, 201
Graham, John, 189, 190
Greimas, A.-J., 31, 36, 44–60, 61, 171, 172, 173, 174, 178, 181
Gruphius, Andreas, 179
Guiguet, Jean, 187, 188, 189, 190
Guillaume, Gustave, 175

Hafley, James, 187
Hamburger, Käte, 63, 65–66, 89, 98, 174, 175, 176, 183

Index

Hamlet, 7, 24
Hegel, G. W. F., 155, 162, 163
Henry, Anne, 132–33, 194, 195
Historiography, 4, 32, 37, 56, 99, 157, 161
History, vii, 8, 29, 30, 31, 32, 56, 60, 63, 64, 69, 70, 108, 113, 117, 128, 130, 158, 159, 163, 176, 183, 186, 195; efficacity of, 164; monumental, 109, 110; philosophy of, 4; as utterance, 63
Hofmannsthal, Hugo von, 179
Homer, 8, 69, 153, 163
Hošek, Chaviva, 164
Hume, David, 12
Husserl, Edmund, 157, 177

Imagination, 23, 90, 164, 166, 183, 184; productive, 3, 19
Innovation, 25, 162
Intelligibility, 26, 28, 29, 48, 60, 131, 158, 169
Intentionality, 187; historical, 159
Intertextuality, 18

Jacob, André, 175
James, Henry, 13, 91, 186
Jauss, Hans Robert, 152, 196, 199
Joyce, James, 26, 90, 156, 179, 183, 187, 188
Judgment, 44, 61, 174

Kafka, Franz, 10, 16, 89
Kant, Immanuel, 3, 59, 174
Kellogg, Robert, 162
Kenny, Antony, 173
Kermode, Frank, 21, 22–27, 162, 165, 166, 167, 168, 170
King Lear, 24
Kucich, John, 165
Kuhn, T. S., 163
Kundera, Milan, 185

Language, 10, 11, 12, 21, 22, 30, 31, 44, 45, 51, 62, 66–67, 70, 72, 97, 107, 109, 117, 118, 119, 120, 163, 164, 165, 166, 167, 168, 170, 171, 175, 178, 186, 199
Latham, Jacqueline E. M., 189
Le Goff, Jacques, 169
Leibniz, G. W. von, 117
Lejeune, Phillipe, 183
Lessing, G. E., 179

Lévi-Strauss, Claude, 34, 35, 168–69, 172
Lewis, Wyndham, 26
Linguistics, 30, 31, 51, 82, 169, 170; textual, 67, 73
Linneaus, Carolus, 33, 35, 37, 38, 169
Literature, 8, 9, 12, 14, 19, 24, 27, 31, 74, 76, 101, 150, 151, 155, 157, 161, 163, 164, 168
Locke, John, 11, 12
Longinus, 164
Lotman, Jurij, 93, 99, 154, 167, 185, 186
Love, Jean O., 189

Macbeth, 24, 166
Macpherson, Jay, 164
Mallarmé, Stéphane, 19, 150, 169
Malraux, André, 177
Mann, Thomas, 74, 76, 80, 101, 112–30, 161, 179, 190, 191, 192, 194, 195
Maupassant, Guy de, 52, 55, 173, 177
Meaning, 24, 27, 31, 48, 49, 51, 57, 59, 62, 66, 67, 73, 74, 80, 84, 86, 87, 103, 109, 111, 127, 128, 131, 137, 138, 143, 144, 145, 146, 147, 151, 160, 162, 168, 179, 181, 182, 186, 194, 195, 196; genesis of, 157
Memory, 11, 12, 64, 80, 83, 85, 87, 89, 93, 99, 104, 105, 108, 131, 133, 137, 138, 139, 140, 141, 142, 144, 148, 150, 176, 187, 188, 196, 197, 198, 199, 201
Mendilow, A. A., 101, 162, 163, 187
Metaphor, 94, 95, 96, 99, 148, 149, 151, 165, 178, 199
Meyer, Hans, 191
Miller, J. Hillis, 21, 165, 167
Mimesis, 12, 14, 65, 67, 75, 88, 89, 97, 153, 154, 155, 156, 180; mimesis$_1$, 62, 63, 101, 156, 164, 173; mimesis$_2$, 3, 4, 5, 8, 20, 27, 62, 63, 72, 153, 156, 164, 169; mimesis$_3$, 5, 20, 27, 62, 74, 164
Mink, Lewis O., 43
Minkowski, E., 112
Moody, A. D., 189
Müller, Günther, 61, 75–81, 84, 87, 178, 179, 181
Muthos, 4, 5, 10, 17, 20, 23, 37, 38, 43, 54, 88, 153, 154, 157, 162, 164, 165. *See also* Plot

Myth, 16, 17, 22, 23, 26, 27, 28, 152, 163, 164, 166, 167, 168–69

Narrative, vii, 4, 22, 25, 28, 30, 31, 41, 42, 43, 46, 47, 50, 51, 61, 64, 70, 71, 82, 153, 172; closure, 20–22, 23, 24, 34, 35, 45, 100, 102, 152, 167; configuration, 3, 4, 5, 15, 20, 28, 31, 43, 69, 72, 95, 96, 100, 101, 156, 158, 165, 172, 177; constraints, 170; conventions, 11, 12, 13, 14, 22, 25, 134; entry into, 66, 69, 98; episodes, 9, 21, 163; fictional, vii, 3, 4, 5, 32, 61, 65, 71, 88, 96, 97, 101, 154, 155, 156, 157, 158, 160, 161; field, 3, forms, 8, 28, 29, 34, 174; function, 4, 14, 15, 28, 29, 31, 32, 176; grammar, 168; historical, vii, 3, 4, 8, 42, 61, 156, 157, 158, 160, 161; instance, 85–86; intelligibility, 169; as ordered, 7, 15, 22, 25, 26, 27, 34, 37, 44, 47, 162, 167; poetics, 61, 72; point of view, 88, 90, 91, 93–95, 99, 113, 154, 163, 176, 182, 184, 186; process, 49, 80, 195; present, 98, 176; schematism, 15, 18, 19, 20, 43; semiotics, 4, 5, 15, 29, 31, 45, 48, 52, 53, 158; sentence, 43, 57, 172; situations, 91–93, 95, 183; statement, 49, 50, 51, 58, 61, 69, 75, 81, 85, 86, 88, 100, 159, 171, 180, 181; story-line, 10, 102, 112, 140; temporality, 5, 47, 85, 158, 181; time, 38, 45, 47, 61, 80, 82, 169, 174, 178, 181, 182; understanding, 4, 7, 10, 14, 15, 19, 20, 29, 31, 32, 38, 42, 47, 52, 56, 83, 157, 158, 159, 162, 172, 181, 185; utterance, 61, 68, 69, 70, 72, 75, 82, 85, 86, 88, 98, 100, 159, 177, 180, 181; voice, 85, 86, 88, 90, 91, 92, 93, 95–99, 102, 104, 111, 112, 114, 116, 117, 118, 121, 128, 134, 154, 176, 178, 180, 181, 182, 186, 187, 189, 193, 195, 196. *See also* Character(s); Time

Narrativity, 42, 43, 48, 49, 56, 57, 58, 60, 69

Narratology, 4, 7, 14, 75, 81, 82, 84, 85, 86, 87, 156, 161, 181

Narrator, 66, 69, 70, 73, 74, 80, 82, 84, 86, 87, 88, 89, 90, 91, 92, 93, 94, 95, 96, 97, 98, 102, 103, 104, 105, 106, 107, 108, 109, 111, 112, 114, 115, 117, 118, 119, 120, 121, 122, 123, 124, 125, 126, 127, 128, 129, 130, 133, 134, 138, 139, 141, 142, 143, 145, 147, 148, 150, 151, 154,

155, 176, 178, 180, 182, 183, 184, 185, 186, 187, 189, 190, 192, 193, 196, 197, 198, 199, 200; implied, 183; point of view, 184

Nef, Frédéric, 173, 174

Nietzsche, Friedrich, 26, 27, 106, 125, 126, 166, 190

Novalis (Friedrich Leopold Freiherr von Hardenberg), 191

Novel, the, 3, 4, 7, 8, 9, 10, 12, 13, 24, 25, 28, 69, 71, 89, 154, 155, 156, 166, 170, 175, 180, 183, 195; polyphonic, 96–97

Ontology, 87, 160

Paradigms, 4, 7, 8, 14, 15, 20, 23, 26, 27, 28, 29, 62, 84, 139, 162, 166, 168, 170, 194

Paradox, 6, 12, 13, 14, 21, 29, 69, 99, 103, 108, 128, 130, 155, 196

Parker, Patricia, 164

Patrick, Julian, 164

Phenomenology, vii, 59, 62, 76, 124; of action, 58, 59, 173; of internal time-consciousness, 5; of suffering, 59

Plato, 145, 175, 180

Pleasure, 10

Plot, 7, 8, 9, 10, 11, 12, 13, 14, 23, 25, 28, 32, 33, 34, 35, 36, 38, 39, 41, 42, 44, 52, 59, 69, 73, 96, 97, 154, 162, 163, 165, 167, 168, 171, 187; time of the plot, 32, 39

Plotinus, 47

Pouillon, Jean, 90, 183, 184

Poulet, Georges, 137, 196, 197, 199

Pound, Ezra, 26

Praxis, 9, 44, 58, 74, 101

Prince, Gerald, 181

Propp, Vladimir, 31, 33–38, 39, 40, 42, 44, 45, 46, 59, 169, 170, 171, 172, 173, 178, 185

Proust, Marcel, 80, 82, 83–88, 89, 101, 130–52, 161, 162, 179, 182, 194, 195, 196, 197, 198, 200

Quest, 19, 35, 37, 46, 47, 48, 55, 104, 119, 131, 132, 133, 134, 162, 170, 174, 190

Rabelais, F., 155

Rastier, François, 171

Rationality, 4, 19, 29, 30, 31, 32, 38, 41–

42, 157, 169; historiographical, 38, 56, 157; narratological, 38, 56, 158, 159, 172; semiotic, 14, 52, 162
Reader, 10, 11, 21, 22, 24, 25, 26, 28, 88, 92, 99, 100, 102, 104, 105, 122, 129, 134, 141, 150, 160, 162, 163, 183, 184, 188, 189; expectations, 24, 25. *See also* World
Reading, 5, 20, 79, 83, 113, 120, 131, 132, 134, 137, 140, 161, 187, 200. *See also* Time, of reading
Reality, 13, 14, 27, 30, 66, 150, 155, 160, 178, 180, 185, 196, 200
Recognition, 54, 146, 149, 151, 172, 200
Redfield, James, 155
Reference, 11, 12, 159, 160, 169; referential illusion, 169
Reid, Thomas, 11
Religion, 27, 164, 170
Repetition, 20, 201
Representation, 10, 12, 14, 40, 44, 58, 70, 91, 155, 164, 166, 179, 180, 185
Reverberation, 105, 112, 115, 189
Richardson, Samuel, 11, 162
Ricoeur, Paul, 161, 164, 172, 173, 174, 178
Rimmon-Kenan, Shlomith, 181
Robbe-Grillet, Alain, 166
Rosenberg, Harold, 166
Rossum-Guyon, Françoise van, 186

Said, Edward, 167, 186
Sartre, Jean-Paul, 166, 184, 187
Saussure, Ferdinand de, 30, 82, 170, 180, 181
Schelling, F. W. J., 133, 195
Schiller, J. C. F. von, 9, 66, 74, 155, 175, 179
Schklovsky, 180
Schlegel, August Wilhelm, 76
Schneider, Monique, 169
Scholes, Robert, 162
Schopenhauer, Arthur, 133, 195
Searle, John, 184
Sedimentation, 25, 28
Segre, Cesare, 180
Semiotics, 31, 32, 51, 54; semiotic square, 49, 53, 54, 55, 56, 57, 58, 59, 60. *See also* Narrative
Shakespeare, William, 24, 106, 109, 111, 164, 188
Shattuck, Roger, 148, 199, 200
Smith, Barbara Herrnstein, 21–22, 165, 167, 168

Soliloquy, 90
Sophocles, 69, 153
Souriau, Etienne, 45, 172, 179
Speculation, 108, 129, 144, 179
Stanzel, Franz K., 91–93, 95, 184, 186
Statement, 5
Sterne, Laurence, 80
Stevens, Wallace, 27, 166
Structure, 29, 30, 31, 34; organic, 31, 33, 38
Style, 14, 15, 19, 20, 26, 28, 29, 31, 32, 87, 95, 148, 149, 151, 159, 163, 168, 185, 199
Synchrony, 30, 32, 95, 169, 186

Tempo, 71, 73, 79, 158, 177
Temporality, 34, 177, 182
Tesnières, Lucien, 45
Text, 3, 72, 73, 75, 81, 83, 167, 168, 176, 185
Thieberger, Richard, 192, 193, 194
Thucydides, 199
Tiffeneau, Dorian, 169
Tillich, Paul, 26
Time, vii, 4, 5, 25, 32, 34, 52, 63, 71, 72, 124, 125, 126, 129, 151, 152, 159, 180, 201; *chronos* vs. *kairos*, 166; clinical, 119; clock time, 108, 112, 121, 130; dated, 122, 123; dimensional character of, 151; embodied, 201; empty, 122; of fiction, 5, 62, 65, 67, 72, 75; fictive, 181; hier-archical, 101; historical, 187; a history, 5, 128, 158; internal, 108, 115, 130, 190; in-visible, 199; of life, 75, 77, 80, 81, 179; lived, 65, 66, 68, 72, 76, 108, 174; lost-regained, 147; monumental, 106, 108, 112, 115, 190; mortal, 110, 190; mystery of, 125; narrated, 81, 103, 104, 110, 113, 114, 125, 163, 178, 179; of narrating, 5, 65, 70, 76, 79, 80, 81, 85, 86, 100, 113, 121, 159, 179; paradox of, 128; public, 107; of the plot, 32; pseudo-time of nar-rative, 83, 84; of reading, 79, 83, 84, 181; of recitation, 155; refiguration of, 103; re-membered, 178; semiotic, 169; sempiter-nal, 166; sense of, 120; specificity of fictive time, 159; of the story, 182; of the text, 70; temporalization, 47; of things nar-rated, 5, 65, 70, 76, 79, 81, 85, 86, 100, 103, 104, 121, 159, 163
Todorov, Tzvetan, 31, 43, 161, 168, 169, 171, 172, 176, 180, 186

Index

Tolstoy, L. N., 9, 96
Tomaschevski, 180
Trace, 200
Tradition, 15, 28, 31, 43, 55, 97, 155, 163, 166; transhistorical, 15, 20
Traditionality, 4, 14, 15, 17, 19, 20, 26, 29, 31, 32, 157, 159, 163, 170
Transcendence, 5, 6, 101, 160, 187, 195
Truth, 3, 11, 13, 27, 55, 71, 131, 139, 140, 145, 150, 158, 160, 176, 182, 199, 200
Types, 7, 8, 14, 20, 29, 157, 162
Typology, 15, 57, 83, 91, 92, 93, 95, 169, 183, 184, 185

Understanding, 32, 60, 99, 183, 184; categorical, 14. *See also* Narrative
Uspensky, Boris, 93–95, 99, 154, 185
Utterance, 5

Valdés, Mario, 161, 186, 187
Valéry, Paul, 168
Vendryes, E., 182

Veyne, Paul, 8
Voltaire, F. M. A., 71

Watt, Ian, 162, 163
Weber, Max, 173
Weigand, Hermann, 190, 191, 192, 193
Weil, Eric, 28, 168
Weinrich, Harald, 63, 66–76, 82, 88, 94, 98, 174, 176, 177, 181, 198
Wilde, Oscar, 27
Woolf, Virginia, 9, 79, 80, 97, 101–12, 161, 179, 187, 188, 189
World, 5, 67, 68, 69, 74, 94, 104, 131, 167, 168, 176, 188; of action, 164; imaginary, 6, 100, 159; narrated, 69, 70, 71, 75, 88, 176, 177; of praxis, 75; of the reader, 5, 6, 20, 99, 100, 160; of the text, 5, 6, 75, 86, 99, 160; of the work, 5, 74, 101, 160, 195
Writing, 201

Yeats, William Butler, 26